Fashion Criticism

Fashion Criticism

An Anthology

Edited by
Francesca Granata

BLOOMSBURY VISUAL ARTS
LONDON · NEW YORK · OXFORD · NEW DELHI · SYDNEY

BLOOMSBURY VISUAL ARTS
Bloomsbury Publishing Plc
50 Bedford Square, London, WC1B 3DP, UK
1385 Broadway, New York, NY 10018, USA
29 Earlsfort Terrace, Dublin 2, Ireland

BLOOMSBURY, BLOOMSBURY VISUAL ARTS and the Diana logo
are trademarks of Bloomsbury Publishing Plc

First published in Great Britain 2021

Selection, editorial matter, Introductions © Francesca Granata, 2021

Francesca Granata has asserted her right under the Copyright, Designs and
Patents Act, 1988, to be identified as Editor of this work.

For legal purposes the Acknowledgments on p. viii and pp. 222–4 constitute
an extension of this copyright page.

Cover design by Adriana Brioso
Cover image: Pat Cleveland in a Halston Fashion Show by Andy Warhol, c. 1970s,
silver gelatin print, 8 x 10 inches. (© The Andy Warhol Foundation)

A catalogue record for this book is available from the British Library.

A catalogue record for this book is available from the Library of Congress.

ISBN:	HB:	978-1-3500-5881-1
	PB:	978-1-3500-5880-4
	ePDF:	978-1-3500-5878-1
	eBook:	978-1-3500-5879-8

Typeset by Integra Software Services Pvt. Ltd.
Printed and bound in Great Britain

To find out more about our authors and books visit www.bloomsbury.com
and sign up for our newsletters.

CONTENTS

ACKNOWLEDGMENTS

I am grateful to a number of people for their support for this book. First and foremost, my gratitude goes to the fashion critics (and in some cases their estates), for agreeing to be included in this anthology. A number of these critics have spoken in my classes and in roundtable discussions at Parsons, thus furthering my understanding of contemporary fashion criticism. I also thank the Andy Warhol Foundation, for letting me use Warhol's image for the book's cover.

The students from Parsons who attended my graduate seminar on Fashion Criticism have been a great sounding board for the ideas in this book, and their enthusiasm for the subject has been a motivating force throughout.

This anthology developed from an issue of *Fashion Projects,* the non-profit journal I edit and founded, on the topic of fashion criticism; I sincerely thank both the issue's interviewees and contributors. The idea for the issue developed in conversation with my partner Jay Ruttenberg, a writer and music critic, whose enthusiasm for the subject of criticism and endless discussions about it were also indispensable to the book—as were his many hours of childcare for our daughter Corinna.

I also would like to extend a heartful thanks to my colleagues at the School of Art and Design History and Theory at Parsons, for their intellectual camaraderie. In particular, I would like to thank my colleagues in Fashion Studies: Hazel Clark, Heike Jenss, Charlene K. Lau, Rachel Lifter, and Christina Moon. A deep thanks also go to the school's deans Sarah E. Lawrence and Rhonda Garelick for their support and enthusiasm for the project. A number of research assistants have aided with the tasks of copyright clearance: Nick Stagliano, Maegan Stracy, and Yannise Jean.

My thanks also go to Van Dyke Lewis, Alice Twemlow, and Susan E. Thomas for inviting me to present on the topic of fashion criticism at, respectively, Cornell University, the School of Visual Arts, and the New York Art Book Fair. Part of the introduction was previously published in *Fashion Theory*, and I thank the journal's editor Valerie Steele. My gratitude also goes to the anonymous reviewers, who gave feedback at the proposal stage and to this full manuscript, shaping this anthology tremendously. In conclusion, I also would like to thank the editors at Bloomsbury and in particular Frances Arnold, Rebecca Hamilton and Yvonne Thouroude for their tremendous and constant support of this book.

Introduction

Film criticism has its Pauline Kaels and Andrew Sarrises, and music criticism its Robert Christgaus and Greil Marcuses—yet fashion remains, in the words of one prominent fashion critic, "culturally beneath regard " (Ruttenberg, 2013, 28). How has such a rich and diverse area of criticism remained so understudied and undervalued?

This question has been percolating with me for quite some time. In 2004, I started a journal titled *Fashion Projects*, with the mission of highlighting the importance of fashion within current critical discourses. A non-profit journal, it was started with the intent to reach beyond the academy. (Unlike academic journals, it is distributed in newsstands and sold at a relatively low price.) In 2013, the same impetus behind starting *Fashion Projects* led me to the topic of its fourth issue: an investigation of fashion criticism, as articulated in journalistic writings. This issue was structured around interviews with fashion critics about the state of their field. Our subjects included Judith Thurman (a staff writer at *The New Yorker*), *New York Times* style writer Guy Trebay, Suzy Menkes (then at *The International Herald Tribune*), and Robin Givhan (*The Washington Post*). The issue was meant to highlight what I believed to be an important yet understudied area of criticism. The richness of the interviews and the interest it generated in publications ranging from *The Columbia Journalism Review* to *Teen Vogue* solidified the importance of the topic and led me to start working on this anthology. (Notably, writing on the topic of fashion criticism has greatly expanded in the relatively short period since the issue was published, further underscoring its importance.[1])

Delay in Legitimization

The central questions that animate my investigation on the topic are: Why has fashion criticism remained undervalued relative to other areas of cultural criticism? What has been its historical development vis-à-vis other fields of criticism? Is its delay in legitimization tied to its gender specificity—by the fact that historically it has been written by and for women?

---

[1]See Peter McNeil and Sanda Miller, *Fashion Writing and Criticism: History, Theory and Practice*, London and New York: Bloomsbury, 2014; Kyung-Hee Choi and Van Dyk Lewis, "Inclusive System for Fashion Criticism," *International Journal of Fashion Design, Technology and Education*, published online February 20, 2017; Monica Titton, "Fashion Criticism Unravelled: A Sociological Critique of Criticism in Fashion Media," *International Journal of Fashion Studies*, vol. 3, no. 2, October 2016: 209–23; and Kate Nelson Best, *The History of Fashion Journalism*, London and New York: Bloomsbury, 2017. *Frock Consciousness: Writing about Clothes from the London Review of Books*, LRB Collections vol. 6, London: London Review of Books, 2019.

Fashion criticism is still undergoing the process of legitimization that other realms of popular culture criticism went through in the 1960s and 1970s, when barriers between high and low culture increasingly came under attack. This process is further complicated by the changes that journalism is rapidly undergoing. Underscoring the field's delay in legitimization is the fact that the Pulitzer Prize board did not bestow the award in criticism to a fashion writer until 2006, when it was given to Givhan, at *The Washington Post*. The jury praised Givhan "for her witty, closely observed essays that transform fashion criticism into cultural criticism," a statement that implies that fashion and its attendant critical study normally reside outside of culture. Perhaps even more symbolically significant is the fact that the esteemed Library of America, with the stated mission "to champion our nation's cultural heritage by publishing America's greatest writing,"[2] has published anthologies of most areas of cultural criticism from food to architecture, yet nothing on fashion to date (Granata, 2019, 554).

Partially explaining this delay in legitimization, philosopher Lars Svendsen points out that critical fashion writing and the developing of a robust field of fashion criticism have been hindered by the fashion press' close relation with the industry. Svendsen argues that genuine fashion criticism sits somewhere between fashion reportage and fashion theory, and is always "rigorous, clearly stated and historically informed" (Svendsen, 2016, 115). Evaluation—the ability to move a positive or negative critique—is central to criticism (Carroll, 2009; McNeil and Miller, 2014; Svendsen, 2016). Similarly, fashion scholars Kyung-Hee Choi and Van Dyk Lewis discuss criticism, in the context of fashion, as "a process of judgment to use a language to heighten understanding and appreciation of a coded object and to communicate discourses on its value system" (Choi and Lewis, 2018, 3). Bemoaning the lack of a critical approach to fashion is hardly a novel idea, as is advocating for it and for the importance of taking fashion seriously. As early as 1845, French novelist and literary critic Jules-Amédée Barbey d'Aurevilly, writing under the female pseudonym "Maximilienne de Syrène," complained in the pages of *Le Constitutionnel* how "fashion reviews are often no more than trade shows of low style, shop windows offering barely more food for the mind than advertisements." And he (as she) adds, "The idea of introducing a degree of objective honesty into these reports came to us out of love and respect for Fashion. […] We do not consider ourselves as frivolous as all that in describing Fashion as a matter of considerable import beneath its apparent triviality" (Maximilienne de Syrène [Barbey d'Aurevilly], [1845] 2015).

Another hindrance to the formation of fashion criticism is the practice of fashion houses to ban fashion critics from shows in retaliation for negative press—a practice that has few counterparts in other fields of criticism (Svendsen, 2016, 109). Recent accounts of such attempts at censoring negative reporting have been noted in relation to Cathy Horyn (then at *The New York Times*). The anthology includes her 2004 review that caused her to be banned from Hedi Slimane's YSL show. Horyn's article reads as a measured assessment of that season's menswear collection in Paris—its alleged affront was hailing the designer Raf Simons and giving a tepid review of work by Hedi Slimane, then designing menswear for Dior. However, the practice of banning critics from attending shows has a long, albeit poorly documented, history. Bill Cunningham reported in his collection coverage for *Details* magazine that in the mid-1980s, *Women's Wear Daily* was banned from the Yves Saint Laurent fashion shows, seemingly for the minor infraction of hailing Lacroix's shows over YSL. *WWD* also had been banned from the

---

[2]Library of America website, retrieved June 8, 2017.

Balenciaga fashion shows from the late 1950s through the 1960s, although continued reporting on it was based on department stores' sketches of the collections. As Cunningham points out, these were not isolated cases, rather it "brings into focus the whole archaic process of commercial fashion houses setting themselves up as untouchable, censoring the press by excluding it from their show, a system that has worked for the smaller, private couture houses since the turn of the century" (Cunningham, 1988, 188).

The attempts at censorship, however, also point to the resilience of fashion criticism. Fashion writing has been published for a long time (at least as early as the late nineteenth century) in broadsheet newspapers, and in high-end general interest magazines such as *The New Yorker*—publications that carefully maintain the wall between advertising and editorial.

Comparison between the development of fashion criticism and other areas of criticism, from theater and literature to the fine arts, is explored by historians Peter McNeil and Sanda Miller, who acknowledge how the development of a critical vocabulary for fashion developed much later than the more traditional "fine" arts, in part due to the historical distinctions between the fields of fine versus applied arts in the European academic traditions, as well as those of high versus popular culture (McNeil and Miller, 2014). What remains perplexing is the fact that the field of fashion criticism remains less recognized than other fields of popular culture criticism such as film or popular music. It is in this distinction where the argument for gender specificity behind this delay in legitimization transpires most clearly. Of course, one could argue that fashion, unlike film or popular music, retains a functional aspect, and yet when compared with architectural criticism, as McNeil and Miller point out, the gap in legitimization is even starker. (The Pulitzer Prize for criticism has been awarded to an architectural critic six times.) A notable exception to the lack of status of fashion criticism is the genre of the fashion exhibition review, which has grown concomitantly with the exponential growth of fashion exhibitions in the twenty-first century. By being aligned with the high-culture space of the museum, the exhibition review has brought fashion criticism to the culture and arts sections of broadsheet newspapers and a range of art and literary publications, thus furthering the legitimization of the field.

As this anthology makes evident, despite its "lower" status in relation to other areas of cultural criticism, fashion criticism has its own distinctive history. Fashion was covered in *The New Yorker* from its inception in 1925 by Lois Long, who, upon her death in 1974, was credited by William Shawn, then the magazine's totemic editor, with inventing the field. And although the title of "fashion critic" was not officially used as a job title until 1994, when *The New York Times* coined it for Amy Spindler, writings on fashion appeared regularly in newspapers starting in the late nineteenth century, when Joseph Pulitzer, the publisher of *The New York World*, is credited with the development of the women's sections of newspapers. This placement contributed to the field's delay in legitimization, as these sections, also known as "women's pages," and often the only places where women could develop journalistic careers, were described as covering the "four F's"—food, fashion, family, and furnishings—and dismissed as the epitome of soft news (Voss, 2018). Thus, while the reasons for this delay in recognition are multiple, the most central one is the gender dynamic of the field. Its association with women and the feminine, which have been, in turn, historically associated with consumption, certainly contributed to its lack of status. This was corroborated in interviews with fashion critics in the pages of *Fashion Projects*. To mention just a few of the comments connecting fashion criticism's lower status with its association with femininity, Robin Givhan pointed out how "there is an incredible amount of sexism at play in the way that the fashion industry is perceived and in the way that the coverage of the fashion industry is perceived" (Labrague, 2013, 12). Echoing this sentiment, Guy Trebay comments on how he was discouraged from writing about fashion, which is considered "feminine, not worthy of masculine attention and regard" (Ruttenberg, 2013, 28).

Aims and Scope

This anthology is meant to rectify, at least in part, the lack of attention given to the field of fashion criticism by collecting in one volume some of the more notable fashion criticism produced from the nineteenth century to present, and thus showing the richness, depth and diversity of fashion criticism. In order to make the project manageable, the book is focused on English language publications produced and circulated for the most part in the United States and the UK.[3] These geographical boundaries start breaking down at the beginning of the twenty-first century, when digital media moved us toward a transnational fashion media culture and English solidified its position as lingua franca. (This is evident in publications such as *Vestoj*, which is based in Paris but written in English and edited by Anja Aronowsky Cronberg, who is Swedish.) Limiting the anthology to English was a particularly fraught decision, as English is not my mother tongue, but a language I only learned later in life. (I spoke Italian growing up and learned German as a child before learning English in my teens.) So I am fully aware of the richness of fashion criticism in different idioms and on a global scale going well beyond the Western sphere. But I envision this book, as its title suggests, as "an" anthology of fashion criticism: one of many possible explorations of this rich form of criticism, which will be hopefully followed by others, with different geographical and temporal scopes.

The anthology starts in the late nineteenth century, as it is during this period that the fashion press was greatly expanded and democratized in Europe and North America (Breward, 1994, 71; Best, 2017, 27–8). Oscar Wilde's journalistic writings on fashion, which open the anthology, illustrate the proliferation of fashion writings across publications. Wilde straddled high and low domain as he wrote about fashion in *The Pall Mall Gazette*—a wide-circulation London-based newspaper akin to the yellow journalism advanced contemporaneously by William Randolph Hearst and Pulitzer in the United States—but Wilde also edited the higher-end monthly women's magazine *The Woman's World* from 1887 to 1889 (Fortunato, 2007). The anthology privileges work published in newspapers and general interest magazines, which are better able to provide unbiased criticism thanks to their relative distance from the industry, and includes only a handful of articles from the mainstream fashion press—such as Susan Sontag's essay for American *Vogue* from 1978, which is republished here for the first time. The anthology also includes selected articles from "niche" and independent fashion and style magazines, starting with *Rogue*—a pun on *Vogue*—an avant-garde "little" magazine from the 1910s.

The majority of the authors anthologized ranging from *The New Yorker*'s first fashion critic Lois Long to the current *New York Times* critic Vanessa Friedman have worked primarily as fashion journalists. But the collection includes several cultural critics who have written about fashion with some frequency, including Wilde, Sontag, and *New Yorker* theater critic Hilton Als. Their writings appear alongside authors who are best known as fiction writers, such as British novelist Angela Carter, whose writings on fashion appeared in the 1970s and 1980s in the pages of *The New Society*; the recently rediscovered Los Angeles writer Eve Babitz, who wrote fashion

---

[3]However, the English has not been standardized; treating the articles as primary sources, we have maintained the spelling and punctuation from the original publications.

criticism in her uniquely personal tone for *Vogue*; and Bebe Moore Campbell, who wrote about fashion and style in the 1980s and 1990s for *Essence* and *Ebony*—two pioneering African-American magazines.

Finally, the anthology includes a handful of examples of academic fashion theorists and historians writing in journalistic settings, thus highlighting the somewhat porous boundaries between media and academic discourse surrounding fashion. In fact, despite the progressive professionalization of the field of fashion studies, which brought with it specialized journals and academic presses, there have been writers who have straddled the two, as is the case with fashion and art historian Anne Hollander, who, from the 1970s onward, published extensively in a variety of publications, including *The New Republic, The London Review of Books*, and *Slate*.

Most of the authors in the anthology are based in New York and London—a fact that underscores the contemporary centralization of US and UK media companies. However, in New York the centralization of publishing predates the contemporary moment, particularly in the case of magazine publishing. As early as the late nineteenth century, two-thirds of magazines with a circulation over 100,000 were published in New York. As historians John Tebbel and Mary Ellen Zuckerman point out, it was then that "a pattern was set up. [...] New York magazines tended to reflect the life of the city [...], while those elsewhere were constantly writing about it" (Tebbel and Zuckerman, 1991, 58). The urbane New Yorker as a woman of fashion, in itself a discursive as much as a "real" entity, was in fact central to the production of New York as the American fashion capital and can be observed in fashion criticism starting at the beginning of the twentieth century.[4]

The book follows a chronological order, even though as fashion theorist Caroline Evans (whose writing is included in the anthology) has so eloquently discussed, changes in fashion and its attendant form of criticism are hardly linear (2003). Themes return throughout the span of a little over a century that the anthology covers. Although it begins in the nineteenth century, the bulk of the work anthologized was produced from the 1970s onward, as it is the period in which fashion criticism took a stronger foothold in the press. The book is divided into three parts, organized chronologically and further subdivided in smaller section. The first part anthologizes work from the nineteenth century to the 1960s—a wide timespan, which sets the scene for the legitimization of fashion criticism to come. The second part starts in the 1970s, acknowledging the deep societal shift that had taken place in the 1960s as a result of second-wave feminism alongside the civil rights movement. Within journalism, the late 1960s and early 1970s are the time during which anti-discrimination lawsuits made their ways through newsrooms, while in fashion journalism, issues of gender equality and race are discussed more openly. The third and final section opens in the new millennium—a period that serves as a marker for the solidification of new media, alongside a veritable proliferation of fashion writing across a variety of media.

Mapping "Interwoven Discourses"

The anthology is further evidence of the existence of a well-developed "fashion media discourse," a type of discourse that Agnès Rocamora, who first coined the term, argues, although specific to the field of fashion, interacts with a number of different discourses. The fashion theorist defines "fashion media discourse" as "a particular instance of fashion discourse. As such, it runs across various texts. It is, for instance, articulated in a set of different magazines, but also in the

---

[4]Parallels could be observed with Agnès Rocamora's astute argument on the centrality *La Parisienne* to French fashion in *Fashioning the City*, London: I.B. Tauris, 2009.

form of fashion features, fashion spreads, newspaper fashion reports or fashion advertisements" (Rocamora, 2009, 58).

As Rocamora argues, "fashion discourse" can be seen "as made up of statements that extend beyond the confines of the field and belong to various discursive formations […] fashion discourse overflows the limits of the field it unfolds in" (Rocamora, 2009, 57–8). This anthology could be read as mapping these "interwoven discourses," across the aforementioned geographical and temporal boundaries.

Reading fashion criticism across a little more than a century, it became evident how "fashion media discourse" overlapped with particular insistence with those surrounding constructions of gender, thus underscoring fashion's centrality to shifting gender roles. This already can be noted in the work of Oscar Wilde and Louise Norton, the latter of whom wrote as Dame Rogue (and later went by Louise Varèse). As early as 1915, Norton, writing in the avant-garde "little" magazine *Rogue*, invoked a unisex fashion, as she proclaimed "trousers, and other things, I hold to be mere arbitrary symbols of sex which I, for one, think obsolete" (April 15, 1915, 17–18).

Discussions of fashion and gender and in particular the shifting of women's social roles increase in frequency toward the end of the 1960s—a time of major cultural and social turmoil. This is also the time when "women's pages" of newspapers began to be transformed into "style sections" as a response to societal changes in gender roles. The changes heralded a relative improvement of the status of these sections, which were, at least theoretically, intended as lifestyle sections meant for a non-gender specific readership, and the fashion coverage within it.[5]

Particularly in the context of the United States, this is also the time that race begins to be discussed in conjunction with gender in fashion writings in the mainstream press. This seems to have been partially spurred by the phenomenon of the Ebony Fashion Fair: a traveling fashion shows started by Eunice Johnson—co-publisher of *Ebony*—which featured African-American models wearing the latest fashion. But it can also be tied to greater societal changes, chiefly the civil rights movement, and points to important intersections between race and gender at this particular historical moment. Unsurprisingly, this is also the time when the anti-discrimination lawsuits, which plagued major newspapers in the United States, start going through the courts (Mills, 1988, 149–73). In addition, *Essence*—a fashion and beauty magazine directed to African-American women, was launched around this time (1970). It is also in this period that Black models started to achieve greater prominence, as is the case with Pat Cleveland (see cover image). However, it is important to note that, as discussed by historian Noliwe Rooks, African-American women magazines covering fashion first appeared as early as the end of the nineteenth century, and thus concomitantly with the general expansion of the fashion press (Rooks, 2004).

The inextricability of discourses surrounding the role of women, femininity, and fashion, which transpires through this anthology, further underscores the extent to which fashion criticism was and still remains central to constructions of femininity and masculinity and played a central role in negotiating shifting gender roles. As Rocamora, after Foucault, argues, discourses are "'practices that systematically form the objects of which they speak.' Media discourses invest fashion—its products, practices and agents—with a variety of values whose 'truth' is as much part of the object of discourse as the material reality it refers to" (Rocamora, 2009, 56). Fashion

---

[5](Harp, 2006, 198). In 1969, *The Washington Post* transformed "For and about Women" into the "Style" section; in 1970, *The Los Angeles Times* introduced "View"; in 1971, *Chicago Tribune* began its section known as "Tempo" and *The New York Times* began its transition to the style pages in the late 1960s (Marzolf, 1977, 200–01; Mills, 1990, 118–19; Israel, 1993; Harp, 2006). *The New York Times* approached its transition to the "style" pages differently than other papers by initially "establishing five rotating sections, one for each day of the week" (Mills, 1990, 119).

criticism not only helped mediate the fashion ideals of those periods, but to the extent to which it was constantly intertwined with discourses outside its fields it produced "truths" surrounding gender, race, and a host of other identity categories. Fashion criticism thus occupied a central role in negotiating shifting gender roles but also shifting understandings of race. This further discredits a facile dismissal of fashion criticism as frivolous, but to the contrary places it in a central position within cultural criticism. Or, as Robin Givhan succinctly puts it: "This is an industry that tells us what is beautiful. And we place an incredible amount of value on beauty. So this is an industry that is helping us decide how much we value different groups of people. And if that's not important, then I am not sure what is" (Labrague, 17).

As the anthology shows, fashion media discourse also frequently interacts with that of politics. The dress practices and appearances of politicians and their spouses are extensively discussed as early as the 1950s by the fashion editor for *The Washington Evening Star*, Eleni Epstein, who wrote about the appearances and wardrobe choices of the Nixon and the Kennedy White House during her time at the Washington newspaper (Voss and Speere, 2013). This overlap between fashion and political discourse has notably increased in the last two decades, as can be observed in *The Washington Post,* where Givhan continued on Epstein's tradition of closely dissecting the clothing choices of those holding political power, while Vanessa Friedman at *The New York Times* has extensively written about the centrality of clothing to politicians' message.

This greater intersection of fashion and political discourse can be attributed to the ever-increasing mediatization of politics and the consequential centrality of image and appearances for politicians. As communication theorist Andreas Hepp explains, mediatization constitutes the molding force that the media exercise in areas well beyond its borders, such as politics. Processes of mediatization in politics have undoubtedly accelerated with the advent of digital media; however, as evident in the writing of Eleni Epstein, it predated them. As Hepp writes "mediatization did not just originate with the establishment of digital media, but is a longer term process" (Hepp, 2013, 31). A number of critics collected in this collection comment on the increased mediatization of the political sphere in the age of digital media, while contributing through their reporting to this process.

In addition, fashion itself from production to consumption is constantly changing through processes of mediatization. These changes have affected fashion criticism in a number of ways and can be clearly observed in the ways critics cover the fashion shows and the importance materiality of clothes occupies in their review. As Rocamora argues, processes of mediatization have transformed the fashion shows into a media event for the internet—first for blogs and then social media (Rocamora, 2017, 509–12). This change has affected the way the shows are covered, as their performative qualities are discussed at length alongside the actual garment. However, the spectacularization of the fashion show as a result of the progressive mediatization of the fashion industry predated the contemporary moment. As *New Yorker* critic Kennedy Fraser commented in 1977: "With all the theatrical fanfare that launches collections these days, how is one supposed to assess the curious hybrid that is the dramatic new fashion show?" (Fraser, 1977, 63).

The progressive lack of attention to the materiality of clothes in contemporary fashion criticism is widely discussed in the literature on fashion media. Media theorist Aurélie Van de Peer talks about a re-artification of fashion in her detailed study of show reviews from 1950 to 2010 in *The New York Times* and *The International Herald Tribune* (2014). This was corroborated by an earlier study of fashion writing in *Le Monde* and *The Guardian* by Rocamora (2001). Even though this shift in fashion media discourse could be read in connection to a desire to intellectualize one's object of criticism (Van de Peer, 2014), it can also be connected to the progressive speed of fashion production and dissemination, modes of circulation that are ill-fitted to the extensive material analysis of clothes, which was the cornerstone of earlier fashion criticism.

Detailed descriptions of garments were central to Lois Long's reviews in *The New Yorker* from the 1920s onward, a fact rendered even more necessary by the magazine's initial policy of not including photographs. Similar attention to garment details and fabric origin characterized the reviews of Eugenia Sheppard in the 1950s and 1960s. However, pockets of resistance to the dematerialization of fashion exist in contemporary fashion criticism, as with Guy Trebay's experiment to review the menswear collections, and suits in particular, by wearing them in his daily routine: a surprisingly rare instance of embodied criticism (2016: D6).

Finally, as the anthology moves into the twenty-first century, it mirrors the increasing transnational nature of the fashion industry, where the geographies of fashion are constantly being renegotiated. As Paul Du Gay writes, "as the link between territory and culture becomes more tenuous, design becomes an increasingly 'global' language, with practitioners in any given 'nation' drawing upon a range of signifiers from all over the world in their work" (Du Gay, 2013, 68). A similar shift has occurred in the media, including the fashion media, which has become progressively deterrrorialized—a process further precipitated by the global reach of digital media in the twenty-first century. "Communicative deterritorialization—Hepp writes—is related to the increased mediatization and globalization of media communication: Ever more media contents are available across diverse territories [...] aimed at a transnational public" (Hepp, 2013: 109).[6]

In conclusion, this anthology is but one of the possible tours and detours one can take in the rich and expanding field of fashion criticism. It is not meant to be exhaustive, its scope and breadth limited by the need for a manageable tome and by the maddening and seemingly arbitrary nature of copyrights laws and costs. What it is meant to be is clear evidence of the richness, diversity, and long history of fashion criticism providing a guided journey through some of the most compelling fashion writing produced over the past century.

Bibliography

Best, Kate Nelson. *The History of Fashion Journalism*. New York and London: Bloomsbury, 2017.

Breward, Christopher. "Femininity and Consumption: The Problem of the Late Nineteenth-Century Fashion Journal." *Journal of Design History*, vol. 7, no. 2 (1994): 71–89.

Carroll, Nöell. *On Criticism*. New York and London: Routledge, 2009.

Choi, Kyung-Hee and Van Dyk Lewis. "Inclusive System for Fashion Criticism." *International Journal of Fashion Design, Technology and Education*, vol. 11, no. 1 (2018): 12–21.

Cunningham, Bill. "The Collections." *Details*, September 1988: 185–283.

de Syrène, Maximilienne [Barbey d'Aurevilly]. First published in French as "Revue critique de la mode." *Le Constitutionnel* (September 1, 1845). Translated by Richard George Elliott, in Ulrich Lehman, ed. *Art in Translation*, vol. 7, no. 2 (2015): 186–99.

Du Gay, Paul, Stuart Hall, Linda Janes, Anders Koed Mdsen, Hugh Mackay, and Keith Negus. *Doing Cultural Studies: The Story of the Sony Walkman*. London: Sage Publications and the Open University, 2013.

---

[6]For an exemplary study of transnational fashion media, see Reina Lewis, *Muslim Fashion: Contemporary Style Culture* (Durham and London: Duke University Press, 2015) and, in particular, chapters 3 and 6.

Fortunato, Paul L. *Modernist Aesthetics and Consumer Culture in the Writings of Oscar Wilde*. New York and London: Routledge, 2007.

Frock Consciousness, LRB Collections, vol. 6. London: London Review of Books, 2019.

Granata, Francesca, ed. *Fashion Projects*, no. 4 (2013).

Granata, Francesca, ed. "Women's Work: An Interview with Judith Thurman." *Fashion Projects*, no. 4 (2013): 31–43.

Granata, Francesca, ed. "Fashioning Cultural Criticism: An Inquiry into Fashion Criticism and Its Delay in Legitimization." *Fashion Theory*, vol. 23, no. 4–5 (2019): 553–70.

Harp, Dustin. "Newspapers' Transition from Women's to Style Pages." *Journalism*, vol. 7, no. 2 (2006): 197–216.

Hepp, Andreas. *Cultures of Mediatization*. Cambridge, UK: Polity Press, 2013.

Israel, Betsy. "The Sexes: Pages of Their Own?" *The New York Times*, October 3, 1993.

Labrague, Michelle. "Fashion Criticism—A Critical View: An Interview with Robin Givhan." *Fashion Projects*, issue no. 4 (2013): 7–18.

Lewis, Reina. *Muslim Fashion: Contemporary Style Culture*. Durham and London: Duke University Press, 2015.

Library of America. n.d. Accessed June 8, 2017. https://www.loa.org/about.

"Lois Long Is Dead, Fashion Editor." *The New York Times*, July 31, 1974: 36.

Marzolf, Marion. *Up from the Footnote: A History of Women Journalists*. New York: Hastings House Publishers, 1977.

McNeil, Peter and Sanda Miller. *Fashion Writing and Criticism: History, Theory and Practice*. London and New York: Bloomsbury, 2014.

Mills, Kay. *A Place in the News: From the Women's Pages to the Front Pages*. New York: Columbia University Press, 1988.

Norton Louise (aka Dame Rogue). "Philosophic Fashion." *Rogue*, March 15, 1915; April 15, 1915.

The Pulitzer Prize. n.d. "Criticism." Accessed June 5, 2017. http://www.pulitzer.org/prize-winners-by-category/213

Rocamora, Agnès. "High Fashion and Pop Fashion: The Symbolic Production of Fashion in *Le Monde* and *The Guardian*." *Fashion Theory*, vol. 5, no. 2 (2001): 123–42.

Rocamora, Agnès. *Fashioning the City: Paris, Fashion and the Media*. London: I.B. Tauris, 2009.

Rocamora, Agnès. "Mediatization and Digital Media in the Field of Fashion." *Fashion Theory*, vol. 21, no. 5 (2017): 502–22.

Rooks, Noliwe M. *Ladies' Pages: African American Women's Magazines and the Culture That Made Them*. New Brunswick and London: Rutgers University Press, 2004.

Ruttenberg, Jay. "This Is Not a Fashion Critic: An Interview with Guy Trebay." *Fashion Projects*, issue no. 4 (2013): 19–30.

Svendsen, Lars. "On Fashion Criticism." In *Philosophical Perspectives on Fashion*. Edited by Giovanni Matteucci and Stefano Marino. London and New York: Bloomsbury, 2016.

Tebbel, John and Mary Ellen Zuckerman. *The Magazine in America 1741–1990*. New York and Oxford: Oxford University Press, 1991.

Titton, Monica. "Fashion Criticism Unravelled: A Sociological Critique of Criticism in Fashion Media." *International Journal of Fashion Studies*, vol. 3, no. 2 (2016): 209–23.

Trebay, Guy. "One Man, Five Designers." *The New York Times*, January 7, 2016: D6.

Van de Peer, Aurélie. "Re-artification in a World of De-artification: Materiality and Intellectualization in Fashion Media Discourse (1949–2010)." *Cultural Sociology*, vol. 8, no. 4 (2014): 443–61.

Voss, Kimberly Wilmot. *Re-Evaluating Women's Page Journalism in the Post-World War II Era: Celebrating Soft News*. Cham, Switzerland: Palgrave Macmillan, 2018.

Voss, Kimberly Wilmot and Lance Speere. "Fashion as Washington Journalism History: Eleni Epstein and Her Three Decades at the *Washington Star*." *Media History Monographs*, vol. 16, no. 3 (2013): 1–22.

PART I

Late Nineteenth Century–1960s

Introduction to PART I

The anthology opens with "Mr. Oscar Wilde on Woman's Dress," which Oscar Wilde (1854–1900) published in *The Pall Mall Gazette* in 1884. The article reiterates Wilde's philosophy of dress, which he had already articulated in his well-received lecture "Dress." Prior to his journalistic career, the legendary raconteur had delivered popular lectures mainly for audiences of middle-class women on topics such as "House Beautiful," "The Decorative Arts," and dress across the United States and the UK (Fortunato, 2007, 19). *The Pall Mall Gazette* had covered one of these lectures, inciting significant reader response, which, in turn, prompted Wilde's article here included (Stokes and Turner, 2013, 228).

Clearly informed by the Dress Reform movement and ideas underpinning the Rational Dress Society, Wilde extols the benefit of simplifying both men's and women's dress in the name of greater functionality and advocates for an end to the use of corsetry and heels for women. This discourse is taken up and further explained in the women's magazine *The Woman's World,* which the Irish author edited between 1887 and 1889.

Wilde was ambivalent about fashion, a view perhaps best encapsulated in his November 1887 editorial that included the now-famous dictum: "And after all, what is fashion? From the artistic point of view, it is usually a form of ugliness so intolerable that we have to alter it every six months" (Wilde, 1887, 40). But he clearly understood the importance of fashion and the need to take it seriously, advocating for not only a new fashion for a new woman, but also the importance to closely chronicle it.

As Wilde scholar Paul Fortunato argues, the writer advanced "a consumer modernism," as his focus on the ephemeral, the feminine, and the ornamental is an attempt at decentering the Western subject:

Wilde takes up these elements, surface, image, and ritual, all as a strategy to force us to reconceptualize our ideas on culture and art. That is, he elevates the marginalized elements—things gendered feminine, considered as bodily rather than rational and often marked as Oriental—in order to de-center the Western rationalist, masculinist subject. (Fortunato, 2007, IX)

Fittingly, the second author included in the anthology is a Wilde acolyte, Louise Norton (1890–1989), who wrote about fashion in *Rogue,* a Dada-influenced New York avant-garde literary magazine that published in 1915 and 1916. *Rogue,* with its title a pun on *Vogue,* was a so-called "little." As the term suggests, the little magazine was a literary magazine with a small circulation. The genre had its heyday in the 1920s and was known to publish artistic and literary work, often aligned with the avant-garde, and thus deemed too daring for a mass magazine audience (Tebbel and Zuckermann, 1991, 217).[1] *Rogue* was started by Norton and her husband Allen Norton, and as argued by literary scholar Jay Bochner, it was steeped in the new advances made by women, taking for granted "the voting, smoking and corsetless woman" (Bochner, 2007, 50).

Norton's witty column "Philosophic Fashions" underlined the importance of fashion, much as Wilde had done. Norton comments on how "Fashion may be to some 'fickle, frail and flighty.' But there are those to whom the rise and fall of petticoats is as momentous as the fluctuations of the market" (March 15, 1915, 17). The fact that Norton quotes the Irish author in her column and is undoubtedly influenced by Wilde's witty writing is evidence of the emergence of a discourse of fashion criticism in the English language.

Another theme that transpires in Norton's column and harks back to Wilde's fashion writing is a call for the end of corsetry and for a unisex fashion. While Wilde had predicted that fashion in the twentieth century would "emphasise distinctions of occupations, not distinctions of sex" (Wilde, 1887, 40), Norton, going a step further, advocates for an "undoing" of gendered fashion:

> But how charming after all, when men grow dainty and women daring! To-day might and to-morrow *will* bring such miracles to pass. Definitions are losing something of their definiteness. Sex is a technicality [...] There are men who wear their hair long; there are women who wear their hair short; and yet there are those who still say, 'a man's a man for a' that!' Trousers and other things I hold to be mere arbitrary symbols of sex which I, for one, think obsolete. (Norton, 1915, 18)

Joy Bochner, writing about Norton's column, defines its nature as "essentially feminine and, for the period, feminist" (Bochner, 2007, 54). Counteracting what he sees as a lack of serious engagement with her work, he claims that in the pages of *Rogue,* one finds "a modernism almost entirely produced by women and perhaps their very ability to be modern was sufficiently doubted as to make their commitment appear without great value" (Bochner, 2007, 49).

Less radical, but equally witty is the fashion criticism penned by Lois Long (1901–1974) in the pages of *The New Yorker.* Long was one of *The New Yorker*'s original staff members, and as early as 1925 wrote a column on nightlife in New York titled "Table for Two" under the pseudonym "Lipstick," as well as one focused on fashion, beauty, and shopping titled "Feminine Fashions," which was signed with her initials. Long epitomized the humorous tone that characterized *The New Yorker* of the 1920s while advancing the discourse on fashion in journalism. In the words of the influential *New Yorker* editor William Shawn, Long "was the first American fashion critic to approach fashion as an art and to criticize women's clothes with independence, humor and literary style" (*The New York Times,* 1974).

Long wrote her column in a user-friendly manner, most often reviewing the French collections only once they arrived in American stores. She did not shy away from criticizing well-known designers in her witty tone, which belied a true understanding of fashion and clothing constructions through a detailed analysis. Writing about the French collections in the Fall of 1927, she did not spare criticism for two of the best-known designers of the time, Coco Chanel and Jean Patou:

---

[1] Tebbel and Zuckermann argue that *The New Yorker* in part proved that these qualities could eventually be found beyond the little, 219.

In the first place, I was disappointed in most of the Patous. The little sweater with three colored stripes around the bottom [...] is all very well, but not very new. The same is true of the Chanel daytime things [...]. Having made a success last year with boleros, belts, pleatings low in the skirts, and tuckings, Mme. Chanel apparently has decided to let well enough alone [...]. My advice is to go slow before paying exorbitant prices for copies, when you undoubtedly have something a good deal like them already at home. (Long, 1927, 60)

Like her predecessors, she often writes about fashion in the context of women's lives, bemoaning the impracticality for working women like her to get custom-fitted clothes which require a great deal of time for repeated fittings, lauding instead the ready-made (March 11, 1933, 48). Long did not regularly travel to Paris to cover the collections. In fact, for a short time in the late 1920s Elizabeth Hawes (1903–1971), later renowned as an innovative American designer, would actually file occasional articles about the Paris fashion shows for *The New Yorker* under the pseudonym "Parasite."

This anthology includes excerpts from Hawes's later writings published in her 1938 collection *Fashion Is Spinach*. Part ethnography, part memoir, the book includes a humorous first-person account of her work as a copyist for a Parisian copy house and of her work as a fashion critic for US publications in Paris, where she had moved shortly after graduating from college. The latter article provided a self-reflective account of what it meant to be a fashion critic in the 1920s and of the difficulties in delivering unvarnished criticism. Singling out *The New Yorker,* Hawes writes: "Anyone who has ever written fashions will, I am sure, appreciate what it means to be allowed to write with no embroidery just what you think about them." To which she adds more explicitly, "The advertising department never raised its ugly head and said that if I thought Patou was no designer, I'd better keep still about it or someone would withdraw its advertising" (Hawes, 1938, 77).

An equally unsparing critical voice was that of Eugenia Sheppard (1900–1984), who started covering fashion in 1940 for *The New York Herald Tribune* (renamed *The World Journal Tribune* in 1966) until the paper folded in 1967. Her column "Inside Fashion" was widely read and highly influential. An outspoken chronicler of post-war fashion, Sheppard provided unsparing accounts of the period's fashion, which in her user-friendly language and descriptive details are reminiscent of Long's criticism.

Further highlighting the existence of a thriving fashion media discourse, Sheppard discusses Elizabeth Hawes's work and her views on fashion in connection to an exhibition of Rudi Gernreich and Hawes at the Brooklyn Museum. Written in 1967, the article, titled "A Mini for Men," praises Hawes's prescient views on women's fashion, which she introduced through her writing and collections in the 1930s, while commenting on the changes to come in menswear.

The last critic to be included in this section of the anthology is Eleni Epstein (1926–1991), the fashion editor for the now-defunct *Washington Evening Star*. Another important chronicler of American post-war fashion, she became the fashion editor at *The Star* in 1948, where she remained in the role until the paper's closing in 1981 (Levy, 1991). Epstein turned being based in Washington, and thus away from New York—America's undisputed fashion center—into an asset, as she covered the local fashion scene alongside the dress of politicians and their spouses (Voss and Speere, 2013). An early awareness of the importance of dress to politics is evident in Epstein's work: a short article she wrote on occasion of the 1968 presidential election describes the most effective ties candidates should wear for various campaign events. An early articulation of the increasing mediatization of fashion and politics, which will inform fashion criticism in the twenty-first century, the article goes as far as discussing the need for accounting for the persistence of black-and-white TV sets in the late 1960s in the choice of candidate's ties.

Bibliography and Further Readings

Best, Kate Nelson. *The History of Fashion Journalism*. New York and London: Bloomsbury, 2017.

Bochner, Jay. "The Marriage of *Rogue* and *The Soil*." In *Little Magazines and Modernism*. Edited by Suzanne W. Churchill and Adam McKible. New York and London: Routledge, 2007.

Fortunato, Paul L. *Modernist Aesthetics and Consumer Culture in the Writings of Oscar Wilde*. New York and London: Routledge, 2007.

Granata, Francesca. "Fashioning Cultural Criticism: An Inquiry into Fashion Criticism and Its Delay in Legitimization." *Fashion Theory*, vol. 23, no. 4–5 (2019): 553–70.

Hawes, Elizabeth. *Fashion Is Spinach*. New York: Random House, 1938.

Levy, Claudia. "Eleni Sakes Epstein, Star Fashion Editor, Dies." *The Washington Post*, January 29, 1991.

"Lois Long Is Dead, Fashion Editor." *The New York Times*, July 31, 1974: 36.

Long, Lois. "Feminine Fashions. *The New Yorker*, September 10, 1927: 60–22.

McNeil, Peter and Sanda Miller. *Fashion Writing and Criticism: History, Theory and Practice*. London and New York: Bloomsbury, 2014.

Norton, Louise [Dame Rogue]. "Philosophic Fashions: Trouser Talk." *Rogue*, April 15, 1915: 15–18.

Stokes, John and Mark Turner. *The Complete Works of Oscar Wilde*. New York and Oxford: Oxford University Press, 2013.

Tebbel, John and Mary Ellen Zuckerman. *The Magazine in America 1741–1990*. New York and Oxford: Oxford University Press, 1991.

Voss, Kimberly Wilmot and Lance Speere. "Fashion as Washington Journalism History: Eleni Epstein and Her Three Decades at the *Washington Star*." *Media History Monographs*, vol. 16, no. 3 (2013–2014): 1–22.

Wilde, Oscar. "Literary and Other Notes." *The Woman's World, November 1887*.

Zeitz, Joshua. *Flapper: A Madcap Story of Sex, Style, Celebrity, and the Women Who Made America Modern*. New York: Broadway Books, 2006.

1

Mr. Oscar Wilde on Woman's Dress

Oscar Wilde

The Pall Mall Gazette, 1884

Mr. Oscar Wilde, who asks us to permit him "that most charming of all pleasures, the pleasure of answering one's critics," sends us the following remarks:-

The "Girl Graduate" must of course have precedence, not merely for her sex, but for her sanity; her letter is extremely sensible. She makes two points: that high heels are a necessity for any lady who wishes to keep her dress clean from the Stygian mud of our streets, and that without a tight corset "the ordinary number of petticoats and etceteras" cannot be properly or conveniently held up. Now it is quite true that as long as the lower garments are suspended from the hips, a corset is an absolute necessity; the mistake lies in not suspending all apparel from the shoulders. In the latter case a corset becomes useless, the body is left free and unconfined for respiration and motion, there is more health, and consequently more beauty. Indeed, all the most ungainly and uncomfortable articles of dress that fashion has ever in her folly prescribed, not the tight corset merely, but the farthingale, the vertugadin, the hoop, the crinoline, and that modern monstrosity the so-called "dress improver" also, all of them have owed their origin to the same error, the error of not seeing that it is from the shoulders, and from the shoulders only, that all garments should be hung.

And as regards high heels, I quite admit that some additional height to the shoe or boot is necessary if long gowns are to be worn in the street; but what I object to is that the height should be given to the heel only, and not to the sole of the foot also. The modern high-heeled boot is, in fact, merely the clog of the time of Henry VI., with the front prop left out, and its inevitable effect is to throw the body forward, to shorten the steps, and consequently to produce that want of grace which always follows want of freedom. Why should clogs be despised.? Much art has been expended on clogs. They have been made of lovely woods, and delicately inlaid with ivory, and with mother of pearl. A clog might be a dream of beauty, and, if not too high or too heavy, most comfortable also. But if there be any who do not like clogs, let them try some adaptation of the trouser of the Turkish lady, which is loose round the limb, and tight at the ankle. The "Girl Graduate," with a pathos to which I am not insensible, entreats me not to apotheosize "that awful, befringed, beflounced, and bekilted divided skirt." Well, I will acknowledge that the fringes, the flounces, and the kilting do certainly defeat the whole object of the dress, which is that of ease and liberty; but I regard these things as mere wicked superfluities, tragic proofs that the divided skirt is ashamed of its own division. The principle of the dress is good, and, though it is not by any means perfection, it is a step towards it. Here I leave the "Girl Graduate," with much regret, for Mr. Wentworth Huyshe. Mr. Huyshe makes the old criticism that Greek dress is unsuited to our climate, and the, to me, somewhat new assertion that the men's dress of a hundred years ago was preferable to that of the second part of the seventeenth century, which I consider to have been the exquisite period of English costume. Now, as regards the first of these two statements, I will say, to begin with, that the warmth of apparel does not really depend on the number of garments worn, but on the material of which they are made. One of the chief faults of modern dress is that it is composed of far too many articles of clothing, most of which are of the wrong substance; but over a substratum of pure wool, such as is supplied by Dr. Jaeger under the modern German system, some modification of Greek costume is perfectly applicable to our climate, our country, and our century. This important fact has been already pointed out by Mr. E. W. Godwin in his excellent, though too brief, handbook on Dress, contributed to the Health Exhibition. I call it an important fact because it makes almost any form of lovely costume perfectly practicable in our cold climate. Mr. Godwin, it is true, points out that the English ladies of the thirteenth century abandoned after some time the flowing garments of the early Renaissance in favour of a tighter mode, such as northern Europe seems to demand. This I quite admit, and its significance; but what I contend, and what I am sure Mr. Godwin would agree with me in, is that the principles, the laws of Greek dress, may be perfectly realized, even in a moderately tight gown with sleeves: I mean the principle of suspending all apparel from the shoulders, and of relying for beauty of effect, not on the stiff ready-made ornaments of the modern milliner—the bows where there should be no bows, and the flounces where there should be no flounces—but on the exquisite play of light and line that one gets from rich and rippling folds. I am not proposing any antiquarian revival of an ancient costume, but trying merely to point out the right laws of dress, laws which are dictated by art and not by archaeology, by science and not by fashion; and just as the best work of art in our days is that which combines classic grace with absolute reality, so from a combination of the Greek principles of beauty with the German principles of health will come, I feel certain, the costume of the future.

And now to the question of men's dress, or rather to Mr. Huyshe's claim of the superiority, in point of costume, of the last quarter of the eighteenth century over the second quarter of the seventeenth. The broad-brimmed hat of 1640 kept the rain of winter and the glare of summer from the face; the same cannot be said of the hat of one hundred years ago, which, with its comparatively narrow brim and high crown, was the precursor of the modern "chimney-pot": a wide turned-down collar is a healthier thing than a strangling stock, and a short cloak much more comfortable than a sleeved overcoat, even though the latter may have had "three capes:" a cloak is easier to put on and off, lies lightly on the shoulder in summer, and, wrapped round one in winter, keeps one perfectly warm. A doublet, again, is simpler than a coat and waistcoat; instead of two garments we have one; by not being open, also, it protects the chest better. Short loose trousers are in every way to be preferred to the tight knee-breeches which often impede the proper circulation of the blood; and, finally, the soft leather boots, which could be worn above or below the knee, are more supple, and give consequently more freedom, than the stiff Hessian which Mr. Huyshe so praises. I say nothing about the question of grace and picturesqueness, for I suppose that no one, not even Mr. Huyshe, would prefer a macaroni to a cavalier, a Lawrence to a Vandyke, or the third George to the first Charles; but for ease, warmth, and comfort this seventeenth-century dress is infinitely superior to anything that came after it, and I do not think it is excelled by any preceding form of costume. I sincerely trust that we may soon see in England some national revival of it.

2

Literary and Other Notes (excerpt)

Oscar Wilde

The Woman's World, November 1887

It is, however, not merely in fiction and in poetry that the women of this century are making their mark. Their appearance amongst the prominent speakers at the Church Congress some weeks ago was in itself a very remarkable proof of the growing influence of women's opinions on all matters connected with the elevation of our national life, and the amelioration of our social conditions. When the Bishops left the platform to their wives, it may be said that a new era began, and the change will no doubt be productive of much good. The Apostolic dictum, that women should not be suffered to teach, is no longer applicable to a society such as ours, with its solidarity of interests, its recognition of natural rights, and its universal education, however suitable it may have been to the Greek cities under Roman rule. Nothing in the United States struck me more than the fact that the remarkable intellectual progress of that country is very largely due to the efforts of American women, who edit many of the most powerful magazines and newspapers, take part in the discussion of every question of public interest, and exercise an important influence upon the growth and tendencies of literature and art. Indeed, the women of America are the one class in the community that enjoys that leisure which is so necessary for culture. The men are, as a rule, so absorbed in business, that the task of bringing some element of form into the chaos of daily life is left almost entirely to the opposite sex, and an eminent Bostonian once assured me that in the twentieth century the whole culture of his country would be in petticoats. By that time, however, it is probable that the dress of the two sexes will be assimilated, as similarity of costume always follows similarity of pursuits.

In a recent article in *La France,* M. Sarcey puts this point very well. The further we advance, he says, the more apparent does it become that women are to take their share as bread-winners in the world. The task is no longer monopolised by men, and will, perhaps, be equally shared by the sexes in another hundred years. It will be necessary, however, for women to invent a suitable costume, as their present style of dress is quite inappropriate to any kind of mechanical labour, and must be radically changed before they can compete with men upon their own ground. As to the question of desirability, M. Sarcey refuses to speak. "I shall not see the end of this revolution," he remarks, "and I am glad of it." But, as is pointed out in a very sensible article in the *Daily News,* there is no doubt that M. Sarcey has reason and common sense on his side with regard to the absolute unsuitability of ordinary feminine attire to any sort of handicraft, or even to any occupation which necessitates a daily walk to business and back again in all kinds of weather. Women's dress can easily be modified and adapted to any exigencies of the kind; but most women refuse to modify or adapt it. They must follow the fashion, whether it be convenient or the reverse. And, after all, what is a fashion? From the artistic point of view, it is usually a form of ugliness so intolerable that we have to alter it every six months. From the point of view of science, it not unfrequently violates every law of health, every principle of hygiene. While from the point of view of simple ease and comfort, it is not too much to say that, with the exception of M. Félix's charming tea-gowns, and a few English tailor-made costumes, there is not a single form of really fashionable dress that can be worn without a certain amount of absolute misery to the wearer. The contortion of the feet of the Chinese beauty, said Dr. Naftel at the last International Medical Congress, held at Washington, is no more barbarous or unnatural than the panoply of the *femme du monde.*

And yet how sensible is the dress of the London milkwoman, of the Irish or Scotch fishwife, of the North-country factory-girl! An attempt was made recently to prevent the pit-women from working, on the ground that their costume was unsuited to their sex, but it is really only the idle classes who dress badly. Wherever physical labour of any kind is required, the costume used is, as a rule, absolutely right, for labour necessitates freedom, and without freedom there is no such thing as beauty in dress at all. In fact, the beauty of dress depends on the beauty of the human figure, and whatever limits, constrains, and mutilates is essentially ugly, though the eyes of many are so blinded by custom that they do not notice the ugliness till it has become unfashionable.

What women's dress will be in the future it is difficult to say. The writer of the *Daily News* article is of opinion that skirts will always be worn as distinctive of the sex, and it is obvious that men's dress, in its present condition, is not by any means an example of a perfectly rational costume. It is more than probable, however, that the dress of the twentieth century will emphasise distinctions of occupation, not distinctions of sex.

Literary and Other Notes (excerpt)

Oscar Wilde

The Woman's World, December 1887

Miss Leffler-Arnim's statement, in a lecture delivered recently at St. Saviour's Hospital, that "she had heard of instances where ladies were so determined not to exceed the fashionable measurement that they had actually held on to a cross-bar while their maids fastened the fifteen-inch corset," has excited a good deal of incredulity, but there is nothing really improbable in it. From the sixteenth century to our own day there is hardly any form of torture that has not been inflicted on girls, and endured by women, in obedience to the dictates of an unreasonable and monstrous Fashion. "In order to obtain a real Spanish figure," says Montaigne, "what a Gehenna of suffering will not women endure, drawn in and compressed by great *coches* entering the flesh; nay, sometimes they even die thereof!" "A few days after my arrival at school," Mrs. Somerville tells us in her memoirs, "although perfectly straight and well made, I was enclosed in stiff stays, with a steel busk in front; while above my frock, bands drew my shoulders back till the shoulder-blades met. Then a steel rod with a semicircle, which went under my chin, was clasped to the steel busk in my stays. In this constrained state I and most of the younger girls had to prepare our lessons"; and in the life of Miss Edgeworth we read that, being sent to a certain fashionable establishment, "she underwent all the usual tortures of back-boards, iron collars and dumbs, and also (because she was a very tiny person) the unusual one of being hung by the neck to draw out the muscles and increase the growth," a signal failure in her case. Indeed, instances of absolute mutilation and misery are so common in the past that it is unnecessary to multiply them; but it is really sad to think that in our own day a civilised woman can hang on to a cross-bar while her maid laces her waist into a fifteen-inch circle. To begin with, the waist is not a circle at all, but an oval; nor can there be any greater error than to imagine that an unnaturally small waist gives an air of grace, or even of slightness to the whole figure. Its effect, as a rule, is to simply exaggerate the width of the shoulders and the hips; and those whose figures possess that statetliness, which is called stoutness by the vulgar, convert what is a quality into a defect by yielding to the silly edicts of Fashion on the subject of tight-lacing. The fashionable English waist, also, is not merely far too small, and consequently quite out of proportion to the rest of the figure, but it is worn far too low down. I use the expression "worn" advisedly, for a waist nowadays seems to be regarded as an article of apparel to be put on when and where one likes. A long waist always implies shortness of the lower limbs, and from the artistic point of view has the effect of diminishing the height; and I am glad to see that many of the most charming women in Paris are returning to the idea of the Directoire style of dress. This style is not by any means perfect, but at least it has the merit of indicating the proper position of the waist. I feel quite sure that all English women of culture and position will set their faces against such stupid and dangerous practices as are related by Miss Leffler-Arnim. Fashion's motto is, *Il faut souffrir pour être belle;* but the motto of art and of common sense is, *Il faut être bête pour souffrir.*

Talking of Fashion, a critic in the *Pall Mall Gazette* expresses his surprise that I should have allowed an illustration of a hat, covered with "the bodies of dead birds," to appear in the first number of THE WOMAN'S WORLD; and as I have received many letters on the subject, it is only right that I should state my exact position in the matter. Fashion is such an essential part of the *mundus muliebris* of our day that it seems to me absolutely necessary that its growth, development, and phases should be duly chronicled; and the historical and practical value of such a record depends entirely upon its perfect fidelity to fact. Besides, it is quite easy for the children of light to adapt almost any fashionable form of dress to the requirements of utility and the demands of good taste. The Sarah Bernhardt tea-gown, for instance, figured in the present issue, has many good points about it, and the gigantic dress-improver does not appear to me to be really essential to the mode; and though the Postillion costume of the fancy dress ball is absolutely detestable in its silliness and vulgarity, the so-called Late Georgian costume in the same plate is rather pleasing. I must, however, protest against the idea that to chronicle the development of Fashion implies any approval of the particular forms that Fashion may adopt.

3

Philosophic Fashions: Who Fell Asleep on the King's Highway?

Dame Rogue [Louise Norton]

Rogue, March 15, 1915

There was an old woman, as I've heard tell,
She went to the market her eggs for to sell;
She went to the market all on a market-day,
And she fell asleep on the king's highway.

There came along a peddler whose name was Stout,
Her cut her petticoats all round about;
He cut her petticoats up to her knees,
Which made the old woman to shiver and sneeze.

When this little woman first did wake,
She began to shiver and she began to shake;
She began to wonder and she began to cry,
"Oh, deary, deary me, this is none of I!"

"But if it be I as I do hope it be,
I've a little dog at home and he'll know me;
If it be I he'll wag his little tail,
And if it be not I, he'll loudly bark and wail."

Home went the old woman all in the dark,
Up got the little dog and he began to bark;
He began to bark and she began to cry
"Oh, deary, deary me, this is none of I!"

Now, who, I should like to know, has in these later days been falling asleep on the king's highway and has ever since then been going about with dresses up to her knees?

Who is she?

She is not old, that is certain, for she does not shiver and sneeze, but bravely walks bare-legged, or nearly, through the snowdrifts of Fifth Avenue, saying softly, "Dearie, dearie, dearie, here is *more* of I."

She is not young, at least not very. No woman under the mid-twenties is clever enough to make a virtue of a fall. And the persona dramatis was egoist enough to set a fashion. It must have been one of those well-known "women of thirty." It is at thirty a woman begins to dress so as to distract attention from her face, which in the early twenties was her only fortune. At twenty a woman is pretty and female, at thirty smart and feminine.

At least she is not a prude. To be certain of this denial you need only to glance at the dyspeptic dresses of prim women. They, like the Queen of Spain, apparently have no legs. But modesty is a variable, very much like beauty. It changes with modernity and is altered by geography. As for legs—they come and go. Sometimes they are taboo, and dresses are long. Again, as now, they are simply conventionalized ornamental flourishes to somewhat retroussé costumes. As to our lady of the street, who has brought ankles *in* again, one sure deduction is that; old or young, she has and knows she has, in the well-worn phrase of our fathers, a well-turned ankle. However, it would appear that it is the cubically counted quantity of displayed person that counts. For any portion newly undraped by fashion, some other bodily feature is forthwith veiled. Thus, now that legs are *in,* necks and arms are going *out* (for streetwear, at least). Sleeves often cover half the hand and collars ascend to the ears—ears which, by the way, are no longer "naked" when worn, so to speak, outside. On the other hand, oh, the immodesty of hats! For instance, the newest pancake styles—have you seen the bright bit of a thing shining through a window in the upper Avenue West, Hindoo-blue and yellow, yellow brighter than even yellow usually dares to be?—these, cocked on one side of the head, leave the hair on the other quite, quite nude. Of course there are veils. They can't be said to hide much, for they are of a transparency, but with their contrasting, flaring bindings of black and white, and I predict, other colors soon, they succeed in distracting the eye from the shamelessly acknowledged hair.

Yet, there may, after all, be something in all this scandal, less accidental or mischievous or vain, than commercial. Fashion may be to some "fickle, frail and flighty." But there are those to whom the rise and fall of petticoats is as momentous as the fluctuations of the market. Think of the psychological capitalists who may be behind this song of a skirt, great minds who understand how to turn feminine failings into masculine millions. This modern Mr. Stout of the Shears, was he not possibly an agent for a trust of dress manufacturers and retailers who, in a panic over the widening circumference of the new skirt, hit upon the above ingenious scheme for reducing the yards of cloth requisite to their making. For the prices of custom-made dresses cannot successfully vary, with the varying width of skirts. It is a curious fact that in the years of our hobbles, dresses were valued as high as they are now in these days of near-hoop. Why? Surely it means that one year the confectioners of gowns suffer and the material manufacturers the next. Undoubtedly they have arranged it between them so that profit swings like the pendulum of a clock—from hoop to hobble, back and forth. Even our highway heroine may not be altogether disinterested.

Perhaps she is a shoemaker's daughter, wife, mother, or "affinity." For as skirts have grown shorter, boots have grown higher—yes, and they have grown *higher,* too! Twenty-five dollars for a pair of those *mousquetaire* boots in Cammeyer's Avenue window, that all of us want and few of us buy! For there is a war abroad and a six-cent loaf at home. We must remember our Belgians and our babies. But there are other shoes, less tall and less high, and almost as chic with lacings any place, up the front, up the back, up the sides—and always and mostly and everywhere there is the spat. Oh, ye ubiquitous white spats! The cubist when he paints a portrait of a woman, paints his memory image of her: a woman getting into a hansom—bulging blueness, a black silk ankle, a horse's tail. If I were a cubist painter my portrait of the woman of today, or any particular woman seen on the street this winter, would be the portrait of a pair of white spats. Have you noticed the Quaker pose of men's eyes these days? Are they really shy or only counting their fortunes on the buttons of your spats?

4

Philosophic Fashions: Trouser-Talk (excerpt)

Dame Rogue [Louise Norton]

Rogue, April 15, 1915

"Man is properly the only object that interests man." – Goethe

Men are such slim creatures these days—even the fat ones. The thin ones look like well-bred eels and the fat ones like well-filled air cushions. I must say they are charming things, some of them, with their narrow-hipped coats, their gloved shoulder blades and their tipped-up tight trousers, outlining ever so discreetly those most lovely of masculine features, the masculine calves! All this is as it should be, but there are other things that are not.

Now it has been man's habit, ever since the day Eve first affected the fig leaf, to make sport of feminine fashions and especially to ridicule the discomforts which ladies endure in the name of—*La Mode. "Il faut souffrir pour être belle"* is axiomatic. But come wonder with me for a moment why no one has been able to comment out of fashion the torturing costume which men have worn these (I'm not good at figures, so say vaguely), these many years. I ask you, are collars more comfortable than corsets? There used to be separate cuffs too! ! ! And shirt fronts (wasn't it Shaw who christened them, "shields of respectability"?) that were wont to squeak like old palmetto trees in the wind! That is over now, thank God! Collars and cuffs are allowed to be soft, and shirts to pleat themselves into millions of dear little tucks and to remain unstarched at the stiffest function. But, alas! masculine clothes-reform advances somewhat after the fashion of the Allies. In spite of the agitation started some years ago to whitewash the character of masculine shirtwaists so that they could be worn abroad without bringing a blush to the sensitive cheek of Mrs. Grundy, coats are still universally worn in and out of doors and season. Men so like sheep in conventionality are just as like donkeys when the goose-step is changed.

No wonder shirts are not more amusing than they are; one sees so little of them except behind plate-glass or "on the jolly wash-line." Why, even a peacock would not spread his tail under a cloak! The story of the ostrich is here reversed; it is as though the "foolish little ostrich" were to sit on his tail feathers to attract admiration. Yet how delightful shirts *have been* in the days of wigs, wags and duels! Then, although as conventionally suppressed quotidianly, they more often were seen because of the modishness of duelling. Recall pictures, *many* pictures, you have seen of two posturing, rapiered gentlemen in blouses and knee-breeches so dainty and debonair as to make any woman as well as envy, as adore. Remember the delicacy of the fabric as it blouses over the satin waist-band and billows from the shoulder to the hand; recollect the coquetry and gallantry of the ruffles at the wrist and the luxury of the lace cascade at the throat. Birlady, 'twould be almost as delicate and discriminating a thing to love such a man as to love the finest lady in the land! For indeed a woman must get most or all of her aesthetic pleasure in love out of the images of her own exquisiteness that her lover in his repetitions keeps ever before her, as the pool holds Narcissus' face up to Narcissus; so that, although in love with a man, a dainty woman of taste does not become careless of in any way coarsened by the contact with his grosser cloth and clay.

Not only do I quarrel with coats that cover shirts and with shirts for their merely negative niceness, but with collars, too, even the reformed ones, because they conceal that detail of the human anatomy which I, for lack of a physiological word, call the *beauty-spot*—that hollow shadowed by the chin that is to the neck what the eyes are to the face and water to a landscape. There is, however, a kind of approvable modesty in the high collar for men. For shame is the acknowledgment of ugliness, and modesty its concealing, so that it was, no doubt, to hide their *Adam's Apples* that men's collars were, in the first instance, cut high. Although it remains an unrecorded legend why the apple stuck in *Adam's* throat and not in *Eve's*.

In those same, aforementioned pictures of the eighteenth century, look behind the parties of the first part and you will see more obscure figures in the loveliest draperies. They, too, are men! Men in cloaks, graceful, although grave. I used to wish that I might have been born in that era when even *men* had taste. "Then Carlo came," as he did in Patagonia, and Broadway smiled (always, when Broadway is uncertain, Broadway smiles), to see him come in the many folds of a military cape out of Italy, buckled with a silver clasp. And when Carlo came again from the shores of the Adriatic he published the fact that, although perhaps in New York it was not noticeable enough to do so, in Venice, at least, he did what the Venetians do and wore their shirts. Such shirts! The collars do just what I said collars *should* do.

As for trousers …. There is so much to say about trousers that I dare not say about them. But this I dare to say, *although the truth,* that trousers make unduly conspicuous the comical bifurcation of man which deformity philosophers and poets have ridiculed ever since the gods made men to be their playthings and court fools; but, surely, now that man is greater than the gods and *privileged* to wear clothes of his *own* design, he should really do something to show himself less absurd. Plato said, "Man is a two-legged animal without feathers." Swift called him, "a forked, straddling animal with bandy legs," and someone else, it might have been Dryden, likened him to "a forked radish with head fantastically carved." More unpleasant still is Herr Teufelsdröckh's definition of man in *Sartor Resartus,* "an omnivorous Biped that wears Breeches," and Montaigne said—what Montaigne said of trousers you may read in the third book of his essays, the fifth chapter, entitled *Upon Some Verses, of Virgil!* Yet, on the other hand, as Homer Croy says, "trousers *are* handy," —sometimes.

Some nations have recognized the awkwardness and vulgarity of trousers. The Scot, who has never been accused of anything worse than virtue and absolute virility, has always worn the kilt; and I read, only a week or so ago, in one of our nice, gossipy Sunday sheets (well up in the Scandal of prehistoric times) that, "the soldiers of Assyrian kings are said to have worn a sort of kilt, while the mountaineers of the Balkans regard it as indispensable" —whether because they thought it decenter or more aesthetic, was not stated.

On the side of the aesthetics there is much to be said for the skirts in preference to trousers as between a mermaid and a terrestrial woman what man, or at least what artist, would pause to choose; though I own that a mere man a mermaid *might* puzzle! Legs seem ironically to ally us to the Colossus of Rhodes and all the animals. They suggest the utilitarian or the monstrous and always the grotesque. I could become reconciled to legs—I could even forget that *legs is legs*—if clothed in knee-breeches. The curves of the calf would then give the needed punctuation to the leg and pause to the eye. Sportsmen, even *English* sportsmen, I adore and *even* sports for their legs' sakes.

And men aren't much better when they get undressed. I should say, when they get *into*, undress, for I am not referring now to their somewhat ridiculous anatomy, but to that which covers it by night—the pajama suit; again, without that economy which nature so loves, in two pieces and again cut above the *beauty-spot*. I am speaking always for the majority of men, for it is the majority who endure these things. With more compassion and comprehension I would acknowledge those who lie in silk and walk abroad in candid collars with handkerchiefs stained in Phoenician dyes (*from Paris*) and steeped in "the costly perfumes of Arabian dew" (*from Paris*). Indeed one brave shop tries, by displaying them in its windows on Broadway and Forty-fourth Street, to popularize a more décolleté pajama suit. It will have to advertise them in *Town Topics* or *The Saturday Evening Post,* and point out before their *choiceness* their *cheapness,* before it can hope to interest the so *tired Business Man,* who is apparently the man inevitably catered to by the commercially sagacious—magazine editors, theatrical managers, publishers and tailors. [...]

But how charming, after all, when men grow dainty and women daring! Today *might* and to-morrow *will* bring such miracles to pass. Definitions are losing something of their definiteness. Sex is a technicality for the consideration of pathology and physiology; the psychologist is after the individual. It is no longer a question of are you a *Man?* or, are you a *Woman?*—the answer is, I am an *Individual.* "I am what I am and so will I be," as the old lines go. There are men who wear their hair long; there are women who wear their hair short; and yet there are those who still say, "a man's a man for a' that!" Trousers, and other things, I hold to be mere arbitrary symbols of sex which I, for one, think obsolete.

Here endeth the third lesson.

5

Philosophic Fashions: The Importance of Being Dressed

Dame Rogue [Louise Norton]

Rogue, July 15, 1915

The custom of wearing clothes is one of civilization's contributions to the difficult art of complicating life.

As Wilde said:

"What is interesting about people is the mask that each one of them wears, not the reality that lies behind the mask. The more one analyses people, the more all reasons for analysis disappear. Sooner or later one comes to that dreadful universal thing called human nature."

That is why to me Henry James is so exciting. When I lose the sweet sensation of complexity in my own life I read "The Awkward Age" and taste again the ultra importance of life among the Philistines. Henry James' style is like those Russian nests of dolls; you uncover and uncover and uncover, and you come, at last, to—another doll. Pater, too, is an intoxicant—the very *best* wine. When life grows stale I can get drunk on "Imaginary Portraits" and "The Child in the House," and occasionally on "Greek Studies." These two, Walter Pater and Henry James, have the magic touch that magnifies.

Someone once sent me some doggerel by somebody, called, "Thank God for clothes!" I remember part of it went something like this:

"Thank God for dress!
"That through the darkest day can send a gleam
"When some long pondered frock comes home a dream
"That glorifies the marriage rites; and, yes
"Lends to bereavement craped becomingness,
"That gives us courage to confront our fate
"Illusion shattered; but our hat on straight.
"Thank God for Dress!"

To me that is a charming poem!

Of course there are those who still dress to cover their nakedness, for the sake of mere comfort and convention, but most of us have subtler reasons for wearing clothes. And what a lot of clever clothes it takes to content some people. Yet although it requires a perfect fit to please "a mighty modish French-like gentleman," I have seen a man put into the identical state of blessedness by the acquisition of a semi-shabby and certainly ungainly suit. The quality of the pleasure, however, is the same. Thank God for clothes!

Then too, if one didn't dress one never could undress. What a tragic simplification to lose the luxury of lingerie! Formerly only a simple smock was worn under the outer garment. So not in the literature of the Dark Ages nor even in that of the Renaissance is to be found the romance of undergarments which is so piquant a part of many writings ever since the advent of complicated underclothing in the middle of the sixth Century. Dear old Papa Pepys once got a peep at a pro tem [for the time being] royal clothesline, about which he writes: "And in the Privy-garden saw the finest smock and linen petticoats of my Lady Castlemaine's, laced with rich laces at the bottom, that ever I saw; and did me good to look at them." Richard Le Gallienne has written an entire romance around a petticoat and a pair of stockings that he saw kicking from a country wash-line in the wind. And how much the silk and laces and fine linens of lingerie do to refine the delicate improprieties of love. Today the greatest artists are giving their genius as much to drawers as dresses. Everybody knows those delicious Paul Poiret combinations. And in all the lingerie of the day there is an ingenuity of design and a catholicity of material that makes me wonder why women bother with gowns. Do you remember the toilet of Helen in "Under the Hill" "La Popelinière stepped forward with the frock. 'I shan't, wear one tonight,' said Helen. Then she slipped, on her gloves." One is often tempted!

But then there are always those gowns which seem to be made for the sole purpose of suggesting the little they conceal. Such gowns are catalogued decolleté, and are considered in good taste after dark. (Please don't misunderstand me—not "in" but "after" dark.)

Corsets are getting back their vulgar uprightness, but for all time the charm of those slim shapeless things we've worn for the past few years finds immortality in Clara Tice's semi-nudes. Clara Tice is the artist of undressing par excellence. With delicacy and deftness she suggests in a few lines all the lyricism of lingerie. One feels that her little ladies fastening garters should be set to music.

In my fashion folk-lore, have I ever quoted Carlotta? No? That is strange, because my friend Carlotta does such queer little different things to bedevil La Mode— yet walks down the Avenue an incarnation of the last word from Paris. For it is possible to avoid following the fashions and still seem to be more à la mode than, a Vogue fashion drawing. That is Carlotta's achievement. Today Carlotta wears her tailored skirts as tight as ever they were worn in the year of grace 1913, and with her short hair and, as the French say, her jollilèe face, she looks like an adorable American Claudine with the last flair of modernity. But that does not prevent her from resembling a Watteau shepherdess when at a garden tea she butterflies in Dresden silk, velvet bodice and limpest leghorn. She is artiste; whatever she wears is à la mode partly because she wears it with an à la mode air and mostly because the accessories are pertly and perfectly Parisienne. "Oh the importance of fanfreluches!" Carlotta used to sigh and say that if the accessories were accurate you could really dispense with the rest; charming picture: a nude descending Fifth Avenue uncriticised because of the correct tiptilt of the hat, the spotless spats, the sparkling shoes, the chic of the wrist bag and watch on her wrist and the necklace of white fox! But maybe Carlotta was joking.

However, let me warn those who desire to be different by being previous. It is worse for you to precede the fashion by a year or two than to lag a little behind. I know! A year before it was the order of the day I cut my hair in a bang, thereby affording rather an excessive amusement to my Alma Mater (or is it Amer mater?). Then it chanced that my grandmother's long ear-rings amused me a few months in advance of a psychological moment, and what hoots I endured along the byways of Manhattan from urchins and truckmen and loungers, those geni that do most insist on the conventions and dote on mediocrity. Learning nothing by experience, in the summer of 1913 I had trimmed with bands of mink a white muslin dress. The "absurdity," the "affection" of wearing fur in summer, people said. And here we are two summers later swathed, as well as trimmed, with fur. What am I to do? I can't repeat a whim and bore myself just for fashion's sake; yet fancy the frumpiness of the summer of 1915 sans fur! I am afraid it all goes to show me what an essentially unsocial person I am. *Hèlas!*

Women think they grow up and put away childish things. But in the midst of their mundane sophistication they play with toys. Clothes take the place of dolls,—and *such* games as they invent for the use of those toys! What a play of fancy some, women show in varying their actions to suit their frocks and fur belows.

Let me tell you A Tale of Ear-rings: One day when I had a new pair of ear-rings, I went at once to show them to my friend Carlotta who used to be famous for her own collection. It was late in the morning, and the girl she lives with was just coming out of the apartment: "Carlotta is in bed," she said, "go in." I went in.

"Look," I said, pointing to my ears with their weight of uncut pendant stones.

Carlotta was really nice about them. I knew she would be. "Who gave them to you?" she asked. I mentioned Josephus, and then asked to see her collection.

"Oh," she said, making a face, "all that's left of it is in that ivory box."

I lifted the jeweled mirror which formed the lid of the box, and saw a dozen or more odd ear-rings.

"But, Carlotta, what a shame," I cried. "What have you done with their twins?"

"Lost," said Carlotta.

I held up a lovely black opal.

"Now, Carlotta, however did you lose the mate to this?"

"The opal?" She paused. "I was coming home one night from the opera with Tommy in a taxi—"

"I see," I said, removing the expression from my face. "And how about this expensive looking Chinese antique? That was a pity!"

"Oh," she said, " that was on my way home from a dance with Dick."

"And this pearl?" I asked, holding up a large baroque.

" I was coming from the Fakir's ball with Harry—"

"In a hansom?" Then I did laugh.

"Carlotta," I said, "you must give up lovers, taxis or ear-rings—there is no other way."

"Oh yes," said she demurely, "there is. I have had my ears pierced." Incurable Carlotta.

"And now," I said, picking up a bit of coral that lay near the pillow next to her, "you only lose ear-rings in bed." Then I asked her if she had read Theophil Gautier's masterpiece. But Carlotta had never heard of Mademoiselle de Maupin.

Now Carlotta is nursing sick soldiers somewhere, and I am sure the soldiers like Carlotta and her ear-rings.

6

Feminine Fashions

Lois Long

The New Yorker, August 28, 1926

A Letter from L. L.—One Reception and Another–How a Mode Is Born

The winter openings of the great couturiers are over, and the American buyers, those lucky devils who get a trip to Europe for nothing are returning to their more or less native land for a good rest in the office.

You would think that a dressmaker's opening would be a great deal like a theatrical affair— weeks of preparation, an anxious bow before the critics, and, after that, failure or a long run. Not so. To a couturier, the strain of opening is prolonged through a series that lasts for days and days, the social status of each being carefully defined. Between the first appearance of the models before the assembled ladies and gentlemen of the press and their bow to all of the buyers who are able to force their way in the next day rests all the difference between a reception *chez* Astor and a subway jam.

Take the initial showing at Lelong, for instance. This, like that of a great many of the good dressmakers, takes place, with great pomp, in the evening. At about nine o'clock, in stream the representatives of the newspapers and magazines—modish as to their evening attire, their pearls, coiffures, and genteel voices. They pour into a series of chastely paneled rooms, with gilt tables placed socially about, laden with bonbons and cigarettes and vases full of roses. The light is becoming. In the near distance the limpid strains of a negro jazz band are distinctly audible. Everybody preens himself, converses sweetly, and watches the casual entrance of the late arrivals.

In due course of time, when everybody is comfortable, the music softens and becomes soulful, and the first of the mannequins make her appearance simultaneously with that of several gentlemen in livery bearing large trays of champagne, wine, and cocktails. These, of course, are refused.

There is a burst of applause for a particularly effective model and the proud creator, hovering in the doorway, smiles delightedly. As the evening wears on and the gentlemen with the trays aforementioned continue their work, applause become more frequent and the entrance of each mannequin becomes more and more like that of a great theatrical star in the middle of Act I. The mannequins burst through the curtains, shoulders back, swinging the hips out of line with each step—there is none of this American show-girl glide nonsense; the French mannequins give All to their public. In return, each acquires her individual claque among the onlookers. (Halfway through the evening, each mannequin has picked a gentleman near the front to smile on, and the ladies of the press are beginning to feel a little shabby.)

At the finish, around 11:30, there is a final burst of applause, a babble of conversation, many congratulations all around, and considerable politeness being shown as to the real opinions of the guests about the excellence and significance of the presentation. The mannequins may be observed in the back room, enjoying what remains of the cigarettes and champagne. And the guests depart, leaving their hosts with a wan and hollow horror of the arrival of the buyers next day.

The next day the buyers arrive. In the street outside (this is for houses like Chanel and Patou and other that represent the buyers' idea of heaven) crowds battle madly to gain the entrance, some waving cards over their heads, others hoping to bluff their way in. The opening is called for 2:30. By two o'clock, seven hundred people (all with reservations) are jammed into three hundred chairs, packed around very small rooms, and every vendeuse has completely lost her head and is running around wildly. At this point, they decide to solve the seating problem by locking the doors outside, ignoring, in the casual French fashion, the fact that Mr. Ginsberg, the most lavish buyer in America, is left raging on the sidewalk.

Inside, the lady buyers settle themselves to look as much like "Lady Goodenough-Goodenough, snapped at Le Touquet" as possible, and the gentlemen lean on canes, in the best boulevardier manner. It gets hotter and hotter and later and later. Our buyers fan themselves with programs and begin shouting across the room at each other. At about four, the mannequins, bored and furious, begin to stalk through the crowded rooms, repeating their numbers over and over again, and being stopped every other step by the clutching hands of gentlemen who want to feel the goods. Nobody has yet ascertained how many telephone numbers are obtained by this simple, businesslike process.

The buyer from Slotzenberg's, mindful of what happened last year when Minsky's made an American success with a model he hadn't bought, warily watches the reactions of the buyer from Minsky's, whose face shows nothing but weariness at his tenth opening of the week. Lemonade appears (sometimes champagne, but not often) and everybody grabs.

The press is reverent. Buyers are never reverent. The mannequins, who understand English, become more and more annoyed as jests about their ankles, morals, and size are bandied about amidst merry laughter. And six, everybody storms out, making appointments for final selections as he goes, and silence settles over the house, until the next day. Thus, my children, a Mode is born.

7

Feminine Fashions

Lois Long

The New Yorker, September 10, 1927

The clothes from the openings for the evening in Paris have reached New York and in a tour of some of the big shops I have seen enough to make one dizzy.

In the first place, I was disappointed in most of the Patous. The little sweater with three colored stripes around the bottom, one of the colors being repeated in the skirt, is all very well, but not very new. The same is true of the Chanel daytime things—of which, I must admit, I saw only a few. Having made a success last year with boleros, belts, pleatings low in the skirts, and tuckings, Mme. Chanel apparently has decided to let well enough alone. In one dress she combines all elements, with the high bolero in front turning into a blouse in back so as to make sure that no successful element of last season is left out. Other original touches consist of making last year's two-piece models one-piece. My advice is to go slow before paying exorbitant prices for copies, when you undoubtedly have something a good deal like them already at home.

But, to be constructive:

Saks-Fifth Avenue has a very good assortment of coats and evening capes. For informal daytime occasions, there is a good deal of tweed. For formal daytime, finished cloths, particularly broadcloth, usually in black. For evening, velvets and brocades, as of yore. A great deal of fur appears on all of these, not only on the collars (the shawl type still seems good, though there are several notched fur collars) but also around the hem. In a coat of black broadcloth from Worth, and in black velvet and white ermine evening coat from Patou, the fur also makes the flare at the closing of the wrap-around. Most of the coats are straight, but a good many fit tightly as far down as the hips and then flare perceptibly. Premet does this in a black coat trimmed with gray embroidery to look like krimmer, and very Cossack in effect. Jenny does it in a tweed that is otherwise absolutely simple; Renée, in a coat of dark gray wool with the inverted pleats that make the flare outlined in fur; and Doeuillet, also on black broadcloth. There is a marvellous tweed from Vionnet, with a shoulder such as only she can make.

For the evening, Vionnet has made a cape of black velvet with inserts of gold and a shawl collar that stays on the shoulder without effort. Doeuillet makes one of three tiers of transparent velvet, the top one, which is shirred around the shoulders below the fur collar, giving a shoulder-cape effect. And there is one of gold lamé and brown velvet brocade from Martial et Armand which is all sleeves and will certainly hitch your dress up above your knees if you dare wrap it. Louiseboulanger contributes a velvet wrap with a scarf collar which flares direct from the shoulders—a trait of hers—and, if not wrapped around, would solve the problem of what to wear over the *robe de style.*

Elsewhere in Saks, Vionnet's new version of the satin evening dress with a swirl of drapery over the tummy, the drapery being, this season, on the side. A Poiret tea-gown of black velvet, wide at the shoulders and slick to the figure below it, possibly heralding a new Egyptian-Persian line. And two blouses that must be worn without a coat to be appreciated—Patou's with fine pleating in back like that on a man's evening shirt; Poiret's with a high band collar, intricate shirrings in front, and wing sleeves outlined in grosgrain ribbon.

At Bonwit Teller, two daytime costumes in particular stood out. The first was an utterly divine sweater costume from Nowitsky, made of a Rodier mixed wool in gray and white with a tiny white stripe effect. The jumper was adorned around the hem with a band, occasionally bursting into circles, of quilted white silk. Bonwit Teller has imported the fabric for copies. The other is a simple little black crepella two-piece from Lanvin, with a bow tie and bands of red and white flannel. Youthful and very wearable. There is a sports costume from Patou, employing a pinkish tweed for the business like coat and skirt. This also trims the irregular V neckline of the pink jersey sweater.

Among the evening dress, Vionnet contributes one marvellous Grecian-drapery affair in pale blue crêpe Roma with bands of blue beading nestling here and there around the neckline and armholes. It is perfect, but should be worn only by a woman so chic that she can be casual without looking dowdy. Louiseboulanger bursts out spectacularly with a dress of very heavy satin, almost like upholsterer's satin. This fits the body like a sheath in front; in back, a long rectangular train and two flaring *poufs* supply the excitement. There is also a straight simple black chiffon from Lelong, with a suggestion of that naked effect at the top and a raggedy edge at the bottom. And a gold lamé from Molyneux, draped up in front and decorated with tiny gold fringe around the hemline.

If you are stern woman who likes flat-heeled shoes and Spitalfield neckties, you may possibly not be interested in the new clothes at Gervais; otherwise, I fancy you might be tempted to bankrupt yourself, chiefly because of a group of Paquin evening dresses. This designer's coats are known everywhere, but his dresses are infrequently copied on a large scale, as they are difficult to wear, the chic is not obvious, and they must be made for the individual or they lose everything. There is one dress of goldish lamé printed in tiny green formal flowers. This is perfectly simple in front, save for the scalloped hemline (most of the Paquin dresses I saw have this feature) and is decorated in the back with a small bow at the V décolletage and at the hip. Another printed lamé is distinguished by a tiny bit of shirring running straight down the front from the waistline to a point a little below the hip. Here it swerves to the right to support a side fullness. One of dark red velvet has a peculiar irregular hemline, also adorned with scallops. And the scallops appear again on a two-piece dress of *gaufré* velvet (this is the wrinkled kind) with a golden girdle. Paquin also contributes a black broadcloth suit, the short jacket flaring perceptibly on one side below the belt, the white satin blouse shirred up the front. Irene Castle would look divine in it.

There is a moire evening dress from Chanel with a fringed hem, and her black taffeta with a deep square neck, a wide bolero, a girdle ending in a flaring bow at the side, and a full skirt.

Shopping discoveries: the Patou tulle evening dress I talked about has been tracked to earth at Olga Frances' 685 Madison Avenue, and costs there $59.50. It does not knock me as gaga as I expected, but there you are. Miss Frances also has transparent black velvet day dresses, adorned with a bit of lace, a bolero, and a buckle, for $39.50. Tailored dresses of F & H covert elfeene, grand for school, $25. And angora sweaters with crepe skirts as attractive as I have seen, $35.

8

Copying a Fancy Name

Elizabeth Hawes

Fashion Is Spinach, 1938

Before the big docks were built, the harbor at Cherbourg was the very nicest place to land in France for the first time. You were taken off your big boat and put onto a tug which sidled into such a pleasant, small, inefficient world. The porters screamed and lost your baggage while you slowly digested the low, whitish houses, red tile roofs topped by long "Tonique" signs, backed by small green hills.

We landed on the fourteenth of July. I felt as if I'd gotten home after all those years. The fourteenth being what it is, the one big national free-for-all fête, our train took fourteen hours getting from Cherbourg to Paris. Ordinarily it takes about five. It seemed the engineer got off at every town to dance in the streets or something.

I loved it. I always relax the minute I hit the French shore. I knew then, as I do every time, that there just isn't any hurry. I know now, as I didn't know then, that the food will be good at every little inn, the wine lovely and the beds divine. I like the land and the people in France. If I had been born French, I would be very happy about it every morning. I wasn't born French so I finally had to come home and be an American, after much had happened. I didn't go to France because it was beautiful and peaceful and full of good food. I went to learn about chic. I learned plenty.

We installed ourselves in a cheap Parisian pension, Evelyn and I. We shopped with our girl-friends and I penetrated those gigantic dressmaking places, the homes of the French couturiers, for the first time. The other girls bought clothes while I watched and felt quite terrified at finally being right in the middle of all chic. I was so scared I didn't really see much, just very large rooms and very smooth salesladies, very thick carpets and very beautiful clothes.

We'd go afterward and have enormous lunches with fifty-four kinds of hors d'oeuvres and wonderful cheese. Then we'd ride in carriages through the Bois, down long, long lanes of trees. I never got used to the idea that a forest should exist without any underbrush, even on the edge of Paris. We had our tea in some treesy place and rather hurried the driver back to the Ritz bar.

There the boys who'd just graduated from Princeton and Yale and Harvard and the whole United States bought drinks for us. "Double Alexandres" I learned to drink at that point. Once after we'd all had three double Alexandres, which I, personally, thought was the name of the drink, we ordered another round. The waiter looked at us very hard and said, "Do you want a *double* Alexandre or just a single Alexandre?"

After a few days, I presented myself at Bonwit Teller's Paris office. The head man, French and fat and shiny, said he didn't know. I might come back a little later.

I didn't have time to be discouraged at all, because Evelyn's mother turned up right away from America. She whipped me around to her dressmaker and muttered a few brief and well-chosen sentences. I was hired. I didn't know for what money or what labor or what kind of place it was, but I had the job. I was to come sometime after the fifteenth of August.

Evelyn and I packed up and went along to Evian on the Lake of Geneva with her family. They had a regulation French villa, red brick, white stone trim, gravel walks, too much furniture. I was so preoccupied with getting back to my job and wondering about it that I recall very little of the visit.

We motored over the Alps a bit. They are a little too high and mighty for my peace of mind. We tried very hard to read *Ulysses* and I failed. We went into Geneva and saw where Mr. Wilson had saved the world for Democracy. I thought it was very wonderful. The French were more skeptical.

Finally the middle of August came around and we scampered back to Paris. Evelyn got a trousseau and went home to be married, I went to work. My place of business turned out to be a copy house.

A copy house is a small dressmaking establishment where one buys copies of the dresses put out by the important retail designers. The exactitude of the copy varies with the price, which varies with the amount of perfection any given copy house sees fit to attain. A really perfect copy of a model costs in a copy house just about half what it cost in the place where it was born.

I am sure that wherever important couturiers have flourished in sufficient numbers to warrant attention, there have been copy houses. Certainly when I was in Paris in 1925 there were plenty of them, and they still continue on their illegitimate way.

Since the depression, the large houses in Paris have lowered their prices and have driven a number of copyists out of existence. The whole matter is of interest, both because it still exists in Paris and because, if retail designers ever rise to any sort of eminence and numbers in New York, we will have our copy houses too. They already exist but are not very virile.

Copying, a fancy name for stealing, is also interesting as an example of what a curious and rather degraded business dressmaking may be. The passion which has been created for being chic leads to almost any thing, probably including murder.

Most copy houses in Paris are upstairs, on side streets, although the one in which I worked was on Faubourg St. Honoré, just a bit up from Lanvin near the Place Beauvais. It was a very good copy house. Our boast was that we never made a copy of any dress of which we hadn't had the original actually in our hands.

The front entrance was through one of those perfectly usual heavy stone-rimmed doors, into a dark and reasonably unclean hall, up a winding stair to a door which bore a brass plate marked with the name of the house, call it Doret. There was a door-bell.

The back entrance was on through the first-floor hall, across a rather dirty court, up a very narrow and definitely dirty flight of stairs to a door with no name on it. That door led to the stockroom. The back stairs continued up to a floor of workrooms, and above that to a kitchen and small dining room where everyone except the actual sewing girls ate lunch together, when there was time to eat lunch.

The house was supposed to be closed from twelve to two for lunch. If a customer was in at twelve, we were stuck until she left. If there was no customer, the front door was locked at twelve, and the loud clarion voice of Madame Doret, resounded through the place, "A table!"

We had very good substantial food, soup, rabbit stew, salad and cheese. There was plenty of red wine and chunks of bread. Monsieur Doret, the only man in the place, was master of the table. He always wore a cigarette stuck behind his ear for lunch, and spoke in Montmartre argot, that lowdown slang which one is not taught at Vassar. It took me a good two months to get to the point of following the luncheon conversation.

Copy houses are not chic in interior decoration. They are in business for the sole purpose of underselling the designers from whom they steal their wares. Our main entrance was usually unlocked, but there was a gong attached to the door so that nobody could sneak in without our knowing it. When there was any suspicion of an approaching raid, the front door was locked. One rang for admittance. Sometimes we answered the bell. If we actually expected a raid, we just didn't. All the old customers knew how to get in by the rear entrance and when the copy-house-seeking police were on the rampage, we didn't want any new clients.

If the customer got in, she entered a small hall with a dingy carpet, walked past a tiny office on the left which was used by the salespeople and the sketcher and, in times of great rush, as a fitting room. On the right was a large office where Monsieur Doret plied his nefarious trade of keeping a double set of books. It appears to me to be especially a French characteristic, not in any sense limited to the dress business, to hate to pay taxes.

Monsieur Doret made a great point of doing all transactions in cash. Although the set-up did not indicate any great amount of profit, it was he, rather than any of my rich American friends, who got the Bankers Trust to open an account for me in which I kept a couple of dollars a month. I gathered he had both a dollar and a franc account there and they respected him.

In Monsieur Doret's office hung such model dresses as we kept to show. There were very few of them. We sold mostly from sketches. The models were not copies. They represented our "front." At the beginning of every season we ran up a few boring little sport dresses for show.

My job was selling Americans who didn't speak French—also bringing customers, if possible. I improved my sketching a bit and helped with that. The hours were nine to whenever you got through, around six, and I received the munificent salary of 500 francs a month, about $20 in 1925.

If a customer arrived without any introduction, or if we suspected her integrity, we showed her our own models and bowed her out. If we knew her, or her introduction was good, we took her into a small salon which contained one large table, a useless fireplace, a dilapidated rug, four or five badly painted imitation Louis XV chairs.

We then got together whatever authentic copies we had, mostly dresses in the process of being made for other customers. We pieced out with the sketch books and made our sales.

Madame Doret was the brains and energy of it all. She had worked in the business under another woman who finally retired and left it to her and Monsieur. She was little, about five feet three, with wonderful legs and feet. Her hair was curly and brown, and her eyes very bright and black. She never walked. She had a sort of abbreviated run which got her everywhere at once. She spent most of her time making lists in the stockroom, and dashing out to see important customers. Her appointments were usually after five, at which time she shut herself up in the salon with a batch of foreign men, or an odd French woman. Out of this we always received a new set of models.

The house was closed for July and half of August. This was to give us a vacation, but primarily to give Lanvin and Vionnet, Chanel and the rest time to get their collections together so we could copy them. I went to work the fifteenth of August, 1925. There were practically no models but they began to appear. By September first we had a nice collection of fifty or sixty perfect copies, exact material, exact color, exact embroidery.

I never got any satisfactory answers as to how they got there, but after a few months I became sufficiently trusted to become embroiled in the business of stealing. It wasn't considered stealing. It was just business. Lots of people wanted Chanel's clothes who couldn't afford them, and we filled the gap.

I discovered, to my great surprise, that we actually bought models. I discovered this because I was sent to buy them. I was American and young and unsuspected. When it became pretty sure that there was a particularly good dress somewhere, and we were not going to be able to get it free, or half price, or by any of the other hooks and crooks which I finally learned, we bought it.

The dress was described to me in detail and usually I was given the number. I then repaired to the couturier's in question, and either used the vendeuse of a friend, or just was very American and had never been to Paris before. If the dress was for an older woman, I bought for my mother, whose measures I had, and to whom I was taking the dress. If it was young enough, I had it made and fitted on me.

I think not more than four or five models a season were bought that way. But there was one more thing to be done at the couturier's. The embroidery men always came around to us with the embroidery for certain dresses from the big houses, particularly Callot, who was successful still. I would go and look up those dresses and see how they were made, if possible. With the exact embroidery, and my sketch, our model turned out pretty authentic.

So where did the rest of the clothes come from? Three major sources: customers, mistresses, and foreign buyers. I don't know how many years it takes a copy house to get the sources, but ours were both good and plentiful.

Some of the richer customers were women who bought a good many clothes directly from the designer. They then filled in their wardrobes chez the bootlegger. They liked the bootlegger and they let her copy their clothes in return for which they probably paid even larger prices, but still only half the price of an original. Perhaps some of them did get really low prices. The matter of price is seldom a fixed one in any dressmaking establishment, bootleg or not.

It made me very proud to have tea at the Ritz and see our customers in their Chanels, exactly like the real Chanels across the table. One of the wonderful things about the chic monde in Paris seemed to me to be their fantastic desire to all have the same dress. In those days, it was always black. It was not smart to be economical, so if you had a copy, it really had to be perfect. We dressed some of the really chic women. Their return favors probably gave us a quarter of our models.

Half of the models came through foreign buyers. This always seemed to me a rather sordid business. I do not know, but I assume, that we paid out some money for the privilege of copying the models. I really felt like a thief the day I discovered how that worked.

I knew that many of the big couturiers delivered clothes just exactly in time to make certain boats, or they tried to. I always thought it was because they were busy with orders. What they really try to do is prevent leaks. But they don't succeed. Some of the better copy houses are run by people who work, or have worked, in resident buying offices. The supply of models is thus assured.

It was during the mid-season showings in November that I was initiated into the mystery of the resident buyer and the copy house. All manufacturers or stores who buy in Paris work through their resident buying offices which attend to everything for them. The resident buyer and his staff arrange for tickets to the openings, attend the home-office buyers hand and foot, day and night, while they are in town, and subsequently receive and ship the purchases to America or wherever.

One of our most frequent visitors, the only one who was ever invited to lunch, was a resident buyer for a large American manufacturer. Madame Ellis was an American who had lived abroad for years. She was about fifty-five, exceedingly attractive, and pretty smart. Anything she lacked in brains she had fully made up for in experience. She seldom got any clothes from us, and I never saw her bring anything into the place. She was obviously an old and trusted friend of the management, and spent a good many weekends at the Doret country place.

I had a very large beaver coat. A fur coat in Paris is quite a rarity among the working class. Mine turned out to have a special value. I was requested to don it one day in November and go to the resident buying office through which Madame Ellis worked. It was toward the end of the mid-season buying, the day before a large boat was to sail.

The buying offices in Paris, excepting a few of those owned and run by American firms, are, like the copy houses and most of Paris, situated in old stone buildings, built about dirty courts. The halls are dark and the stairs wind you up to the offices.

I went up to Madame Ellis' office. She was there, alone, with a large pile of boxes from Chanel. The boxes were hastily opened, dresses pulled out and shaken from their tissue paper covers. "Put them under your coat," said Madame, "and get them back here as fast as you can."

I automatically obeyed, delighted to be in the process of verifying this source, flew downstairs, into a taxi, to the Faubourg St. Honoré, up our backstairs, and shed my booty on the floor of the stockroom. The workgirls had gone home. The fitters were there. They took the clothes and made accurate patterns of them, while I made accurate sketches.

Madame Doret even more accurately examined every line, made notes on buttons, belts, cut bits of material from the seams, and looked over the finishing. We had six or eight new Chanels to sell.

Someone was sure to say, however untruthfully, during the examination, "How Chanel has the nerve to deliver clothes made this way! Look, it's all cut off the grain. The inside seams aren't even finished."

But, well or badly made, the idea was there, we had it, and the clothes went back under my fur coat. I went back in a taxi to my waiting Madame Ellis. The models were put back in their tissue paper, and off they went to New York on a fast boat.

That was the only office I ever went to for that purpose. But it was by no means the only office from which we got models. That happened to be an order for New York. We got a great many clothes from a Dutch buyer who probably got a cut on the profits, or some such thing. And there was also a German who did a good deal of running in and out with packages.

There was a regular business of buying muslin patterns of dresses. The patterns began to appear as soon as the workrooms of the big designers got going on a new collection. They were often not authentic, so we didn't buy many. These patterns were, of course, stolen by the sewing girls who worked in the ateliers of Vionnet, Lanvin, etc., and copied as the new designs were made up.

A more picturesque source was the mistress. Our best mistress was kept by the manager of a famous designer. She got all her clothes from the big house. Then she rented them out to various copyists to turn an honest penny on the side. This source always rather pleased me, but Madame Doret didn't really like it much because those particular models got into the hands of every copy house in town.

One couldn't help thinking that all of this might be stopped. It might have. But, for one thing, I doubt if the fabric houses wanted it stopped. They could have simply refused to sell the materials to copyists. They didn't. At least, we always bought direct and I was never aware of any difficulty. The fabric houses must have sold as much to copyists of certain materials as they ever did to the originator of the model. And there is an old tradition in Paris that the day a designer isn't copied, he is dead.

However, efforts were made to close up copy houses from time to time. The general bootlegging atmosphere always prevailed at our place. Models were never left in sight, and everything was constantly kept in readiness to be hurried out the door.

This may have been because a few years before I went there, the place had been raided. The whole story is typical of the devious ways in which the copyists continue their existence against any odds. The house was raided by the police, acting for a combination, which I remember included Lanvin and Callot, and, I think, one other large couturier.

There is a special organization in Paris which is maintained by the couturiers for the purpose of protection against copying. Lanvin, Callot, et al., on suspecting a certain copy house, turn the matter over to this bureau who in turn calls in the police of the district to pull a raid. The copy house must be caught with the actual and perfect copies on the premises before it can be prosecuted.

Madame Doret was caught with the goods, perfect copies, and a suit was brought. But it all came out okay, and why?

The intelligent little Madame Doret had once been very kind to a customer. The customer had gone motoring with a gentleman, and was hurt in an auto accident. The gentleman with whom she was motoring was not the gentleman who was paying her bills. How she landed on the hands of her copyist at this point, I do not know, but Madame Doret got her off into hiding, and took care of the whole affair, so that not a word ever got about. The gentleman who paid her bills just happened to be a minister in the government.

So, when the copy house was raided and faced with disaster, by a simple gesture Madame Doret got the lady she had befriended to get the minister of the government to do something. The copy house was fined a few thousand francs and closed up—for two months.

If couturier designers, people who design for and maintain their own dressmaking establishments, ever rise to a sufficient prominence in New York, we will have our Dorets to organize the copying for the individual. At the moment, copying is not very serious—in this field. It is done by inefficient people who have not discovered how to get the originals. Even when they do copy, their workmanship is apt to be bad.

Of course, when I say there is no copying in New York, I only mean to imply that we don't do things in a small way. We have mass production!

9

News ... News ... News ...

Elizabeth Hawes

Fashion Is Spinach, 1938

My first sketching season ended in February 1926. I went into it penniless and came out with $500 in the Bankers Trust. I'd been in Paris eight months and was at last solvent. I still believed firmly that all beautiful clothes were made in the house of the French couturiers and that all women wanted them.

I took one fifth of my capital and invested it in a lovely little suit at Callot where I got a special price. I got a special price because I had purchased things there for Madame Doret. My saleslady at Callot thought they were for my mother. She always felt I should have something for myself so I took advantage of her innocence.

Subsequently I dressed myself at Callot for some time, getting some beautiful bargains in stylish clothes which lasted me for years. I had an extra fondness for Callot because the American buyers found her out of date and unfashionable. She was. She just made simple clothes with wonderful embroidery. Embroidery wasn't chic.

The occasion of my extravagance was my mother's coming to Europe. I hadn't had a new rag to my back since I left America. I met my mother at Cherbourg the first of March, dressed in my new suit and feeling very fine. I proceeded to initiate her into life as I had seen it in Paris, including the food at the Foyer Feminine.

She proceeded to initiate me into taking taxis, eating good food, taking a bath every day, and otherwise enjoying the fine things of life. We traveled around Normandy and Belgium.

When she left I still had most of my $400. I also had reacquired a desire for an American standard of living. Another buying season was knocking at the door, mid-season April 1926, in the shape of Madame Ellis, who expected me to sketch for Weinstock.

I sketched, filled many outside orders. I banked $750 on May first and hated myself a little and all American buyers much more.

The minute that season finished, I leapt onto a bicycle and spent three weeks touring Brittany with Bettina Wilson. As a foil for the dressmaking racket, it proved eminently successful.

All you can take with you on a bicycle trip is a sweater, an extra set of underclothes, and a toothbrush. You have a perfect and intimate view of the scenery coupled with just the right amount of exercise. At the end of your easy-going thirty miles a day, you invariably find that delectable supper and wonderful bed for which the French are so justly famous.

At the end of three weeks, you are exceedingly healthy and so utterly filthy that a return to the fashionable life is all you ask. True, after ten months in Paris, I was not yet fed up on clothes, style, fashion, the Ritz Bar, Montmartre or the Bois de Boulogne.

The buyers appeared to me to be a horrible phenomenon created by God to disgust me and all the French couturiers. I saw that it was worth it to the French. Obviously, it was worth it to me. Otherwise I should not have had my bicycle trip.

After the bicycle trip, I still had time and money to get myself to Italy where I joined up with an old college friend. We were motored from Florence to Venice and the lakes. We ended in Geneva where I enjoyed my first look at the Council of the League of Nations in action. I found I was getting like the French, skeptical.

Back in my same 800-franc Paris room, I found myself with a few hundred francs and my diamond ring. It was the middle of July 1926. The buyers were about to descend again. I decided to have another season of sketching, replenish my finances.

While flitting from opening to opening like a bird of prey, I developed an idea for the future. The future was definitely still Paris to me. I loved it. I had acquired friends, both male and female. I wanted to travel more in Europe. Being thrown out of Miller Soeurs having brought me up sharp on the business of stealing sketches, I must find another means of support.

My plan involved going back to New York to start it. The idea was very simple. I saw that there was only one set of fashion news from Paris. I had been feeding bits of it to the store in Wilkes-Barre. They liked and used it. They sent me copies of ads which said that their Paris representative told them everything was blue this season—"and on our fourth floor you will find *our version* of blue, done with the new flared skirt which our Paris representative tells us is all the rage."

I decided that there must be hundreds of small department stores, who could use this news, who had no direct contact with the source of all fashion. I couldn't think how they ever got on without Paris news every week. I figured that a service could be syndicated and sold to such stores for a reasonable figure.

With no further knowledge of small department stores in middle-sized cities than my brief reporting for Wilkes-Barre, I built up my idea, went back to New York, sold it to a syndicate. It was no more unreasonable than most fashion reporting ideas.

It took me three months to get my syndicate. I kept being sent from one friend on a newspaper to a friend on a magazine to a friend in a store to a friend in a syndicate to another friend in another syndicate. All one really requires for putting anything over is enough energy and resistance to keep on plugging the idea. Someone will eventually fall.

A very large and grandfatherly gentleman was running a syndicate called Cosmos. He gazed down upon me from his great height and bulk and listened with extraordinary interest. He was syndicating a weekly fashion feature from Paris. It was a story with pictures which went to the *Post* in New York, the *Detroit Free Press,* the *Baltimore Sun* and other papers of equal standing.

This feature was being run by a boy in Paris who, I was told, was doing a remarkable job. However, it was too much work for one person. The boy screamed by every boat for an assistant. Why shouldn't I be sent, first as an assistant, secondly to work out the syndicate store service idea?

While the old gentleman considered that thought, I happened into the newly born *New Yorker* office. Lois Long was doing their fashion column. Lois Long went to Vassar. The *New*

Yorker had no Paris fashion news. It was arranged in the twinkling of an eye. I was to send them one cable a month and one five hundred word story. For this I would get $150 a month.

The Cosmos Syndicate seemed greatly impressed by this news. He hired me. I was a fool. I figured everything in francs. I told him $25 a week would be plenty until we got the store syndicate started. He played poor, but he did send me back to Paris. He had to. I didn't have a nickel left.

I returned to Paris rich enough in prospects for my taste, anyway; $250 a month was around 7,000 francs, twice what a French midinette gets in a year. Eagerly I sought out Sylvestre, my boss, the other employee of the Cosmos Syndicate.

Sylvestre's was a typical Paris fashion idea. Sylvestre was a typical 1926 Paris fashion reporter.

What Sylvestre told me was this: He was half French. He knew all the great French designers intimately. He understood chic as no one ever had before or since. The great designers would tell him, Sylvestre, things they would never tell an ordinary reporter. He could get advance information. He could obtain sketches never given out to any other reporter.

This is the usual case with fashion reporters in Paris. Each one has some magic way of finding out what no one else can. Either the reporter has a cousin who is a Duke or a rumor floats around that the reporter is very intimately connected with the Count de Falderol. Sometimes, my dear, they say that certain reporters are the bastard daughters of English peers. Anyway, no Paris fashion reporter is quite an ordinary mortal. One couldn't employ just humans to tell about miracles.

The grains of truth in Sylvestre's story unfolded themselves to me in the next month. Sylvestre was half French. Sylvestre knew Jenny quite well. Jenny was a couturier who was of little interest to the fashion world. Sylvestre knew the manager of Redfern well. Redfern was about dead. Sylvestre knew Charlotte intimately. Charlotte designed for the house of Premet. Premet had nice young clothes which were of no particular importance.

The first day I met Sylvestre, he gave me a rendezvous at some hotel on the Champs Elysées for tea. He told me that everyone was going to wear gray that season and that this was a very smart hotel. I told him that nobody ever went there for tea and besides that, gray was never very much worn because it was too unbecoming.

We left the hotel and went back to his apartment where we drank Jamaica rhum and became friends. Sylvestre was not very interested in the store project but he took no time at all in winding me into his newspaper story.

His little reporting racket was perhaps the easiest ever worked out. We had to send out one fashion story a week. Each story was about one designer and carried with it six sketches. We got absolutely no information that anyone else couldn't also get.

It worked this way. On Monday we realized that a fast boat was getting off Wednesday. Sylvestre called whatever big designer we had next on the list. He called the press agent whom he had already contacted and to whom he had explained all, mostly how he was the most important newspaper person in Paris.

The press agent was being paid to get his designer into the papers so it wasn't very difficult for him to lay his hand on six sketches. It was particularly easy for him because Sylvestre never cared what sketches we got. All we wanted was six of them with explanations.

I would go around and pick up the sketches sometime Tuesday. I usually rounded into Sylvestre's apartment late Tuesday afternoon, sketches in hand. We had a drink. Then we had dinner. Then I sat down at the typewriter and wrote two news columns about the six brand new things in question, things which may have been designed any time during the past four months. At first I often couldn't see anything new about them.

Sylvestre taught me to observe every line and pocket. He taught me that everything I saw was new. He taught me how to write a fine lead on the subtlety of Vionnet's rhythmic line or the delicate softness of a Jenny gown. In the beginning I often had to do the whole thing over twice, but eventually I got so I could vomit out the stories in an hour of concentrated hyperbole.

After that, we went out for a drink. The next noon I got the stuff off on the boat train. We repeated it the next week. When I felt forehanded, I got several stories done in a day and left town for a couple of weeks.

Once we decided we ought to go to the Riviera. Sylvestre knew Frank Harris and it began to seem that our reporting needed a new note. Frank Harris happened not to be at his villa near Nice and we really didn't have much money. We spent some time in Marseilles and some more time in very cheap night clubs in Nice. One day we went to Monte Carlo by bus. We sent quite a glowing report of the new things on the Riviera that spring.

Of course, if you are a conscientious reporter, you don't behave like that. You get up in the morning and go from one hat place to another bag place to the Ritz for lunch. You cultivate the right people, your cousin the count, or your rich friend who has a villa in Cannes.

You night-club in the right places. You follow the ponies to the races and the chic monde all over the lot, from London to the Lido. And you suffer.

The minute you persuade yourself or some newspaper or magazine in America that there is fashion news in Paris or anywhere else on the Continent every week, you are in for a life of hell. Unless you're blessed with a good healthy imagination and no inhibitions, you get looking like all other fashion reporters in Paris.

Most of them are quite gaunt. Their skin is dry and they have a pinched look around the mouth. They are the dowdiest looking bunch imaginable. They don't make enough money to buy expensive clothes and there isn't anything else in France.

Only four times a year is there really fashion news in Paris. Two of those times, it's big news, all the summer or winter clothes, shoes, hats, bags, jewelry which Paris can think up, and that's plenty.

The other two times, it's mid-season collections, small fill-in showings of advanced spring or fall clothes, tossed out for foreign buyers. There really isn't much in those showings, but the clothes are new and one can legitimately report them as news.

In between times, the reporter must manufacture brand new fashion ideas. If you feel like it, you can go to Biarritz or Cannes or the Lido or wherever you can see real, live society women wearing the clothes you formerly saw and have already reported from the previous openings.

You can report it all over again as something to scream over. If you're at all bright, you know perfectly well when you see the clothes on the mannequins at Chanel's which ones are going to be seen later at different resorts. If you want to, you can find out from the saleswomen in the various dressmaking houses who bought what. Then all you have to do is watch the society columns to see where the women go and report them there, in the clothes.

Even if you go all the places and do all the things, you are still faced with those dreadful weeks when the chic monde seems to have evaporated. The couturiers seem to have buried themselves. It rains. There is nothing new under the sun.

You rewrite old columns in a new way. You find eleven different ways of telling the world that women in Paris are wearing two silver foxes around their necks. You concentrate on details to such an extent that all the world begins to hinge on whether The Duchess de X had on heels an inch high or one and a half inches high.

After piling it on thicker and thicker, you send it off to your newspaper syndicate. In a week or so, all the women in the United States are informed of the major events in life. They are left in no doubt but that, unless they can get two silver foxes, they are absolutely out of fashion. They are bombarded with news of what the chic monde is wearing for bathing at the Lido. They don't know where the Lido is or what it looks like and they go to Jones Beach every Sunday, wearing whatever kind of bathing suit Gimbel chose to provide that season.

There must have been over a hundred American fashion reporters in Paris in 1926. Many of them conscientiously sent out news regularly to American newspapers. From what I see now and again in the news columns, a lot of them are still there, turning out the same stuff.

However, it is my impression that the American newspaper situation in re Paris fashions is cleaning itself up. The U.S. newspapers have discovered that it is not really good business for them to have in their columns fashion news about things which can't be bought on the spot. They now incline toward columns with a little box at the bottom saying that if you will write in, you will be told in what local store the item mentioned can be bought. The local fashion girls are having their day.

In 1926 there were many Paris offices devoted to the business of sending news to the various fashion and women's magazines in America. Of those, *Vogue* and *Harper's Bazaar* were the largest. They are now about the only offices left. They have a unique position in Paris, being recognized as the most important publicity agents the French can use. The French couturiers and these two magazines are in business together, in business to promote chic and keep the world of fashion spinning.

As with the newspapers, there is a vast difference today in the amount of French news crowding the pages of *Harper's Bazaar* and *Vogue*. In the late '20s, 90 percent of the drawings and photographs were the work of the Parisian couturiers, often elaborate creations, which nobody ever wore anywhere. Now those pages are filled only with such French designs as actually come to America and are, for the most part, manufactured here. Many pages in both magazines are devoted to clothes created in America for American life.

Many of the offices which worked from '25 to '29 for American magazines have been closed. The *Ladies Home Journal*, the largest woman's magazine in the United States, now has no Paris office, and all because they hired a very bright lady as Fashion Editor about 1932.

The lady had worked previously for a department store and also for *Harper's Bazaar*. She said she saw no reason why the *Ladies Home Journal* should maintain an expensive Paris office. She said that magazine catered to middle class American women who never actually saw a French original design. She thought her public was interested in news of what existed in fashion in America, whether it had been originated in Paris or on Seventh Avenue.

In 1926, however, America thought it needed Paris fashion news and Sylvestre, myself, and a hundred others were all busy supplying the need. We were doing our best to build up the French legend.

When I had thoroughly mastered the business of writing Sylvestre's column for him so that he had literally nothing to do but draw down about $200 a week from the syndicate, I went at him about the store service. I explained to him that all the small department stores needed to know directly what was going on in the big center of fashion and that we were there to do it.

At first Sylvestre wouldn't bite, but as he began to see the matter in terms of additional royalties, he reflected.

He realized that he and only he could get confidential information from the big designers. He got worried about the stores not realizing the fact. Finally he became so intrigued, he told me to go ahead and work out the form and content for the service. He would go to America to see that the Cosmos Syndicate sold it properly.

I, therefore, began to compile short reports for stores. I made thumbnail sketches and resuméed everything weekly: shoes, hats, bags, gloves, belts, clothes, colors. I indicated what was very new, less new, going out.

Sylvestre got to New York and the thing began to sell. I was rather harassed because I had to continue turning out the fashion column and make an effort to cover the entire Paris market weekly for the store service. It wasn't more than a full-time job, but I could have used a secretary.

After about six weeks, Sylvestre returned triumphant. The store service, my brain child, had been sold to Lord and Taylor. Lord and Taylor already had a large office in Paris with plenty of employees who could tell them all. However, Sylvestre had convinced them about his private resources.

I was so busy being appalled by Sylvestre's salesmanship to Lord and Taylor, I forgot that some small stores out of New York had bought the service, too. I was so sick of writing the horrible fashion story weekly, I decided the time had come for action.

My action was quick. I found that Dorothy Shaver, a vice president of Lord and Taylor, was in Paris. I called upon her to make sure my ideas on the matter of the store service were right. She grimly agreed with me that I was correct. It was nothing for Lord and Taylor. I thereupon gave the idea to Sylvestre with my blessing and retired from the Cosmos Syndicate.

I could retire gracefully because there was the *New Yorker*. One hundred and fifty dollars a month was enough to live on until something else came along. Writing news for the *New Yorker* was my favorite fashion job of all time. Even my nom de plume now gives me a small laugh. "Parasite." Someone suggested it at a party given in honor of a brown dress suit, whose I don't recall. It epitomized the whole fashion business much better than I, in my innocence, realized.

Anyone who has ever written fashions will, I am sure, appreciate what it means to be allowed to write with no embroidery just what you think about them. Practically nobody in Paris knew I wrote for the *New Yorker*. I never used it as an entrée to see the collections until shortly before I quit the job.

Not a soul on the *New Yorker* ever gave me a kind word during the three years I sent in my pieces. On the other hand, no one ever complained. The advertising department never raised its ugly head and said that if I thought Patou was no designer, I'd better keep still about it or someone would withdraw his advertising.

After burbling for the *New York Post*, the *Detroit Free Press*, et al., that everything was divine, glamorous, chic, gorgeous, as Sylvestre had taught me, I would retire to the fastness of my own little apartment and tell the *New Yorker* readers that Molyneux was a good safe designer with not too much originality; that Patou thought he'd designed a coat if he put enough fox fur on it; that Talbot had her tongue in her cheek when she made baby bonnets. The *New Yorker*, ladies and gentlemen, is the only magazine I ever saw which had the guts to let its fashion reporters speak their minds. I expressed myself freely in its pages, and through those pages I was made to face facts from time to time. When the printed copy of the magazine came to me in Paris, along with some of my reports, I'd read L.L.'s comments on the new, oh so new, things I'd written up.

Those jersey bathing suits which took my eye at Biarritz existed a whole year ago in the good old U.S.A., said Miss Long. Those daisy little sandals which Dufeau just put out were shown six months ago in Delman's. Patou's newest tennis dress differed very little from one of Best and Co. last summer.

Slowly an idea began to penetrate my mind. All beautiful clothes are designed in the houses of the French couturiers? Well …

10

Fashions from Paris: A Suit Story at Balenciaga

Eugenia Sheppard

The New York Herald Tribune, March 18, 1951

Big Daddy Balenciaga didn't take the crown from Marc Bohan of Dior this afternoon. American buyers are beginning to believe the great Balenciaga means what he says. He is designing for private customers and doesn't care whether buyers and manufacturers come or quit.

A sampling of opinions telephoned at the end of today's opening goes like this: "Pretty but unexciting." "Not one of the greatest." "No news but the suits." "A tired collection."

Many buyers, after seeing Balenciaga's, think more kindly of Givenchy's collection which, they say had more color. Some grumble that the two collections ought to be combined, since there are so many repeats in fabrics and details. One commented that the hottest thing at Balenciaga was the room temperature, which hovered consistently around 102. Many were sore at being forced to stay over in Paris for a week to look at what they are calling a double anticlimax to the season.

Comparing the two collections, buyers call Givenchy's coats terrific and his suits dull. Balenciaga's suits are rated wonderful but his coats nothing to write home about. Dresses are on a par. Both collections show more floor length ball gowns than other Paris houses.

Both buyers and designers are delighted with Balenciaga's suits, said to have a completely new mood. "They caress the body," said one spectator, while another found in them a subtle suggestion of Chanel.

Balenciaga's suit jackets come in all lengths, including longish cardigans with no fastenings at all. They are worn open to show their overblouses, not only down the front but at the necklines. Specially mentioned are a black suit with a double-breasted overblouse of white pique and a white wool, bound in navy blue braid. Shorter jackets, like little boleros, are buttoned at the neckline and cut away in a curve.

Almost no suit skirts are straight. Many have big pleats front and back that look like panels. They give the fluid skirt movement Paris craves. A few skirts wear patch pockets.

Balenciaga shows both straight and cape back coats. Shoulders are less wide than Givenchy's. Lengths are mostly three-quarters.

Slightly longer skirts are especially noticeable in daytime dresses, most of which are sleeveless and belted at the normal waistline in fabric or leather. Hems often end in modified flares and ruffles, suggestive of what went on yesterday at Givenchy's across the street.

Small patterned prints are used for many dresses and jacket costumes. Buyers praise them as lovely and ladylike, dubious compliments in today's fashion world.

Hats are attractive. They come in all sizes from a tiny black patent leather artichoke in honor of Alexandre's latest hair-do to larger hats of lacquered coque feathers and absolute lampshades of draped silk. One of these has a ribbon across the top and tying under the chin.

There are almost no cocktails dresses except flowered chiffons. Stunning at-home costumes combine mandarin jackets over tunic tops and easier slacks.

Evening gowns are floor length and skinny and worn with heavy necklaces in contrasting colors. Jewels are often set in hair-do's.

Many evening sheaths are wrapped diagonally like Balenciaga's best selling dinner dress of last season. Lots of artful drapery is used.

Balenciaga brings back the long print silk evening gown. One has a three-cornered shawl of the same fabric that falls to below the waist behind.

Evening gowns are lightly beaded, including a version of Givenchy's Spanish shawl flowers. Little evening jackets are beautifully glitter-embroidered on gauze. Curved slits in the fronts of tight skirts give them a Marlene Dietrich allure.

The dress that brought down the house today was shocking pink silk organdie, double-ruffled around the hem and worn under a slightly shorter ruffle-edged cape. Even a socialite gray poodle in the audience burst out yapping when this model breezed in.

"I won't write another number until the dog barks again," quipped an American manufacturer.

The poodle slept through the rest of the show.

11

A Mini for Men?

Eugenia Sheppard

The World Journal Tribune, February 1967

Are men on the way to wearing skirts?

Art Buchwald made a gag of the notion last summer, but fashion designer Elizabeth Hawes is dead serious.

"I'm making a skirt for men," she said in her room at the Hotel Chelsea. The skirt will be on view the first week of April, part of a show she is sharing with Rudi Gernreich at the Brooklyn Museum. Though the exhibition is billed as retrospective Hawes, at least, can't resist throwing in a few prophecies.

Elizabeth Hawes has always been loudly and defiantly ahead of her time. In 1938, she was a hot name in fashion. She was designing free, swingy clothes. "Mrs. Chase (Edna Woolman Chase, then editor of *Vogue*) had a terrible time with me," she says. She had also written a book with the world's catchiest title, "Fashion is Spinach." It was the first less than reverent approach to fashion and was anti-establishment, to say the least.

Since she and her partner, Narcissa Vanderlip closed their dress salon on Madison Avenue, Hawes has been living on the West Coast. She packed up and drove herself out in a Peugot, re-discovering America all the way.

It was on the West Coast that she met Rudi Gernreich, another free thinker who likes to speculate on the fashion future. They became great friends.

She has kept a few clients, like Mrs. Louis (Eleanor) Gimbel, who swears by her. She is borrowing back some of their clothes for the 70 percent of the show that will be retrospective. Her room at the Chelsea is full of dress dummies, wearing her favorite circular tweed capes and a hostess caftan, made of different sample lengths of satin brocade put together like an abstract painting.

The Brooklyn Museum, which has always been strong for American creative talent, already owns quite a collection of early Hawes.

Though Hawes seemed big and formidable in her Spinach days when she spoke at The Fashion Group (women in the fashion industry) or tossed off one wise crack after another at her openings, she is actually a small, bright-eyed woman who looks more like a college professor than a fashion designer.

"Do you realize that this is the first time in history that women have been able to wear anything they feel like?" she asked, opening a drawer and pulling out a white yarn wig that she made for herself.

"It's adorable, isn't it? Every woman who sees it wants one." She's so right. The wig would have looked great at Susan Stein's party for the King of Morocco's sister the other night.

What really fascinates Hawes at the moment, though, is this business of men's fashions. "It's just ready to bust loose," she says.

Hawes felt the beginning back in 1938 when the look of gayer shirts and looser clothes started filtering down from Harlem. She put on a men's fashion show that year, she says. Paul Draper, the dancer, and Bill Chadboutne were among the eight models. In the show Hawes predicted many fashions like lace cuffs that have come true on London's Carnaby Street.

The same year she wrote "Men Can Take It" commiserating with men on what they have to wear. Thurber did the illustrations.

Since she lives in Berkeley, Hawes has been doing scientific research on the campus there. "Most of the boys are terribly conservative in their clothes. The time is ripe, though, and I know it's going to crack."

So you won't be caught dead in a skirt and neither will any man you know?

Hawes predicted that women's fashions would become free and funny, and goodness knows they are.

She has a record for being right, but about thirty years too soon.

12

A Campaign Issue—Clothes?

Eleni Epstein

The Washington Evening Star, September 16, 1960

We fully expect the next political directive to come not from the political candidates but from their wives.

It may amount to a "cease and desist" order on any future discussion of how much each spends on her wardrobe, where she gets her clothes, and whether or not she's pro-American in fashion.

Mrs. John F. Kennedy, eyes flashing, prettily hatted, and maternity dressed in a $29.95 number of black silk, answered her fashion critics who declare she's "too chic, spends some $30,000 a year for clothes in Paris along with her mother-in-law."

That's hitting below the belt, says Mrs. Kennedy in her pert inimitable way.

What's more, when she was interviewed in New York at the Waldorf Towers, reporters saw a book of Norell dress sketches sent with fabric swatches, on a coffee table.

Mrs. Kennedy is an open admirer of the talented Norell, and has often bought his clothes. Not directly from him but through stores.

Questioned last week as to whether he had been designated as "the American designer who has lined Mrs. Kennedy up" after she was reportedly told to buy only American, he said, "I don't know a thing about it."

Questioned yesterday, Mr. Norell told us he had just gotten in from Boston and was delighted with the report that his sketches and swatches were on the table for Mrs. Kennedy's perusal. "I'd be happy to make clothes for her. Who wouldn't? She's a dream to dress."

"I don't know how they got there," he explained. The explanation came our way later in the afternoon from Adolph Klein, a former president of the Couture Group of the New York Dress Institute, and now a vice president in the Norell firm.

"Eleanor Lambert (fashion publicist for the New York garment industry) called and asked us to send over Norman's sketches and swatches. Without question we shot them over to her and that's how Mrs. Kennedy got them," Mr. Klein said.

Mr. Klein mentioned, Mrs. Kennedy has always admired Norell, and since she has always lived and dressed in, that design orbit, there is no reason why she shouldn't dress expensively.

"I see no reason why our political figures have to look like they came straight from the poorhouse."

The Washington dressmaker Mrs. Kennedy referred to yesterday is probably Mrs. Norman Paul of Saint-Aubin in Georgetown. It's been about a year since any dresses were made for Mrs. Kennedy there, but "she did come in for a hat to wear to one of the de Gaulle parties," Mrs. Paul said.

Another young Washington designer, Patricia d'Arascu who was formerly with the Saint-Aubin salon about three years ago made several things for her at that time.

One was a Nile green organza strapless gown with an entire bodice of lilies of the valley with a matching green stole.

The other design was a Chanel-type suit of beige and black tweed. "We have many mutual friends in Paris." Mrs. d'Arascu mentioned. Mrs. Kennedy mentioned to her that she would drop by her Georgetown shop, Vogue de Paris, when things became less hectic.

"Maybe when she returns next week," she added, "I will get in touch with her again."

13

Candidates in a Tie on Fashion's Slate

Eleni Epstein

The Washington Evening Star, April 10, 1968

By his tie ye may know him! It's doubtful that the Presidential race will end in a tie but the candidate who ties on a tie of distinction may get more votes than he figured.

To make certain that presidential candidates putting out their necks do so in style, the Men's Tie Foundation is presenting the three announced candidates (and any Johnny come-latelys) with tie wardrobes.

The Total Image concerns the politician and the candidate can state his political position with ties that bolster his conservative, flamboyant, or grassroots appeal.

The bi-partisan president of the foundation, Myron H. Ackerman, has come up with these tips for the politics:

TV APPEARANCES — Though there are many with color sets the candidate must keep in mind that there are so many more black-and-white sets which won't show the subtle tones and hues of a color or pattern. Stripes are better. They come across to an audience with forcible impact.

COLLEGE CAMPUS GROUP — Relate. And since stripes are the prevailing favorite of the on-campus group, follow the scene.

OUTDOOR RALLIES — Red, white and blue goes over big. A brighter pattern and color is great for the "regular guy" mood the candidate may wish to establish.

FUND RAISING — No nonsense here. A serious attitude with a bit of banking sobriety establishes the need for funds.

LADIES' GROUPS — Women who pick their husbands' ties will all be mentally selecting one for their favorite candidate. It should be remembered they love patterned neckwear.

SMALL GROUP APPEARANCES — A casual, intimate, but still informed air will be expressed by the nubby weaves that some ties possess.

FORMAL EVENTS — As specified, either black tie with dinner clothes or should the occasion come up white tie and tails.

What kind of a tie does a candidate wear to a "happening"? Well, if authenticity is what propels him, he will call his teenage son or friend, who'll dig one up that may have belonged to the candidate during the real "Bonnie and Clyde" era.

PART II

1970s–1990s

Introduction to PART II

The book's second part covers the period from the 1970s to the end of the twentieth century. It was a particularly rich period for fashion criticism (and for cultural criticism more generally), when issues of gender and racial identity as articulated through fashion came to the fore, thus fully embedding fashion criticism into larger socio-cultural concerns. Although these shifts started in the 1960s, they did not make their full effect felt with the genre of fashion criticism until the 1970s. As discussed in the introduction, the early 1970s are when most newspapers transformed their women's pages into style sections, and it was also not until the 1970s that feminist thought and writing, now identified as second-wave feminism, entered fashion criticism.

Part II opens with an article from 1975 by the British writer Angela Carter (1940–1992) written for *New Society,* an intellectual magazine dedicated to social enquiry. Founded in the 1960s, the magazine was acquired by *The New Statesman* in 1988. Carter is best known for her surrealist fiction, but she contributed a number of articles on fashion for *New Society*. The piece included in the anthology, "The Wound in the Face," is clearly informed by feminist thought, discussing fashionable make-up as mediating changes in femininity and women's social roles. In a lyrically written passage, Carter bemused a short-lived moment in the 1970s when black lipstick and red eye shadow graced fashionable faces on and off magazines pages as a visual resistance to conventional feminine beauty:

> Because black lipstick and red eyeshadow never "beautified" anybody. They were the cosmetic equivalent of Duchamp's moustache on the Mona Lisa. They were cosmetics used as satire on cosmetics, on the arbitrary convention that puts blue on eyelids and pink on lips. Why not the other way round? The best part of the joke was that the look itself was utterly monstrous. It instantly converted the most beautiful women into outrageous grotesques; every face a work of anti-art. I enjoyed it very, very much. (Carter, 1975, 214)

Also, from the 1970s is Kennedy Fraser's article assessing that season's fashion shows. The New York-based English born writer succeeded Lois Long in 1970 as the *New Yorker*'s fashion critic and is equally unsparing in her articles. This particular article, a review of the New York 1977/1978 Fall collections, rather than simply discussing clothing, focuses on the shift of the fashion show into a performance, and the new role occupied by the models as performers. The article also discusses the increased diversity in fashion, in the context of the runway shows. The 1970s, in fact, saw the rise of a number of Black models, such as Alva Chinn, Bethann Hardison, and Pat Cleveland (see cover) among others.

The cultural critic Susan Sontag (1933–2004) wrote about fashion for *Vogue* in 1978 on occasion of an exhibition and catalog of the work of Richard Avedon. The article provides a critical assessment of fashion; unfortunately, it has not achieved the attention it deserves, as it was not included in Sontag's essay collections and, to my knowledge, has never been republished until now. Deceptively titled "Looking at Avedon," her article engages in a sustained critical discussion of fashion and its meanings, prior to discussing Avedon's fashion photography. According to Sontag, "fashion concerns itself with dematerializing the material world. In particular, the body itself is made as incorporeal as possible. [...] The flesh," she adds, "becomes itself a garment, to be presented in mint condition." (Sontag, 1978, 461) The increasingly visual import of fashion, according to Sontag, is what placed fashion photography at the center of the fashion "world."

Following Sontag's neglected essay is an article from 1982 by another incisive cultural critic, Bebe Moore Campbell (1950–2006). The American author remains best known for her novels, which unpacked topics including racism (her first novel, 1992's *Your Blues Ain't Like Mine*, was based on Emmett Till's murder), and later mental illness. However, Campbell also had a prolific journalistic career, writing among other topics on fashion and beauty for prominent magazines intended primarily for an African American audience, such as *Essence* and *Ebony*. The article in the anthology, originally published in *Ebony*, is titled "What Happened to the Fro?" and is steeped in the awareness of the ways "hairstyles have social, cultural, economic and political implications" (Campbell, 1982, 84)—particularly so for Black women. At times using moving personal recollections regarding her own adoption of the Afro in the late 1960s, Campbell recounts and speculates on the shifts in popularity and meaning of the hairstyle: how it went from "a rowdy, revolutionary symbol" in the 1960s to a fashion statement in the 1970s and had begun to lose in popularity in the 1980s.

The subsequent section belongs to the renowned fashion critic Holly Brubach. Originally published in *The Atlantic* in 1987, it is an ambivalent assessment of the work of Ralph Lauren, focusing on the designer's elaborate constructions of wealthy WASP utopias through his advertisements, stores, and clothing. In 1988, Brubach joined the staff of *The New Yorker*, where she wrote on fashion. Originally published in *The New Yorker* in 1989, "In Fashion: Modernism Outmoded" is a critical review of that season's Milan collection which singles out for praise Franco Moschino and other Italian designers.

The next article, by the writer and academic Elizabeth Wilson, was published in 1989 in *The New Statesman*, a British cultural and political magazine. Ironically titled "Haute Coiffure de Gel," a play on words on the gelatinized hairstyles popular in the 1980s, the essay discusses how the political conservatism of the 1980s was mediated through fashion. Writing at the end of the decade—it ran in December—Wilson takes stocks of the period's fashion in the wake of Thatcherite Britain and looks forward to the next decade.

Another rebuff of the 1980s fashion and its politics is brought forth by Eve Babitz. In her 1992 article for *Vogue*, "Hippie Heaven," the California author discusses fashion's hippie revival in the early 1990s through personal anecdotes of her life and dress in the 1960s, intertwined with the cultural history and changing topography of Los Angeles. Surveying the new hippie-inspired stores peppering East Hollywood, which are part of the burgeoning 1990s indie scene, she discusses the endless recycling of fashion history.

Although best known as an academic writer and curator, Valerie Steele has also written for fashion magazines and newspapers. Included in this anthology is "Calvinism Unclothed," a detailed assessment of Calvin Klein published in 1992 in *Design Quarterly*, a magazine published by the Walker Art Center (Minneapolis, MN) from 1946 to 1996 to explore societal impact of design. Steele's article juxtaposes Calvin Klein's minimalist clothing to his highly sexualized advertising, which brought male sexuality and beauty to the mainstream, alongside the more conventional use of sexualized female bodies.

Unlike with other fields of cultural criticism, the title of "fashion critic" was not officially used as a job title at *The New York Times* until 1994, when it was coined for Amy Spindler (1963–2004). The American journalist worked at a time when fashion itself came to be seen as having a theoretical and critical edge. It is around this time that the term "deconstruction fashion" came to be used in the English language. Spindler was influential in defining this movement in the pages of the *Times,* discussing, often critically, other significant aesthetic shifts in the fashion of the 1990s.

Despite being the first journalist at the *Times* to acquire the title of fashion critic, Spindler has not been discussed within the academic literature on fashion criticism—an omission likely due to her career having been cut short by her untimely death at forty. Her criticism was notable for its coverage of fashion as part of greater cultural shifts of the 1990s. As Cathy Horyn, Spindler's successor at the paper, noted: "Ms. Spindler was never interested in simply putting a dress on a page or talking about hemlines. She recognized that fashion was as important a cultural barometer as music or art and that it should be—demanded to be—covered as rigorously as a political campaign" (Horyn, 2004). Spindler's article included in this anthology is a detailed assessment of deconstruction fashion, which describes its sartorial vocabulary of raw hems and frayed edges. Contextualizing deconstruction in fashion, Spindler argues that the movement came to signify a certain rejection of luxury: "a backlash against established 80s excess [...] a sort of asbestos suit against the bonfire of the vanities" (Spindler, 1993, V9).

Although best known as a historian of art and fashion, Anne Hollander (1930–2014) wrote for a number of publications celebrated for their cultural criticism, such as the *New Republic,* the *London Review of Books*, and the *New York Review of Books.* The anthology includes two short extracts from her book *Sex and Suits,* first published in 1994. Here, Hollander discusses the significance of men's and women's suits in the construction of femininity and masculinity in Western fashion. She then chronicles a move toward an androgynous look, which she praises for its liberating effects on sexuality:

> The intense power of deliberately androgynous looks has lately asserted itself publicly among adored popular performers, visually confirming the ancient idea that pleasure in sexuality may be richer if the two sexes are allowed to acknowledge their erotic affinities and are not kept stringently divided. (Hollander, [1994] 2016, 138)

Lynn Yaeger, currently a contributing fashion editor for *Vogue,* is perhaps best known for her long tenure at the *Village Voice*—the iconic weekly alternative paper that chronicled downtown culture from its founding in 1955 until ceasing its print edition in 2017. Yaeger, who was at the *Voice* for thirty years (fifteen of those writing about fashion), was known for her democratic approach to fashion. Her first article in the anthology, titled "The Eastern Bloc," surveys the mid-1990s offering of East Village independent boutiques; its humor and user-friendly nature are reminiscent of *New Yorker* critic Lois Long's surveys of New York stores—although, through Yaeger's lens, geared for a downtown *demimonde.* Her second article here, "Avant Guardians," continues the explorations of the experimental downtown New York fashion scene, this time through emerging designers shows.

Hilton Als is a longtime *New Yorker* writer perhaps best known for his theater criticism, for which he won the Pulitzer Prize in criticism in 2017. The Pulitzer board prized Als for placing theater in cultural context, "particularly the shifting landscape of gender, sexuality, and race." The same could be said for Als's writing on fashion, much of it from the late '90s. Included in the anthology is Hals's 1994 *New Yorker* profile of André Leon Talley. Suggestively titled

"The Only One," it captures the theatrical persona of Talley while exploring the complexities of the subject's position as an extremely successful Black American in the fashion industry. Finally, the article lays bare the persistent racism in the Parisian fashion circles in which the famous editor circulates. In his second article here, from 1996, Als critically engages with fashion photography. The writer perfectly captures the dominant look of 1990s fashion photography, later to be known as "heroin chic," best articulated in the work of the late British photographer Corinne Day's work: "Day's world unfolds in broad expanses of grimy nature, or in dingy council flats that one associated with post-Thatcherite Britain, and the type of girl Day was attracted to was not unlike her: awkward, thin, disconsolate."

Concluding this section of the anthology is an article by Suzy Menkes, one of fashion criticism's most celebrated figures. Currently, at *Vogue*, Menkes spent the meat of her career at *The International Herald Tribune*, where she covered fashion from 1988 until 2014, shortly after the paper morphed into *The New York Times International Edition*.[1] The London-based Menkes is known for her uncompromising coverage of the collections and her deep knowledge of the fashion industry and its histories. An example of her exacting criticism, Menkes's article, from 1996, dissects with her usual precision the military look, which was an undercurrent of that season's international collections.

Bibliography and Further Readings

Als, Hilton. *White Girls*. San Francisco: McSweeney's, 2013.

Brubach, Holly. *A Dedicated Follower of Fashion*. London: Phaidon, 1999.

Campbell, Bebe Moore. "What Happened to the Afro?" *Ebony* vol. 37, no. 8 (June 1982): 79–85.

Carter, Angela. "The Wound in the Face." *New Society*. April 24, 1975: 214–15.

Carter, Angela. *Shaking a Leg: Collected Journalism and Writings*. New York: Penguin, 1998.

Fraser, Kennedy. *The Fashionable Mind: Reflections on Fashion 1970–1982*. Boston: D.R. Godine, 1985.

Fraser, Kennedy. *Scenes from the Fashionable World*. New York: Knopf, 1987.

Frock Consciousness: Writing about Clothes from the London Review of Books. LRB Collections, vol. 6. London: London Review of Books, 2019.

Hollander, Anne. *Sex and Suits: The Evolution of Modern Dress*. New York and London: Bloomsbury, 2016. First published 1994 by Alfred A. Knopf (New York).

Horyn, Cathy. "Amy M. Spindler, Style Editor of Times Magazine, Dies at 40." *The New York Times*, February 28, 2004.

Lamb, Yvonne Shinhoster. "Bebe Moore Campbell." *The Washington Post*, November 28, 2006.

Rollyson, Carl. *Understanding Susan Sontag*. Columbia SC: University of South Carolina Press, 2016.

Sontag, Susan. "Looking with Avedon." *Vogue* vol. 168, no. 9 (September 1978): 460–1, 507–8.

Spindler, Amy. "Coming Apart." *The New York Times*. July, 25, 1993.

---

[1] A Paris-based English language newspaper, it began in 1887 as *The Paris Herald* and soon morphed into the international edition of *The New York Herald Tribune*; in the 1960s, upon *The New York Herald Tribune's* demise, the international paper became jointly owned by *The Washington Post, The New York Times,* and Whitney Communications.

14

The Wound in the Face

Angela Carter

New Society, April 24, 1975

I spent a hallucinatory weekend, staring at faces I'd cut of women's magazines, either from the beauty page or from the ads—all this season's faces. I stuck twenty or thirty faces on the wall and tried to work out from the evidence before me (a) what women's faces are supposed to be looking like, now; and (b) why. It was something of an exercise in pure form, because the magazine models' faces aren't exactly the face in the street—not low-style, do-it-yourself assemblages, but more a platonic, ideal face. Further, they reflect, as well as the mood of the moment, what the manufacturers are trying to push this year. Nevertheless, the zeitgeist works through the manufacturers, too. They do not understand their own imagery, any more than the consumer who demonstrates it does. I am still working on the nature of the imagery of cosmetics. I think it scares me.

Construing the imagery was an unnerving experience because all the models appeared to be staring straight at me with such a heavy, static quality of *being there* that it was difficult to escape the feeling they were accusing me of something. (How rarely women look one another in the eye.) Only two of the faces wear anything like smiles, and only one is showing a hint of her teeth. This season's is not an extrovert face. Because there is not more to smile about this season? Surely. It is a bland, hard, bright face: it is also curiously familiar, though I have never seen it before.

The face of the seventies matches the fashions in clothes that have dictated some of its features, and is directly related to the social environment which produces it. Like fashions in clothes, fashions in faces have been stuck in pastiche for the past four or five years. This bankruptcy is disguised by ever more ingenious pastiche—of the thirties, the forties, the fifties, the Middle East, Xanadu, Wessex (those smocks). Compared with the short skirts and flat shoes of ten years ago, style in women's clothes has regressed. Designers are trying to make us cripple our feet again with high-heeled shoes and make us trail long skirts in dog shit. The re-introduction of rouge is part of the regression; rouge, coyly re-introduced under the nineteenth-century euphemism of "blusher."

The rather older face—the *Vogue* face, as opposed to the *Honey* face—is strongly under the 1930s influence, the iconographic, androgynous face of Dietrich and Garbo, with heavily emphasised bone structures, hollow cheeks and hooded eyelids. Warhol's transvestite superstars, too, and his magazines, *Interview,* with its passion for the tacky, the kitschy, for fake glamour, for rhinestones, sequins, Joan Crawford, Ann-Margret, have exercised a profound influence. As a result, fashionable women now tend to look like women imitating men imitating women, an interesting reversal. The face currently perpetuated by the glossies aspires to the condition of that of Warhol's Candy Darling.

The main message is that the hard, bland face with which women brazened their way through the tough 1930s, the tough 1940s and the decreasingly tough 1950s (at the end of the 1950s, when things got less tough, they abandoned it) is back to sustain us through the tough 1970s. It recapitulates the glazed, self-contained look typical of times of austerity.

But what is one to make of the transvestite influence? It is that the physical image of women took such a battering in the sixties that when femininity did for want of anything better, return, the only people we could go to to find out what it had looked like were the dedicated male impersonators who had kept the concept alive in their sequined gowns, their spike-heeled shoes and their peony lipsticks? Probably. "The feminine character, and the idea of femininity on which it was modelled, are products of masculine society," says Theodor Adorno. Clearly a female impersonator knows more about his idea of the character he is mimicking than I do, because it is his very own invention, and has nothing to do with me.

Yet what about the Rousseauesque naturalism of the dominant image of women in the mid-1960s? Adorno can account for that, sociologically, too. "The image of undistorted nature arises only in distortion, as its opposite." The sixties face was described early in the decade by *Queen* (as it was then) as a "look of luminous vacancy."

The sixties face had a bee-stung under lip, enormous eyes and a lot of disordered hair. It saw itself as a wild, sweet, gipsyish, vulnerable face. It's very lack of artifice suggested sexual licence in a period that had learned to equate cosmetics, not with profligacy as in the nineteenth century, but with conformity to the standard social and sexual female norm. Nice girls wore lipstick, in the fifties.

When the sixties face used cosmetics at all, it explored imports such as kohl and henna from Indian shops. These had the twin advantage of being extremely exotic and very, very cheap. For purposes of pure decorations, for fun, it sometimes stuck sequins to itself, or those little gold and silver "good conduct" stars. It bought sticks of stage make-up, and did extraordinary things around its eyes with them, at about the time of Flower Power. It was, basically, a low-style or do-it-yourself face. Ever in search of the new, the magazines eventually caught up with it, and high-style faces caught on the flowered cheeks and stars on the eyelids at about the time the manufacturers did. So women had to pay considerably more for their pleasures.

The sixties look gloried in its open pores and, if your eye wasn't in to the particular look, you probably thought it didn't wash itself much. But it was just that, after all those years of pancake make-up, people had forgotten what the real colour of female skin was. This face cost very little in upkeep. Indeed, it was basically a most economical and serviceable model and it was quite a shock to realise, as the years passed, that all the beauty experts were wrong and, unless exposed to the most violent weather, it did not erode if it were left ungreased. A face is not a bicycle. Nevertheless, since this face has adopted naturalism as an ingenious form of artifice, it *was* a mask, like the grease masks of cosmetics, though frequently refreshingly eccentric.

At the end of that decade, in a brief period of delirium, there was a startling vogue of black lipstick and red eyeshadow. For a little while we were painting ourselves up just as arbitrarily as Larionov did before the Revolution. Dada in the boudoir! What a witty parody of the whole theory of cosmetics!

The basic theory of cosmetics is that they make a woman beautiful. Or, as the advertisers say, more beautiful. You blot out your noxious wens and warts and blemishes, shade your nose to make it bigger or smaller, draw attention to your good features by bright colours, and distract it from your bad features by more reticent tones. But those manic and desperate styles—leapt on and exploited instantly by desperate manufacturers—seemed to be about to break the ground for a whole new aesthetic of appearance, which would have nothing to do with the conformist ideology of "beauty" at all. Might—ah, might—it be possible to use cosmetics to free women from the burden of having to look beautiful altogether?

Because black lipstick and read eyeshadow never "beautified" anybody. They were the cosmetic equivalent of Duchamp's moustache on the Mona Lisa. They were cosmetics used as satire on cosmetics, on the arbitrary convention that puts blue on eyelids and pink on lips. Why not the other way round? The best part of the joke was that the look itself was utterly monstrous. It instantly converted the most beautiful women into outrageous grotesques; every face a work of anti-art. I enjoyed it very, very much.

However, it takes a helluva lot of guts to maintain oneself in a perpetual state of visual offensiveness. Most women could not resist keeping open a treacherous little corner open on sex appeal. Besides, the joke went a little too near the bone. To do up your eyes so that they look like self-inflicted wounds is to wear on your face the evidence of the violence your environment inflicts on you.

Black paint around the eyes is such a familiar convention it seems natural; so does red paint on the mouth. We are so used to the bright red mouth we no longer see it as the wound it mimics, except in the treacherous lucidity of paranoia. But the shock of the red-painted eye recalls, directly, the blinding of Gloucester in *Lear*; or, worse and more aptly, the symbolic blinding of Oedipus. Women are allowed—indeed, encouraged to exhibit the sign of their symbolic castration—but only in the socially sanctioned place. To transpose it upwards is to allow its significance to become apparent. We went too far, that time. Scrub it all off, and start again.

And once we started again, red lipstick came back. Elizabeth I seems to have got a fine, bright carmine with which to touch up her far from generous lips. The Victorian beauty's "rosebud mouth"—the mouth so tiny it was a wonder how it managed to contain her teeth—was a restrained pink. Flappers' lips spread out and went red again, and the "generous mouth" became one of the great glamour conventions of the entire twentieth century and has remained so, even if its colour is modified.

White-based lipsticks, colourless glosses, or no lipstick at all, were used in the 1960s. Now the mouth is back as bloody gash, a visible wound. This mouth bleeds over everything, cups, ice cream, table napkins, towels. Mary Quant has a shade called (of course) "Bloody Mary," to ram the point home. We will leave our bloody spoor behind us, to show we have been there.

In the thirties, that spoor was the trademark of the sophisticate, the type of Baudelairean female dandy Dietrich impersonated so well. Dietrich always transcended self-pity and self-destruction, wore the wound like a badge of triumph, and came out on top. But Iris Storm in Michael Arlen's *The Green Hat*, the heroines of Maurice Dekobra, the wicked film star in Chandler's *The Little Sister* who always dressed in black to offset her fire engine of a mouth—

they all dripped blood over everything as they stalked sophisticatedly to their dooms. In their wake, lipstick traces on a cigarette stub; the perfect imprint, like half a heart, of a scarlet lower lip on a drained Martini glass; the telltale scarlet letter, A for adultery. On a shirt collar on the kitsch poetry of it all!

Elizabeth Taylor scrawls "Not for sale" on her bedroom mirror in her red, red lipstick in *Butterfield 8*. The generosity the mouth has given so freely, will be spurned with brutal ingratitude. The open wound will never heal. Perhaps, sometimes, she will lament the loss of the tight rosebud; but it has gone forever.

The revival of red lipstick indicates, above all, I suppose that women's sense of security was transient.

15

Feminine Fashions: The Fall Collections II

Kennedy Fraser

The New Yorker, July 18, 1977

To judge by all the theatrical fanfare with which these collections are launched these days, audiences are to be discouraged from forming impressions of fashion shows which are based on the clothes alone. In many cases, the productions have become far more elaborate than the simple, graceful clothes being widely produced for fall. How, then, is one supposed to assess the curious hybrid that is the dramatic new fashion show? To apply the standards of the theatre, the dance, or the art gallery is patently absurd, however designers may seek to cloak their efforts in the trappings of grander and more widely respected art forms than the craft of clothing manufacture. The form whose criteria would seem most applicable is the public-relations happening, but this is scarcely a helpful guideline, having historical roots even shallower than those of fashion shows, and being a genre that by its nature makes no provision for critical analysis on the part of its audience. One is supposed to have one's attention alerted (often in some very nebulous way) by a P.R. event, or perhaps to be staggered by the expense it involves, but one is not intended to judge it, compare any one with any other, or refer to a tradition. Each example bubbles up and then sinks back into its own moment.

But as one experiences the motley events that are the new fashion shows, one aspect of the whole does seem to present itself as a valid object of critical scrutiny—the performance of the models. This is a surprising development, because no spectator at a traditional fashion show was ever particularly tempted to think of these young women as performers, let alone as people bent on expressing themselves. Their emanations, when not completely neutral, used to be vaguely animal-like. They were gazelles and, in some cases, jungle tigresses at first; when, five years or so back, they started dancing down the aisles in youthful-looking fashions instead of gliding by in mature ones, they became more like puppies. But now models seem anxious to be seen as human beings, in some direct and equal relationship with the human beings who come to gawk at them, and they are encouraged—in varying degrees, according to the designer's taste—to project their personalities. Fashion shows have become more elaborate in part because the job of modelling, within its own peculiarly circumscribed range, has started to evolve. It was perhaps inevitable that in our age of individuality and "creativity"—and long after practically every other kind of woman has learned to stand up for herself—models should begin to assert their right to be more than objects, and to behave like people. In the field of fashion photography (a career separate from showroom modelling, although the same woman is sometimes in demand in both), the new concern for the model's self-respect is reflected in current talk of listing—along with the photographer, the designer, and the manufacturers of accessories—the name of the woman who is shown wearing the clothes. It is now common to see showroom models greet friends in the audience they parade before; and at the end of the show they gather round the designer to bill, coo, and applaud his work as affectionate show-business equals. Even designers who used to be known for the sedateness of their clothes now permit models to prance, flirt, mime, jog, or ham things up with spoofs of the model's traditional struts and turns. Watching the show put on by Carol Horn, one felt like some indulgent nanny on the sidelines of a creative playground where models got up to a hundred cutely self-expressive stunts, from playing the flute, knitting, and waving lighted flashlights to applying lipstick to each other's mouths.

The show presented by Anne Klein and Company in the Grand Ballroom of the Plaza was one of the most comprehensive of the season's examples of the new fashion spectacle. Throughout the show, the senses of the huge audience were remorselessly manipulated by dramatic changes of lighting and music. (The first group of clothes appeared in a semi-darkness that was chopped up by the flicker of one of those discothèque light machines which make their victims feel they have a terrible malfunction of the eyelids or have wandered into a Buster Keaton film.) And the models in the show were given a lavish opportunity to spread their performer's wings. Complex choreography sent them out in groups, weaving in and out in a Busby Berkeley flow, or else captured them temporarily in static spotlit friezes of kneeling and stretching poses, like figures on a Grecian vase. The show's finale wholeheartedly abandoned the pretense of making the clothes look remotely the way they would look on Anne Klein customers in their normal lives. The models—or at least, those among them who were capable of taking a stab at such activity— were transformed into ballet dancers who happened to be wearing Anne Klein designs. This was clearly the models' big moment. Each in turn got to make a dramatic entrance, leaping out from behind the gold-and-white Ionic columns of the ballroom's stage; to flit down the long runway essaying balletic twirls, twists of the wrist, and chassés; and then at the end to retreat into the wings with a ballerina's limpid lingering backward gaze. The audience, which thought that it had come to see a mere fashion show, rooted valiantly for these more high-flown performances, and it seems a mite churlish to observe that most of the models made simply awful dancers. (Among the few things that inspire the same sinking feeling as clumsy dancing are an ice skater coming a cropper and a horse misjudging a fence.)

One sometimes yearns, as one trudges round the collections from this extravagant entertainment to that stimulating performance, for the days when fashion shows were fashion shows, and models, instead of performing other jobs with an amateurishness that is supposed to be endearing, did their own work with a superbly professional grace. They are beautiful women, for the most part, with elegant models' bodies, which are of quite a different build from the bodies of dancers. But the psychological tide may have turned for them irrevocably; it is probably impossible for them to put on a completely bland act again. They look really happy now only when the show is grand, the crowd is huge, and they can feel themselves to be the active stars of a noisy success. In smaller, more traditional shows, when they are simply walking down the runway in new clothes, their expressions betray the prickly defensiveness characteristic of people who feel overqualified for their job. But, in the end, the possibility of models' developing themselves through their work will always be limited. Even though attempts are being made to emphasize their personalities, models must always remain subsidiary to the clothes they display and serve as litmus paper for the designer's tone. One of the most interesting aspects of attending lots of shows is witnessing how utterly different the same top models, who go the rounds of them all, can look and behave in different circumstances, according to their outfits, their perception of the atmosphere around them, and the degree to which they are encouraged to display their newly discovered sense of self.

While it seems futile to judge fashion shows solely on their presentation and difficult to judge them solely by their clothes, it seems fair to demand that there be some semblance of harmony between the two. One of the most charming of the season's smaller shows was that given by the designer Joan Vass—it was her first such effort—in her own apartment, on West Twenty-fifth Street. Mrs. Vass's clothes are all made by hand on cottage-industry lines. Many of her styles are given names, as though they were family pets—there is the Alexander Nevsky coat, the Sierra Club muffler, and the Christopher Robin hat. Her show was on an equally intimate and human plane. The apartment where it took place is a huge, shabby penthouse, a cross between an artist's loft and a greenhouse. The "models" included her daughter and her three sons and a group of young dancers whom the designer had discovered in Riverside Church. These dancers had their own inexperienced and very free interpretation of what was called for in displaying clothes. Their spontaneity made a welcome change from the artificiality of the models the audience had watched for hours and days at a time in other showrooms. The dancers were not exactly the same as average women, but they had, in several cases, the rounded curves that ordinary customers are often endowed with and real models never possess.

Along with harmony between form and content, the audience at fashion shows ought to have a right to expect some consistency of tone and some evidence of editing in the designer's presentation of his styles. Many shows are unnecessarily padded out with multiple examples of the same idea or with styles that will never actually be produced for sale in the stores. But this season Perry Ellis, Charles Suppon, Bill Haire, Richard Assatly, Gil Aimbez, and Alice Blaine (or the firms who employ these designers) were responsible for sound and generally well-edited collections. Their presentation was often fairly lavish, but the clothes were usually able to match the vitality of the display. Giorgio Sant'Angelo presented a hopelessly rambling show, yet he may be excused for that, because he is among the few really artistic talents around, and his collection had some perfectly brilliant ideas in it. But my favorites of the several dozen shows I saw were those of Calvin Klein, Geoffrey Beene, and Mrs. Harriet Winter. Each of these collections had a markedly different tone, but among them they sum up the new fall fashions at their best. In all three cases, the clothes had a private, unostentatious character and were presented with relative modesty and restraint in the designers' own showrooms.

Getting in and out of the Calvin Klein show was one of the most nightmarish experiences of the whole season, and the near riots that erupted in the aisles and at the elevators on that day have become notorious in the annals of the fashion world. But once the audience was squeezed into the room (at least, those of the invited guests fortunate enough not to be blocked in the lobby or trapped in the elevators) it saw a show whose models instinctively comported themselves to match the clothes they wore—with a fine combination of delicacy and arrogance. Klein's style is more controlled and conservative-looking than either Beene's or Mrs. Winter's, but his work has developed and lightened considerably from the strictly tailored sportswear with which he rose to prominence—a tailoring that used to seem too cramped and inhibited for my taste. A general feminizing of Klein's tailoring was exemplified in this collection by the little jackets with which he has replaced his famous but more masculine-looking blazers. (Little jackets, cropped even shorter than Klein's, showed up elsewhere, too—notably in Richard Assatly's collection for the firm of Gino-Snow, in Patti Cappalli's for Jerry Silverman Sport, and in Ralph Lauren's show.) The Klein jacket is narrow-torsoed, squarish-shouldered, single-breasted, and short—of a length somewhere between bellhop and hipbone. It is a silhouette that flatters more women than the longer, double-breasted blazer does. Although any mention of thrift shops is as taboo in the professional fashion world as the irresponsible boosting of miniskirts, the pre-New Look fashions to be found in such places have certainly had an influence in the reshaping of contemporary jackets. And Klein's extremely feminine, beautifully detailed blouses, used in combination with relatively masculine tailoring, are a modern version of a fashion idea that is several decades old. Sometimes his jackets appeared with skirts that fell to some three inches below the knee, but they looked their self-confident best in combination with sinuous, long-legged pleated-front trousers. (Klein's loyalty to the elegance of well-cut trousers is refreshing at a time when other designers are to be seen turning resolutely to skirts for their greater softness" and "femininity"—the often mindlessly employed shibboleths for the new fall clothes.) Outfits were assembled in gentle combinations of the colors of nuts and fruits and in interesting textural contrasts—tops of velvet, fine tweed, or cashmere over blouses of cotton, silk broadcloth, Charmeuse, or handkerchief linen. Blouses had delicate tucks and discreet ruffles, or more of the scalloped collars and cuffs that Klein used so successfully in his spring collection. Often, these scallops were turned down at the wrist to extend beyond a jacket sleeve and frame the hand, or turned up at the collar and ringed round by a silk kerchief for a swan-neck effect. This was tied in a bohemian bow tie that Klein's written release characterized as "very George Sand." Other new-looking toppings included hipbone-length cardigan jackets that were collarless and buttonless and had the savoir-faire of early Chanel; body-hugging wraparound sweaters of fine cashmere; and cashmere pullovers with necklines that followed the collarbone. All these trim sweaters held their own against the big, bulky, hand-knit monsters one saw in profusion elsewhere around town. I had less sympathy for Klein's cashmere sarapes, slung pointlessly over one shoulder (shawls of every kind will be seen ad nauseam in the fall, it seems), and for his use of foulard-printed challis, which also threatens to be part of the obligatory uniform of slaves of fashion. I liked the way Klein used Charmeuse in blouses combined with tops and bottoms of more robust textures but relished the fabric less when it appeared alone for long or short evening gowns. This slithery, satinlike material was used in many of the collections, and designers often played up its overtones of boudoirish sinfulness. To Klein's credit, his choice of colors and style generally mitigated the lingerie connotations. In the main, his collection was notable for its dignity and clarity.

Geoffrey Beene's collection differed from any other by a quality rare among fashion designers, who are on the whole an instinctive breed. (The innovators, of whom there are very few these days, create with instinctive flashes of inspiration. The assimilators and imitators, who form a far larger group, react instinctively to those flashes of inspiration and pass them along at just the right moment.) The distinctive quality of Beene's work—which at the same time reflects an immediate sensuous response to the color and texture of beautiful fabrics—must be characterized as a variety of intellectualism. This is of a kind different from and more deep-seated than the smattering of cultural crosscurrents which has become common in the written releases and statements of "philosophy" that many designers now launch on the world together with their collections. Such releases draw on increasingly ambitious sources these days in their attempt to interpret as well as describe new clothes. Designers rightly perceive that the psychological and cultural atmosphere attaching to an outfit is of as much significance to shoppers as details of its shape, hem length, and color. This atmosphere is what will first capture the customer's imagination and put her in the mood to buy. Descriptions of clothes released by designers have become more fanciful than ever in an attempt to conjure up symbolic images and correspondences between clothes and the arts. At the simplest level, this greater literariness gives colors more inventive names. Perry Ellis's clothes came in, among other things, "pink dust,/blue ridge" hopsacking, "birch" melton, "quail" corduroy, and "true " tweed. Bill Haire listed his outfits as "movements" in "Copen blue and ash" or in "port and clay," and labelled his pastels "Monet blue" and "Degas pink." Devotion to the ballet, fascination with Byron and Shelley, and the influence of Dumas's *The Three Musketeers* were listed as the sources of inspiration for the designer's collection. Credits these days no longer restrict themselves to the names of those who provide shoes, makeup, and hairstyles for fashion shows but stretch to include those responsible for their "poetry" and "choreography" as well. Donna Karan, one of the designers for Anne Klein, referred not to groups of clothes but to various "idioms" and "moods," and she gave credit to Martha Graham and Jane Austen. Before long, we shall doubtless see designers' programs filled with academic footnotes, and their clothes described, like Whistler's paintings, as symphonies in color. But Geoffrey Beene's brand of thoughtfulness goes beyond semantic dabblings and historicist parlor games. It is a sincerely reflective response to women's image of themselves and to the society in which they live.

Beene shows a solid understanding of the principle that if clothes make a psychological and sociological statement about their wearer no woman of intelligence and complexity would wish that message to be a monolithic, single-minded one—particularly if it was drafted on her behalf by a designer who had assembled the same package of self-expression for a thousand other customers. Beene is a master of contrasts and contradictions within a single outfit. In his new collection, he used an infinity of contradicting textures and colors of fabrics—silk under corduroy, bulky hand-knitting over fragile sprigged cotton, shearling jackets over flimsy evening clothes, quilted cotton over velvet, to name a few. Most of his skirts floated wide and full to the graceful low-calf length. But then he slid away from the romantic effect of such skirts (which are also styled for comfort, since one may sprawl or sit cross-legged in them as readily as in pants) by combining them with touches of clumsiness. These touches of self-parodying buffoonery—whose presence always conveys an essentially youthful message—included funny brimmed hats jammed low on the brow, dumpy flat-heeled boots, and pink ballet slippers worn with cream-colored hand-knit legwarmers that rippled into wrinkles round the ankles. (Beene is one of many designers to have been influenced this season by dancers and the dance.) His standard of workmanship is high, and he uses superb and exclusive fabrics. Price—sat least in his couture collection—are considerable. (Those of Beene Bag, his sportswear department, are more moderate.) But the customer who would wear the clothes from his fall collection is not the sort to flaunt her ability to pay for them, and they are pregnant with ironic mixed messages about their value, besides being combined contradictions of style. Other designers showed flashy furs and metallic fabrics that throbbed like Times Square neon with information about their cost. But when Beene showed a luxurious looking coat with deep sable cuffs (there was something of the Balenciaga years in the generosity of its cut) the coat itself was made of a relatively humble chocolate-colored corduroy. The collection was distinctive, too, for its abundance of interesting details and playful accessories: a sausage of trapunto trimming the armhole of a jerkin; gloves and stockings in homespun-wool knit; and belts that were a study of textural contrast within themselves. One belt was a twisted combination of fat noodles of hessian and turquoise silk wound with strings of glitter. Some of the belts were further enlivened by a sprig of eucalyptus or a jaunty teasel.

Harriet Winter's clothes have a style different again from either Beene's or Klein's, but, like theirs, they are bathed in an imaginative atmosphere that feels just right. Her designs for Yesterday's News have a self-contained, almost introspective tone, and a sense of secure, unfrilly femaleness. They have a palpable aura of peace. Skirts in the collection fell gently to boot length and were made of fluid crêpes and jerseys. Her colors were well chosen and well combined, and detailing was interesting without seeming gratuitous. Many of the details, in fact—wrapped and gathered waists; loops of fabric forming ties on jackets; knots at the back of the ankles of loose-limbed pants; and seams that were exposed on the outside of the garment—also performed a function and were an integral part of the structure. (Only in the case of the drawstrings that she used in several styles did Mrs. Winter's tireless investigation of the possibilities of this structural detailing come close to running amok and marring the simplicity of the whole effect.) She also used details with no particular purpose beyond their allure—the superposed double and triple Peter Pan collars she has long favored, and handkerchief schemes of self-fabric falling softly around the throat. Mrs. Winter has said, with a more sincere understanding than many men designers who express similar opinions, that all clothing is an extension of a woman's psyche. She has also described her own designs and techniques as being "machine couture." Between them, these two observations encompass the essence of her style. Her clothes are ladylike without being pompous, and they represent a misty, streamlined dream.

The most compelling new fashions often incorporate the principle of mixed messages, and the new hairstyles and accessories are instrumental in the expression of these contradictions. Although clothes have eased and softened from the rigidly classic sportswear that was around a few seasons back, many of the new clothes can still look "straight" and fairly boring if they are worn with hair and shoes that match their style exactly. But if they are worn with the new crazily sprouting hair-styles or with the eccentric foot-and-leg gear that is around, the effect, though somewhat schizophrenic, is more satisfying. For the most fashionable young women, heads and feet have become prime vehicles for the expression of fantasy. The most interesting styles for these extremities set out not to look flattering but to look witty. One still saw, in some of the shows, hair that had been set on rollers or else blown dry into Waspy-looking pageboys, and nice little flat-heeled pumps or sexy high-heeled evening sandals worn with natural nylons. But all these looked tired and timid beside the freewheeling notions that other designers explored— hair that had been rumpled with the fingers and left to dry naturally under heat lamps; hair set into intricate braids when wet and either left that way or unleashed into a fluffy thatch of Botticelli frizziness; strange-colored combinations of hose and boots, worn in layers over each other; and rumpled, old-mannish socks over hightop sneakers, medieval sandals, or Chinese-cotton Mary Janes.

Giorgio Sant' Angelo's show— although badly in need of editing, one of the season's most imaginative—explored to the utmost the contradicting possibilities of styles for heads and feet. His shoes were uniformly well chosen (credit for them was given to Judie Buie, Sasha, Maud Frizon, Charles Jourdan, and Reed Jay Evins), and they often deflected or scrambled the message of the outfit they accompanied. The lacy refinement of an embroidered Ultrasuede skirt was combined with dark stockings and ankle-high boots with hippie-style Indian fringes at their cuffs. A fringed blanket coat of fire-engine-red mohair, with overtones of wintry, log-fire coziness, appeared with opaque red stockings and matching but distinctly summery sandals. A wispily glamorous evening dress was worn with high heels and thick purple stockings. The hairstyles in the show were equally original. (Credit for these was given to a hairdressing firm called Christiaan Laboratory.) They often involved very intricate braiding that began at the roots of each section of hair and then wound itself close to the scalp to give the effect of a small head. Hairdos like these, when created for the fine and very often blond hair of white models, not only embody a witty contradiction between themselves and the more formal outfits they accompany but also play on the styles of different races. The effect of braids close to a small, neat skull obviously derives from the often exquisite patterns of cornrowing that are seen on the heads of young black women—and on young black men, too.

The most interesting new fashions in hair—and probably in clothes as well—owe much to the coming together of black-and-white styles. Where five years ago black designers and fashionable young black women had their own quite distinctive and separate brand of élan, they have now brought it into something more like the mainstream, and often give to fairly classic, conservative, and expensive styles their own special flair. It is significant that the new hairstyles—whether braiding or unleashed Pre-Raphaelite fullness—may be practically effected on the very different textures of white and black women's hair. The effect is somewhat different in the two cases, but it is equally spectacular. If the new frizz is perhaps some distant descendant of the Afro, it is a gesture of stylishness rather than politics, and its shape—with fullness in the back and sides below the ears rather than on top of the head—is radically different. But the simple unravelling of wet-braided hair into a downy isosceles-triangle shape is not the end of the tale. The locks that come foaming forth like a bush of spirea are then sometimes partly recaptured in a braid that hangs down over one eye, or wholly caught up in a lunatic tuft, sprout, or ponytail set off-center on top of the head or at any other place that takes the wearer's fancy. And then these caught-up sprouts (or the whole bush) are taken a stage further and decorated with what might look to an unsympathetic observer like bits of rubbish. (Although sprout decoration was seen in various places and on many white women, it is true that it was seen at its most stylized in the show given by Scott Barrie, a black designer, who employed a greater proportion of black models than did most of his colleagues on Seventh Avenue.) Flowers and combs in the hair have now been so widely adopted and have such uncompromising, uncontradictory messages of sugary femininity that they are beginning to look passé. Instead of these, the new hair ornaments are dime-store barrettes; fishing flies; strings, loops, and streamers of metallic ribbons, beads, or pearls; funny bits of feather and fur; and sets of bows made out of twisted candy wrappers. The image the new hairstyles bring most readily to mind is of Christmas trees lying in the streets at the end of the festive season and strewn with windblown, rain-tangled remnants of tinselly trimmings.

16

Looking with Avedon

Susan Sontag

Vogue, September 1978

Haunting commerce! Irrepressible art! Fashion is more than the propaganda of couturiers, department stores, makeup firms, or even fashion editors. These efforts to get women to buy more clothes and makeup are also a repository of immobilizing fantasy, of useless delights. Many fashions are more avidly followed than heeded. The industry's feverish, inventive, ever-so-calculating propaganda for the erotic and beautiful has an often indirect, even perverse relation to what people actually *wear*.

Fashion is an acute mentalizing of the erotic. Its subjects are beautiful women, and women comprise most of the audience for these images when they first appear in magazines: women scrutinizing images of women—for an idea of the erotic. Like art generally, fashion concerns itself with dematerializing the material world. In particular, the body itself is made as incorporeal as possible. Skin is transmuted into ivory, its texture purified of imperfections by makeup and lighting. The face is smooth; the silhouette is refined, pared down. The flesh becomes itself a garment, to be presented in mint condition. Always intent on providing an idea of the erotic, fashion transposes the erotic into an image. The ideal would be something very close and quite inaccessible, an image both realistic and preposterous, titillating and chaste, nude and in drag.

Fashion deals out a succession of imperious images, but fashion itself is, first of all, a way of seeing. And not just a way of seeing that is crassly emulative, hooked on staring and shopping; but also disinterested, often ironic, one of civilization's more agreeable excruciations. It is about appreciation, or connoisseurship, based on the recognition of the profundity of surfaces. But a series of statements which assert the superiority of appearances cannot decline to indicate *which* appearances are superior. Hence, the dismaying imperfection of all such attempts to view the world in a superior way.

A superior way of appearing, when it is named, becomes what people understand as a style. Of course, to name a way of appearing as a style dooms that way of appearing to an all-too-predictable morality. Its destiny is to be *seen through*, to cease to fascinate, to become obvious, then forgotten and to be replaced by another, no less perishable, style. But styles are now granted a kind of immortality. Once dead, a style can be scheduled for a number of posthumous appearances. When revived, it can be cherished in a fresh way.

Similar rules of succession govern the scope of fashion as such. Since for a long time fashion centered on how people looked indoors in formal settings (at the Court, at a ball, at a theater, at a reception), it became necessary that a vocabulary of fashion for outdoor informalities (on the street, at the beach) be developed. After fashion photography came to be typified in static posing, it was inevitable that it would want to show exaggerated, improbable movements. So far as fashion models looked romantic or poetic or at least dignified, someone was bound to come along and make them droll, grimacing, self-mocking. The minimum achievement that defines fashion: that whatever is will be allowed to generate its opposite or its complement.

Once fashion meant a rivalry in reckless ostentation, an all-consuming sport of the upper class. Eventually, fashion also came to mean something more solemn, more anxious, more middle class: the seriousness of the consumer, accumulating well-made products on intelligently planned shopping expeditions, concerned not to be ridiculous or feel deprived, eager to conform. The more fashion came to mean seriousness, the more it was inevitable that in the late twentieth century it would promote liberating frivolity, playfulness, a salutary vacation from looking "right." Fashion becomes the discovery that anything is all right—if worn by the right person.

But fashion hardly died, as is sometimes said, just because "the world of fashion" (a phrase first used in England in the early eighteenth century)—that is, the upper class; later called "society"—has been democratized. That fashion could no longer be understood as a singular directive, a standard to conform to or take one's distance from, did not kill fashion. As transformed, to mean what fashion must in a consumer culture, it is as strong as ever. Fashions exist to be contradicted, to negate themselves. And fashion is a mix, an anthology. Fashion is no longer a "world"—but a flux of enticingly juxtaposable, often interchangeable images.

This ongoing transformation of fashion, its so-called death and its rebirth as a much larger subject for photography, explains much of the shape of Richard Avedon's prodigious and varied activity. Many other photographers of fashion have produced memorable images; none has a body of work which deploys so intelligently all the powers and ironies of fashion photography. Endlessly knowing about and loyal to fashion as spectacle (the theatricalization of beauty; the erotic as artifice; the stylization of appearances as such), Avedon has taken pains to show that fashion photography is not limited to fashion—a development that now seems inherent in fashion photography itself.

Fashion photography is the record of fashions but it is not about fashions. It is about appearances that fascinate. But fascination tends to exclude identification. (It would be as easy to identify with the woman in Avedon's 1953 photograph of Marella Agnelli as with a Brancusi statue.) Fashion treats the world as decor—like the still intact pre-war Paris of the late 1940s to mid-1950s one can glimpse in the backgrounds of Avedon's famous photographs, behind the visiting angels modeling their New Looks. Dovima posing with elephants, in front of the pyramids in Giza, cavorting with cape in a Paris square: the body and face in their perfection are seen in sharp focus against the (usually) out-of-focus "picturesque."

Much of the earlier Avedon photographs—bodies preening, prancing—have something of the unremitting jollity or languidness of Balanchine's *Union Jack* or *Vienna Waltzes;* the models look impeccably beautiful and overbred, in the way that ballerinas are supposed to look. The women in fashion photographs are not partnered, as in ballet; they do the "lift" themselves.

The image shows a woman caught at the peak of some audacious, improbably movement—swooning or vamping; a skittish, rather than an unabashed, romanticism.

Avedon's photographs of the last decade or so are likely to have less background, if any. The subject occupies an ideal, therefore unspecifiable, space. Beauty is freestanding; it does not need to be validated or explained or commented on by a decor. These isolated figures are capable of looking pensive, as well as euphoric and sly. Movements and static poses are less obviously choreographed. Beauty is no longer perfect; it includes Tina Turner, not just Lena Horne. June Leaf, all grainy character, an emblem of anti-glamour, looks out from the page facing the picture of Marella Agnelli; and that juxtaposition pointedly closes Avedon's new book surveying three decades of work in and near fashion photography. The idea of fashion is less a noun, an entity that is, at any given moment, fixed. It is adjectival, a free-floating commendation that can be attached to anything.

How it went according to older idea of fashion: someone, usually well-born or rich, looked marvelous (through meticulous grooming, expensive clothes), was seen in the right places, became fashionable. Now: someone is marvelous, because of some power or energy or aura; therefore, what that person looks like becomes a standard of fashion. When people started deploring the death of fashion, what they meant is that fashion seemed no longer to be fashionable. But the norms of fashion have adjusted to take care of the threat. Now, fashion—to be fashionable—must include what is *not* fashionable: the ungroomed, the inexpensive. So Avedon includes women artists and writers in the uniform (man's shirt and jeans) of those who dress "down" instead of "up." Being well-dressed can make one fashionable, but one can be fashionably dressed without being well-dressed. Whatever fashionable people wear tends to look "right." Thus, many images that show nothing to emulate, nothing to buy, are still part of fashion. The gestures that create or inspire fashions are defined by the camera. It is the photograph that confers celebrity, that makes something fashionable, that perpetuates and comments on the evolving idea—that is, the fantasy—of fashion.

Originally, fashion meant a current usage or a mode of action, demeanor, air. Even when the word acquired the meaning of exclusiveness, and was connected to class and snobbery, fashion continued to embrace conventions of both dress and behavior. Being fashionable was not only a matter of appearance, a particular choice of clothes. It covered general deportment, etiquette, style of speech, diction, accent, skill at forms of social and artistic performance. Fashion referred to how people behaved, as well as how they looked. Now, fashion is hardly at all about what people do but almost exclusively about how they appear—and where they are seen. It has become something that is almost entirely visual—that is, photographic. As fashion becomes pure appearance, it finds its perfect summing-up in photographs. What people understand of fashion is now mostly set by photographic images. More and more, fashion *is* fashion photography.

The greatest fashion photography is more than the photography of fashion. With photography, context is almost everything. But the photography can never be locked into one context, any more than it can remain something cut out of, or saved from, the mutations of time.

The camera stops time. But what our reactions to photographs principally register is the passage of time. It is fashion photography that most vividly represents photography's perennial impulse to record the perfect, to glamorize reality. But an important part of what the photograph is as an object—that it dates—is also expressed acutely in fashion photography. The abiding complexity of fashion photography—as of fashion itself—derives from the transaction between "the perfect" (which is, or claims to be, timeless) and "the dated" (which inexorably discloses the pathos and absurdity of time).

The pictures themselves change. Avedon photographs once published in *Vogue* change because the new places—a book, a museum—invite us to look in a different, more thoughtful, more abstracting way. Time has changed them, too. Seen in this retrospective form (compiled in a book, on the walls of a museum), images that started out as fashion photographs become a commentary on the idea of the fashionable. Everything seems, is, dated—faces and bodies as well as the clothes. What was fashion photography is now a manneristic branch of portrait photography, whose strenuously imagined subjects continue to fascinate. In Avedon's work, fashion—a reflection on clothes as costume, on the face as mask, on styles as signs—becomes a reflection on the nature of seeing and posing; that is, a reflection about art.

17

What Happened to the Afro?

Bebe Moore Campbell

Ebony, June 1982

In the '60s and '70s, the Afro was more than hair; it was the symbol of Black pride, a silent affirmation of African roots and the beauty of Blackness. Neither Black men nor Black women made the transition to the Afro casually, but for women, more mental undoing was involved. Even prior to the '60s, most Black men wore their hair *natural* (unless it was conked), just very short. To acquire an Afro, all a brother had to do was grow more hair, throw away his can of Nu Nile and retire his stocking cap.

As they sat in front of a kitchen stove and breathed in air redolent with Dixie Peach and frying hair, many little Black girls learned that the words "nappy" and "kinky" were part of a derogatory description; the offending texture had to be burned into submission. It wasn't that straightening made a Black woman more attractive; the transformation into wavy, curly and straight hair made her presentable. Without a hot comb treatment, many were ashamed of their hair. In the '60s, women who contemplated making a radical departure from the beauty standard they'd accepted from the cradle to adopt a look that glorified their natural, unprocessed hair, had to loose the straightening comb's hold on their minds.

Madame C. J. Walker is credited with inventing the straightening comb in the early twentieth century. An old neighbor of mine in Philadelphia remembers Madame's sales force coming door-to-door in her native South Carolina, selling hot combs and hair pomade. "Colored women was buying them like hot cakes," is how my neighbor put it. Before Madame, who was the first Black female millionaire, my neighbor says women used to wrap their hair with heavy-duty sewing thread. "You take down that thread and your hair would be just as soft and pretty and straight," she told me.

There has been no systematic examination of the beauty practices that survived the middle passage, but we know from old photographs and from scattered references in slave narratives and scholarly surveys that nineteenth century Blacks used various methods including braiding and styles similar to the modern Afro in caring for their hair. Although there is need for further study, it is evident that, gradually, for many of us, "fixing our hair" came to mean approximating the beauty standards of the dominant culture.

"How many burned ears do I remember," says Pam Proctor, a thirtyish Washingtonian.

How many missed opportunities to swim or participate in sports because my hair would 'go back.' I can't count the number of tepid baths I took at my mother's insistence, so as not to steam my newly straightened hair. I must have spent my entire adolescence wanting a Toni Home Permanent, not knowing why it wouldn't work for me. I do remember realizing that the girls on TV with the permanents were all White.

The old definitions were a tiny, suffocating box filled with self-hatred: good hair looks Caucasian, bad hair looks African. The lid came off in the '60s. It was time to get in the water, unafraid. Time to boogey down and make wild love without fear of sweating back. Time to change the definition of nappy and kinky to mean good. Real good. But it wasn't easy. It took more than a phone call to the hairdresser asking for Shirley Temple curls, the flip, a new look; adopting the Afro, at least initially, required making an appointment with oneself.

A Black woman could find a lot of support for her decision. The voices of Nikki Giovanni, Sonia Sanchez, Don L. Lee (now Haki Madhubuti) and "The Last Poets" urged Black people to rediscover themselves, claim their heritage, rejoice in the natural beauty of skin that ran the rainbow gamut, features that were warm and full, hair that defied gravity. In cities and on campuses across the nation, dashiki-clad brothers with mile high 'fros and wild, unexplored beards would coax undecided women, "Say, Sis, when you gonna get your 'fro?"

I remember the day in 1969 when I got my 'fro. My roommate came in, and as soon as she saw me she exclaimed, "Girl, you did it! Right on, Sister!" And she hugged me. Word got around, and by noon at least half a dozen people had crowded into the room to look, touch and admire; Sister Be had crossed over.

Way on the other side was my mama, otherwise known as the unvanguard. Far from the very insulated world of the revolutionary campus, it was a whole 'nother scene. When my mother and grandmother opened the door and saw six inches of born-again Blackness, they were immediately struck with amnesiastutteritis. "Who, who, who … ?" Finally my grandmother managed weakly, "Your hairrr." I had to give both of them glasses of cool water and instruct them to sip it slowly, but they kept on choking.

Not that all young women accepted the Afro and all older ones rejected it. There were plenty of gray naturals in the crowd, while lots of the young heads remained pressed and curled. Still, if Black people ever had a generation gap, the Afro was it. The young vanguard's goal was to get the old folks to embrace the beauty of natural Blackness. The parents were trying to get their child to a hairdresser, a shrink or a spiritual advisor, as soon as possible. In my house it was a stand-off. In the end, my folks stopped beginning every sentence addressed to me with, "Won't you please … " and I stopped calling them "Sister Mother and Sister Nana." But every once in a while, my grandmother would look at me, shake her head and wail, "But you used to be so particular about your hair." And every now and then, I just couldn't resist my soap box. "If y'all had any Black pride and weren't ashamed of your African heritage, you'd stop straightening your hair and get an Afro." I would rant and rave until I noticed that my mother had left the room and Nana was humming *Amazing Grace*. Very loudly.

It took me a while to realize that beyond not appreciating my aesthetic transformation, my parents were grappling with a very real emotion: fear. When "militant" became the rallying cry for calling out the National Guard, big naturals made good targets. "Now, girl, don't you be starting any trouble up at that school," Nana told me.

Then a funny thing happened, quite predictable actually. The Afro went on sale for $29.95. Overnight it moved from radical symbol to style with blow-out kits and wantoo wazuri to keep it fashionable. Sisters with heretofore "good" hair washed their locks in vinegar and Ajax and prayed for kinks. White women started wearing little fuzzy 'fros. My folks and many of the people who hadn't wanted to be associated with a rowdy, revolutionary symbol, began giving the *style* another chance. "Well, it's not so bad," my grandmother told me. "Just cut it down a little so it looks curlier, like the wigs do." I tried to explain that she was missing the point, that the cultural revolution had been co-opted, that this wig business was just another trick the whit ..., but then I realized that they were offering the only kind of acceptance that they could. "Sure," I told them, "I'll cut it. Short 'fros are relevant."

By the early '70s, there were two kinds of female Afro wearers: the vanguard and the fashionable. Those who got on board to be stylish didn't necessarily see their hair as a social statement as did those who'd shucked off the weight of the straightening comb because of firmly felt convictions "I took a vow," recalls one such sister. "I swore my hair was going to be natural for the rest of my life."

I wore my Afro for eleven years. I wore it long, parted and with braids in the front. I braided it all over. I put henna in it. I had my barber cut a V in the back and when that started looking raggedy, I had it squared off. I wrapped my head in African cloth. I cut my hair down to less than an inch. I let it grow 10 inches high. I got tired of my Afro. Even though, intellectually, I knew that with straightened hair a Black woman could feel the same pride and love of self and people that she'd felt wearing an Afro, the day the hairdresser took my 40 bucks and I swiveled down from the high chair looking like Sister Slick, I felt like Sister Sell Out. In time my guilt faded and my curiosity grew, as I saw more and more sisters crossing back over.

"In Jackson, Mississippi," says Billie Jean Young, the thrityish director of Southern Rural Women's Network, "not too many sisters are wearing Afros. By far, the curly look is the most popular, and then come perms. Most Afros are very short."

"You still see some big Afros, but I think there are far more perms and curlies out here," asserts Francine Greer, thirty-two, who teaches in Los Angeles. "Now tell the truth," Ramona Phillips, thirty-two, from Philadelphia asked me, "if you saw a woman with a great big Afro, wouldn't she look dated to you?"

Symbols, style and trends don't happen in a vacuum and their effects aren't isolated either; hairstyles have social, cultural, economic and political implications. "I needed a change," say most women who've made the transition. But what does it mean that Black women are making the switch from natural to chemically treated hair, from big to short 'fros? Are Black women abandoning the feeling of self-pride they first realized in the '60s or are they secure enough to wear their hair in any "style" and still feel that Black is beautiful? There were reasons that the Afro was introduced in the '60s and there are reasons for its de-emphasis now.

Prior to the '60s, Black hair care was in the hands of the Black community. In the last decade, Big Beauty (an arm of Big Business) had discovered that there's cash in kinks, or rather in straightening and curling them. An estimate on how much money Black women spend in hair care ranges from $300 to $500 million annually. Hair care companies, both Black and White, are vigorously campaigning for that cash, wooing women with ads, giveaways, advanced technology and psychology. Big Beauty seemed to read the minds of the guilt-prone Afro wearers; the curly perms developed in their labs were designed to ease the Afro-wearer back into the beauty shop with natural looking, but processed, curls. As curly perms grew out, hairdressers would gradually suggest touch-ups or straighteners. Black beauty parlors, which suffered during the Afro's heyday, are doing a brisk business these days, but now there is White competition such as Seligman and Latz, a White company from New York, which owns salons operating under the names Soul Scissors and Soul Set.

Some say the new trend is fostered by a tight job market and the rigors of career competition. The rule of thumb is big 'fros impede climbing up the corporate ladder, while shorter Afros are more acceptable. "White people accept us more if we look like them," says Lisa Fisher, twenty, a Howard University student from Silver Springs, Md. People in both races find processed hair more appealing. Renee Poussaint, an anchorwoman on Washington D.C.'s WJLA-TV News, wears her hair in a short natural. "I've been told by a number of White males in the industry that the Afro is a harsh style that makes features look harder on camera. I've also had calls from Black women who've told me that if I had any pride I'd straighten my hair," she says.

The social climate, some say, isn't conducive to wearing an Afro. Afros don't elicit the compliments they once did and there is little reinforcement for remaining natural, other than a woman's own feelings. Long earrings, dashiki dresses, head wraps, accessories that accentuated the beauty of African hair have all but disappeared. Says Young, "I think there's a conspiracy among clothing designers. All the clothes look terrible with big Afros."

Women in most societies are taught that they must be attractive to win a man and that they must have a man at all cost. Many women feel that Black men, who actually initiated the natural look in the '60s, no longer care for the Afro. "Black men love long, straight hair," says Young. Poussaint doesn't see long hair as necessarily a Black male hang up. "Generally speaking, American men like long hair, a more traditional look. It's part of the 'little woman' concept. Black men are American," she says. Algea Othella Harrison, Ph.D., a psychology professor at Oakland University in Rochester, Mich., says, "I think Black men have matured to a point where a variety of hairstyles appeals to them." Habibatu Bey, a thirtyish social worker from Pittsburgh who recently got a curly perm, revealed her boyfriend's reaction to her new style. "He told me to cut this mess off and wear my hair in a short natural. He's no super militant; he just prefers me in a short 'fro."

"I prefer a woman in a short natural,' says John Dale, thirty-four, a jazz-loving Washingtonian.

To me that style communicates that she is a down-to-earth woman who doesn't have a lot of pretentiousness about her. When I see a woman with processed hair, I see a lot of superficiality. All of us are affected by European standards, and I realize that it's arrogant to tell anyone how to wear her hair, but there's room for Afro-American standards too. Are there any left?

The question is one that poet Sonia Sanchez, author of "I've Been a Woman," and a woman who is still very much the epitome of the Black cultural vanguard, is concerned about. While she feels positive about the future of Black people, she doesn't see the new hair trend as a good one. "I think there's a retrenchment on being Black in America. This country understood that, if you look a certain way and feel good, you internalize positive. Part of their program to return us to the second Reconstruction is to define how we look and think as a way of controlling us."

Dr. Harrison, who has done research on Black women's inner role conflicts, feels that the current trend may not be bad. "We (Black women) have to give ourselves credit for not being monolithic," she cautions. "We need to push ourselves toward saying, 'I dare to be me. My Blackness is inner.' The more we try to define who and what is Black, the more we get hung up."

Says Sanchez, "I think that when people say they want a new style, there is a new style in a natural way. If the only way you can change is one which burns and destroys your hair, it says something about noncreativity."

"Traditionally," says Dr. Harrison, "we've always put ourselves last. Maybe Black women are saying, 'I make enough money to go to the hairdresser and I'm worth it. I'm free enough to choose my hairstyle and I don't have to make a social statement.'"

Sanchez feels that women who really benefitted the most from the '60s automatically choose natural hair now, but she doesn't disdain those who wear their hair in other ways. "I don't attack people for not having naturals, but I will attack them for not doing the work to change this country and the world."

In the face of an advertising blitz and a conservative political and economic climate, it's a wonder that more Black women haven't made the transition to chemically treated hair. Some refuse to, for a variety of reasons.

"I've just had a 'one inch all over' cut and I love it," says Proctor. "The thought of rollers, perms and hair dryers makes me cringe."

Says Poussaint,

I've been wearing my hair this way for 20 years. It's part of my self-expression. It used to bother me (that more Black women weren't wearing naturals) when I was convinced that one's hair was important in making a statement about one's Blackness, but I have some very together Black friends whose hair is straight; it depends on the individual. I'd love to see more Black women comfortable with Afros; I think our hair is lovely.

Some of the vanguard want to change the topic and move on to other problems. Says Ntozake Shange, author of *For Colored Girls Who Have Considered Suicide/When the Rainbow is Enuf,* "Black women have so much on them right now. I'm not going to bother them about their hair. Let them do what they want."

Making up their minds presents a conflict for many, "I was up in New York and my sister pulled out her curling irons," says Young, with a soft, southern chuckle.

She's been dying to fix my hair for months, so I let her put in a few curls. When she finished, my hair looked so good; the curls softened me. I wore my new 'do back on the plane to Jackson, but you know how unruly hair is; by the time I got home, my curls were gone. It was a big temptation not to go out and get it fixed, but I fought it because I just don't want to have to go through everything, you know, the mental changes, that goes along with having fixed hair. It took me too long to accept my natural hair. I was one of those sisters who wore an Afro wig before I wore my own hair naturally. I'm going to keep my Afro.

Young can find eloquent reinforcement for her decision. In *Primer for Blacks,* published in 1980 by Brooks Press, the nationally acclaimed poet Gwendolyn Brooks addressed an encouraging message "To Those of My Sisters Who Kept Their Naturals," closing with these lines:

... "But oh the rough dark Other music!
the Real,
the Right,
The natural Respect of Self and Seal!
Sisters!
Your hair is Celebration in the world!

Black women must put the revolutionary slogans, the television images, the concern about job mobility and male response, even the poetry into personal synthesizers and choose a hairstyle, a philosophy or both. Whether a Black woman rolls or braids her hair at night, combs or picks it out in the morning, in the final analysis she must live with her decision, at least until it grows out. Not all Black women will continue to make social and political statements with hair, but if they are those who choose to straighten or curl, everyday there are others who go natural for the first time, and those who discover they needn't be locked into either choice. I see a number changing up whenever they feel like it. More and more women are recognizing and are exercising their options, and for that we must credit the successful cultural awareness movement of the '60s. Perhaps the natural growth of the '80s will serve to reinforce a message that will never be alluded to in television commercials and might even have been drowned out in the din of the very social movement that should have underscored it: all hair looks better when heads are held high.

18

Ralph Lauren's Achievement

Holly Brubach

The Atlantic, August 1987

In the little more than a year since Ralph Lauren's flagship Polo store opened in the old Rhinelander mansion, at Seventy-second Street and Madison Avenue, in New York, it has become a cultural landmark, an "instant classic," to borrow a term Lauren's publicists once used to describe the success of his women's perfume. Tourists overheard planning their rounds of the Upper East Side museums now include the store on their agendas: "Today we're doing the Whitney, Ralph Lauren, and the Frick …." On any given afternoon its many rooms are filled with people milling distractedly about, their steps slow, their eyes anxious for fear that they might miss something. They are, to all intents and purposes, on a house tour. They call each other's attention to the antique steamer trunks stored high on shelves above the display cases, to the violin resting alongside a scroll of sheet music, to the antique Waterford crystal chandelier; they admire the art deco green glass panels etched with polo players (relics of the Westbury Hotel's Polo Lounge, before its recent renovation) and the gilt-and-mirror vitrine (from Cartier in Paris); they smile when they come to the boys' department, where antique model racing cars are strewn on the bottom of an armoire, like toys on the floor of a closet; they climb the magnificent hand-carved mahogany staircase, its walls lined with gilt-framed hunting scenes and portraits of somebody's ancestors; they sign the guest book, lying open beneath an enormous arrangement of fresh flowers on a table in the entrance hall. Every last detail is perfect, right down to the books left scattered about as if someone had just been reading them: the leather-bound *Nicholas Nickleby,* resting on a table next to the elevator; the three-volume *Birds of the British Islands,* stacked on an ottoman in the boudoir; the collectors' edition of the works of Eugène Sue, standing on the mantel. Throughout the store young, pink-cheeked men and women greet the crowds, seeming less like salespeople than members of the family, quietly steering visitors away from the private quarters. "How are you today?" they say, or "Good morning," but never "Can I help you?" With tidy fires burning in every grate, the beds (on the top floor, the home-furnishings department) turned down for the night, the teacups on the end table, the house looks lived in, like a home. One begins to wonder what it must be like after closing, when the soigné inhabitants surely retire to their rooms and dress for dinner, reconnoitering for drinks among the men's shoes in the library before going upstairs to dine among the suits.

This house is the grand seat of Lauren's far-reaching empire, a monument to his phenomenal success, which has been praised by some people and decried by others, often for precisely the same reasons. He is either an impassioned connoisseur or a shameless plagiarist, appropriating objects, eras, and styles and signing his name to them. (Last December, *The New York Times* ran a story about "the Laurenization of New York," documenting his influence on other merchants' displays, as if the notion of Victorian Christmas had never existed until Lauren discovered it.) Either he has brought the classic virtues of men's tailoring to bear on women's clothes or he has consigned women to wearing modified versions of the clothes that men wear. He epitomizes American fashion either at its best, easygoing and glamorous, derived in equal parts from the great outdoors and Hollywood movies, or at its worst, contrived, based on received notions and images, with no affinity for the body and no flair for design. Either he is the Great American Success Story (a biography is under way), a self-made man, now personally worth more than $300 million, living in a world he has envisioned, outfitted, and furnished, or he is a playactor, a Jew pretending to the life of the landed gentry.

Lauren was born Ralph Lifshitz, in the Bronx, in 1939, and raised in a four-room apartment overlooking Mosholu Parkway. His surname was changed when he was seventeen—by his father, according to some versions of the story, by Ralph and his brother Jerry, according to others. He studied business at the City College of New York, worked as a salesman at Bloomingdale's and Brooks Brothers, and peddled ties. In 1967 he persuaded Beau Brummel, a men's clothing manufacturer, to let him design a line of neckties, which were four inches wide at a time when the standard width was two and a half, and made from patterned silks that looked like upholstery fabrics. Building on the ties' success, Lauren branched out into a line of men's wear; then women's wear; and eventually fragrances, linens, leather goods and luggage, shoes, and— last year—furniture. Apart from a financial crisis in 1978, which prompted him to restructure the business, Lauren's expansion has been brisk and uninterrupted. And as his business has expanded he has consolidated his image.

Lauren's men's wear was admired early on for its quality (he insisted on all-natural fibers at a time when other designers routinely used synthetic blends) and its cut, which seemed to be for an opinionated Brooks Brothers customer who had traveled the world and brought home a few improvements. For the movie of *The Great Gatsby* he outfitted Robert Redford as Jay Gatsby, the man with shirts by the dozen. Lauren established himself as an authority in men's tailoring just as the notion of androgyny was beginning to seem sexy and appealing. Women dressed in men's tuxedo shirts and pants, ties, and hats, as Diane Keaton did in *Annie Hall*, wearing clothes designed by Lauren. He offered women scaled-down models of fine men's shirts, fitted tweed hacking jackets, skirts pleated at the waist like men's trousers.

In the early seventies Lauren also laid claim to the western style, with chambray shirts, corduroy prairie skirts, separates in denim, chamois, and suede—a rugged, casual look that celebrated the frontier spirit and nicely dovetailed with a then widespread longing on the part of thousands of city-dwellers for a pair of cowboy boots. Soon Lauren appeared in his own advertisements, silver-haired, suntanned, smiling, wearing a work shirt and faded dungarees, at home on the range. The folk-artsy, loving-hands-at-home side of his work—sweaters depicting a schoolhouse, lace-collared blouses—has gradually merged with this western look in a category that might best be labeled Americana, perpetuated now in a separate collection, called Roughwear.

Lauren is still turning out high-class haberdashery for men and women, but lately its style has come to be indistinguishable from his Anglophilia. Lauren's English phase got off the ground around the time of *Brideshead Revisited* and has run right up to the present, seemingly encompassing such cultural milestones as *Chariots of Fire, Out of Africa,* and the "Great Treasure Houses of Britain" exhibition at the National Gallery of Art, in Washington.

Lauren occasionally works in other veins, among them a bright-colored, splashy printed style of resort clothing that at its most casual suggests the beach in the Hamptons and at its most formal calls to mind Rick's Bar in *Casablanca.* In some years, some seasons, his references are pointed. In others they are as generic as the monogram embroidered last spring on his women's blouses, a tangle of lines that look as if they ought to form letters but don't. Still, time and again Lauren returns to the tunes he knows best—one an American anthem, the other a stately hymn to the upper class—and it is in these that his voice is heard most distinctly.

Lauren has persistently denied that his clothes are fashion, and while it's true that he doesn't engage in the seasonal variations on hemlines and silhouettes that occupy most couturiers, there is something disingenuous about this claim. More, perhaps, than any other designer of our era, he has anticipated our collective longings with such split-second timing that he has managed to produce what we wanted next, just before we realized that *that* was what we wanted. In this sense his work has consistently been at fashion's very height. Lately our appetite has been for tradition, as we've struggled to make the past somehow continuous, to keep it alive in the moment at hand. This effort manifests itself in any number of ways, from campaigns to preserve our architectural heritage to a newfound enthusiasm for debutante balls to the rediscovery of silent films. For his part, Lauren makes clothes distinguished by a certain dapper stodginess, reprising a style long associated with old families and old money, and designing furnishings that appear to be antique but nonspecific, so that they manage never to look like exact reproductions.

But neither do they have any life of their own. Wandering through his store, one can't help but be struck by how incidental the clothes, which are totally lacking in "hanger appeal," seem to the overall picture. Even his home furnishings are best seen in context. It is the setting that makes sense of them for us. In fact, the full complement of Lauren's achievement can best be seen not in his products but in his advertisements and his stores, in which he fully articulates the vision he is marketing.

Lauren's ads, ingeniously photographed by Bruce Weber, depict fair-skinned, fine-boned people of all ages—or rather little girls, young women, and men of all ages—but none of the Third World types chosen to be the Benetton stores' ambassadors to the public, or the frowsy white trash that inhabits the ads of Georges Marciano. The scenarios, which generally run to ten or twelve pages, have in the past included a visit to a family swathed in pinstripes, herringbones, Harris tweeds, silk paisleys, and fur-collared cashmeres, as they lounge about what looks to be one of the stately homes of England, complete with chintz slipcovered chairs, back issues of *Country Life,* a canister of walking sticks in the hall, and two resident yellow labs; and an African safari, the slightly sunburned participants resplendent in straw hats and khaki, white linen, and suede, the tea table set with a silver service, a Land Rover in the background, a cuddly lion cub draped over one man's shoulders. The most recent was a field trip to an artist's weathered studio somewhere in the tropics (in the grand tradition of Gauguin's sojourn in Tahiti, perhaps), a room strewn with old rattan furniture and picture frames, a half-finished canvas on the easel, the painter himself wearing a shirt and tie, Prince of Wales plaid trousers, and navy-blue Keds-style sneakers, the woman at his side (his model, his muse?) in a strapless flower-sprigged sundress and thongs. In stark contrast to the freneticism that prevails in most fashion photography, Lauren's people exude dignity, tranquility, and preoccupation—their minds are elsewhere, far from the clothes they're modeling. They look as if they've simply been observed during the quiet course of an average day—at home, at the club, on vacation. They are, clearly, private people, not in the least flamboyant, and yet when faced with the camera's gaze, they meet it steadily; at other times they stare off into the middle distance, deep in thought.

In advertisements for Lauren's Home Collection there are no people. Still, the rooms look less like decorators' showrooms than like living quarters conveniently glimpsed when the occupants were out. Among last winter's designs was one for a slate-blue room dominated by a huge Victorian carved mahogany bed, dressed in paisley, pinstripe, and windowpane-plaid sheets and topped with a claret velvet comforter, on which a fur coat is nonchalantly draped; in the background stands a zebra-patterned wing chair, a pedestal displaying a marble sculpture of a man's head, and a grand piano topped with pictures in silver frames and a vase filled with white peonies. One half expects to see Noel Coward seated at the keyboard. But whether the rooms are empty or occupied, the approach is the same—always photojournalistic, persuading us that this world we see before us actually exists, that events are taking place in it even as we peruse a magazine. These pictures are the visual equivalent of eavesdropping and, better than anything else he has produced, they illustrate Lauren's conscientious efforts to create what he has called "the whole atmosphere of the good life."

The message telegraphed by these ads is that Lauren's clothes are for people whose lives are privileged, satisfying, comfortable, tasteful, leisurely, even luxurious—in short, better than the average person's life may be at the moment, but not beyond imagining. Here is a paradise, but one that is possible on earth, inhabited by people who qualify as aristocrats—if not by their blue bloodlines, then by their refined and sensitive natures. They are also WASPS. Not since Mainbocher dressed the young society matrons of the forties and fifties has a designer explicitly invoked such snob appeal in his clothes. Some critics have roundly condemned Lauren for marketing a fantasy package of the WASP life, as if it were his to sell; some have looked the other way. But deep down there seems to run a current of resentment, grounded in the bitter notion that a Jew from the lower middle class isn't entitled to the style of the Connecticut gentry. One executive of a tweedy New York men's store told me not long ago, "We *are* what Ralph Lauren is trying to be." Remarks like this have a dismayingly anti-Semitic sound, but they also beg a question: Is it objectionable for someone to affect a style he admires, if he wasn't born to it? It is, after all, a free country.

When Lauren recreates the look of an English country house, or of the Adirondack "camps" that were wealthy New Yorkers' wilderness retreats in the early part of the century, or of the manor houses on the north shore of Long Island, the result is always recognizably Lauren's, not to be mistaken for the real thing. His renditions are more emphatic and spiffier than the originals, his colors bright instead of faded, his effects a little too studiously achieved. Like a lot of Americans, he probably formed his first impressions of the world beyond his immediate neighborhood at the movies. One imagines that his Paris is the Paris of *Gigi,* his Wild West that of *High Noon,* his Main Line Philadelphia the house where Katharine Hepburn lived in *The Philadelphia Story.* His career may indeed be the Great American Success Story, not so much because he rose from hand-me-downs to vast riches as because he has recreated the world according to his imagination and then recreated himself as the sort of person who would live in it.

"I was a New York kid playing basketball, playing baseball," he told one interviewer. "The clothes were a dream … a setting, part of a world." He told another of his job as a glove salesman, driving around Long Island with his box of samples strapped into the passenger seat of a used Morgan: "I was twenty-two, and I was wearing custom-made suits. I thought I was Douglas Fairbanks." At one point he considered becoming a history teacher, because he liked the idea of dressing in tweed jackets with suede patches at the elbows and smoking a pipe.

"My clothes sell," he contends, "because I'm the consumer, and I haven't lost touch with that." What makes his images so resonant is not only that they embody our fantasies of what it must be like to lead a certain kind of life but that they seem to embody his fantasies too. His inspirations are intensely personal. His Home Collections have closely paralleled his own houses: a tropical retreat in Jamaica, a six-thousand-acre working ranch in Colorado, a beach house in Montauk, an apartment in Manhattan. Those who know him report that he has never lost his childlike delight in a new toy. On the desk in his office are miniature models of the racing cars he owns.

Lauren is in a sense the quintessential designer for the newly rich, proving by his own example that enough money can buy anything, including the semblance of tradition, a facsimile past—not a pedigree, perhaps, but the things pedigreed people own. And that is what counts, according to Lauren's view of the world. The crux of a person's identity, the experience of being that person, the aura of urbanity or erudition or sportsmanship that surrounds him, resides in the trappings, not in the person himself. There are shortcuts. One needn't ride to the hounds, for example, to wear jodhpurs. (Lauren wore them to cut the ribbon at the opening of his New York store last year.) One needn't be well read, so long as one surrounds oneself with books. One needn't play the piano, so long as one has a piano. In short, one can be whoever one wants to be. Or—more accurately—one can seem to be whoever one wants to be. There is in all of this something touchingly naive.

In the window of his store on Madison Avenue, on a royal-blue flag edged in gold silk fringe and draped over a table, Lauren displays his Achievement. According to W.A. Copinger, in *Heraldry Simplified,* a man's Achievement is defined as his "coat of arms with all the exterior ornaments of the shield, together with the quarterings duly marshalled in order," and it signals his identity and ancestry to any passing armorist. According to a friend in London, an amateur expert, the motif—or, frankly, heraldic pastiche—Lauren has chosen for himself would be entered in the registers of Garter King of Arms, kept at the College of Arms, on Queen Victoria Street, in London, in these terms:

Crown. A circle of gold, issuing therefrom four crosses patée and four fleur-de-lis, arranged alternately: from the crosses patée arise two golden arches ornamented with pearls, crossing at the top under a mound, surmounted by a cross patée, also gold, the whole enriched with precious stones. The cap is of crimson velvet.

Arms. Quarterly: first, Azure, two lions passant in pale, or; second, Gules, a gridiron, or; third, Or, a bend sinister, azure; fourth, Azure, three fleurs-de-lis in chevron, or; the whole encircled with a garter, azure, ensigned "EST MCMLXVII," or.

Compartment. A triumphal wreath of laurel, argent.

Motto. POLO.

Lauren's Achievement was probably pieced together by one of his art directors, whose concerns, we may imagine, were purely graphic. Nevertheless, it is laden with meanings, among them the implication that Lauren's ancestry on his father's side can be traced to two lions (a variation on the Romulus and Remus story, perhaps); the improbable claim that his mother is somehow descended from Saint Lawrence, a martyr grilled over red-hot coals (the gridiron) and a monk; the assertions that Lauren is also descended from a bastard (the bend sinister) and, lastly, from a roly-poly Capetian king of France. In heraldry, groups of three are almost always laid out in a triangle, reflecting the coat of arms' origin as a medieval T-shirt—two symbols at the top, indicating the width of the shoulders, the point of the triangle at the waist. Lauren's arrangement in the fourth quarter—one fleur-de-lis at the top, two at the bottom—is upside-down, thereby conjuring an image of Humpty-Dumpty.

Lauren apparently takes it for granted that by divorcing symbols from their contexts, he can unburden them of their specific meanings and yet somehow leave their general sense intact. If his coat of arms isn't meant to be taken literally, its suggestion of aristocratic glamour surely is. Likewise, he strips objects and clothes of their function and expects them to retain their integrity. But a ranch hand wears dungarees because they're practical for roping cattle, not because he likes the way they look; an English country gentleman wears flannels and tweeds because they're suited to his climate and his leisure; an artist wears what's comfortable; a fisherman, a golfer, or a huntsman wears the gear appropriate to his sport. At first glance Lauren's approach to these many genres strikes us as purely superficial, but on second thought it seems to spring from some deep restlessness and discontent. Like a lot of people who make their living in the fashion business, Lauren is ironically enamored of people for whom clothes are not a self-conscious means of expression but a function of the lives they lead. Oh, to be all caught up in something other than fashion and still have style! The instinct behind this notion is, I think, a sound one, an attempt to affirm that there's something more to life than clothes. But, sadly, Lauren's only notion of how to go about getting beyond clothes to whatever else life might have to offer seems to be to dress the part of someone who never gives clothes a second thought. This, of course, changes nothing.

Lauren is not so much a designer as a connoisseur, calling our attention to the things he appreciates. Other designers, masters of fashion, like Yves Saint Laurent, Emanuel Ungaro, Valentino, Galanos, Geoffrey Beene, trade on images that are specifically upper-class but work in terms that are inventive and abstract. Lauren deals in the familiar, and his terms are loaded. One looks at an outfit by Saint Laurent and is informed by the sophistication of its cut and sumptuousness of its fabric that the woman wearing it must be wealthy. One looks at an outfit by Lauren and concludes that the woman wearing it is wealthy because that is the way wealthy women supposedly look.

In books like Sinclair Lewis's *Dodsworth* and almost anything by Charles Dickens, in movies like *Alice Adams, The Promoter,* and *Stella Dallas,* in *Pygmalion* and, more recently, in *Me and My Girl,* people imitate their betters, only to be punished for their ambition (sometimes) and to learn that their betters aren't really better off after all in any of the ways that matter. In Lauren's version of the story, however, upward striving not only goes unpunished, it is applauded as the apotheosis of a self-made man. He ascends to the realm of the rich and discovers it to be a far nicer world than the one the middle class inhabits; he savors its every detail. This is the romance, an American parable in the manner of popular fiction like *Ellis Island* and confirming that America is still the land of opportunity, that the path to the top may be narrow but it's open. We look at Lauren in his various poses and think, Oh, come off it, but all the while some sentimental voice in our head is saying, Well, good for you. And the moral to be drawn from his story is reassuring: if he has acquired all this for himself, then it's accessible to us, too.

Lauren plays on our ambivalence about the upper class. We grant him the license to pretend to a grandeur that isn't his by birth because we are disillusioned with the rich. The trials of Claus von Bulow, the contest over Seward Johnson's will, the indictment of Ivan Boesky, and *The Two Mrs. Grenvilles* have taught us that the upper class is corrupt. The rich, who occupy that place on high that the rest of us have been striving to get to, are steadily slipping in our esteem, disinheriting themselves from the appurtenances of their class. These people, we think, don't deserve what they've got. Their houses, their clothes, their antiques, their cars, should be in the hands of people who can appreciate them. If the rich won't play their part as stewards of the finer things in life, then those things should be awarded to people who will. This is, appropriately enough, the age of "the democratization of polo," with members of "a new breed of wealthy people" taking lessons at the Greenwich Polo Club, according to a recent article in *The New York Times*. Lauren picks up our fantasy of the rich where the rich themselves have left it off. Look, he says, good news! The things you've always coveted, things that in the past belonged exclusively to a privileged few, are now in the public domain. Help yourself. It is up to you to carry on this exquisite tradition.

And yet there is something faintly absurd about the people who heed this call, and about Lauren himself. Their presumption may go unpunished by us mortals, but built into the unwritten laws that govern this life is the gods' revenge: that a working ranch and dungarees do not make a cowboy or an estate and a walking stick a country gentleman; that the trappings of another person's life cannot impart the dignity of his experience; that an identity is not acquired but earned. In the end there is something oppressively sad about the flotsam of the upper class that has washed up on the deck of Lauren's flagship: the photographs of prep-school crew teams, rows of staunch—looking boys whose names nobody knows; the now meaningless trophies that must once have loomed terribly important; the lovingly chosen presents to commemorate some special event, the people and the day long forgotten. In a showcase on the first floor, in the men's department, is a horn tobacco canister, silver-trimmed, on the front of which is engraved, "To father on the occasion of his silver wedding, 15th October 1910." It is for sale.

19

In Fashion: Modernism Outmoded

Holly Brubach

The New Yorker, November 20, 1989

At the Fiera, in Milan, where the spring Italian ready-to-wear collections—the first clothes for the nineteen-nineties—were being presented a few weeks ago, the talk between shows kept turning to the U.F.O. that, according to Tass, had landed in the Russian city of Voronezh. In the *International Herald Tribune,* witnesses were quoted as describing three aliens, ten to thirteen feet tall, "but with very small heads," who disembarked, along with a robot, took a turn around the city park, then got back on board the spaceship and flew off.

"Well, it makes perfect sense to me," one woman told another as they waited to get into the Gianni Versace show. "I mean, why should we be the only intelligent form of life in the universe?"

"Yes," the other woman answered distractedly, surveying the crowd. "There *must* be interesting men *some*where."

Had the aliens landed in Milan that week instead, they might have gone home with tales of the controversy surrounding the twenty thousand dollars Cindy Crawford, a voluptuous brunette routinely featured on the cover of *Cosmopolitan,* was purportedly paid to model in Versace's show; or with reports of having sighted Tina Turner at the Giorgio Armani show wearing an uncharacteristically loose fitting khaki pants suit (by Armani) and uncharacteristically flat lace-up shoes; or with a review of the party for Versus, Versace's second line, for which a photographer's cavernous studio had been transformed into a discothèque peopled by Jane Fonda and a throng of what one fashion editor called "male chicks"; or with descriptions of one of the week's most poignant moments, at Gianfranco Ferré, when the models, their Barbie-doll bodies the very standards by which so many earthling women measure their shortcomings, sashayed hurriedly down the runway in bathing suits cut high on the leg, nervously swishing towels behind their seats as they walked, as if they felt self-conscious about baring the backs of their thighs; or with an account of Versace's curtain call, heralded by an announcer—a gesture so preposterous that it begged for Ed McMahon to call out, "Heeeere's Gianni!"

It would take someone from another planet to find most of the clothes in Milan this season interesting. During a week that featured forty-one fashion shows presented under the umbrella of the Camera Nazionale della Moda Italiana, a trade association, and fifteen or twenty independent productions, the most common complaint—delivered with a shrug, in a resigned tone, in response to the standard question "What did you think of So-and-So's collection?"—was "Just clothes." The vehicle that is the Italian ready-to-wear shows began to seem like a runaway train. The P.R. machinery was in high gear, fuelled by huge amounts of money. The buyers and the press in attendance numbered some five thousand and were from all over the world, and then there were the pirates and the groupies who had bought their tickets on the black market—an elaborate network with connections in the major hotels, where invitations have lately had a way of "disappearing." There's no question that clothes that are "just clothes" have a place in the world and in people's lives, and they may even do better business than the clothes that qualify as fashion. But do they merit being paraded on a runway in a theatre, with a wall-to-wall audience, to the sound of "Satisfaction," "In the Mood," and arias from "Tosca"? The majority of the clothes shown in Milan this season would be better viewed in a showroom at close range, the way they will eventually be seen on the racks in the stores. Nevertheless, most companies insist on a staged production, because of the prestige attached to it—as if by simply mounting a fashion show they could establish themselves as "fashion houses."

Franco Moschino, the Italian designer who in his clothes has been trying to tell the fashion world that something's gone awry, says he can't believe that there are so many companies in America paying the airfare of so many buyers to come to Milan to buy so many clothes. He thinks that it's time the system was changed: maybe designers should present new collections only once a year or twice every three years. But the fashion people don't want to accept such changes, he says, and he explains,

> Fashion is a shield, and they are hidden behind it, because even if it's fake it's proving that they are richer or more avant-garde—that they are in the fashion places, the right restaurants and clubs. So if you start to discuss and criticize this shield they feel naked. Losing this shield would mean losing not only a job or a profession but a personality, a private identity.

One of the most popular shows of the recent week in Milan was Moschino's. As usual, he called a lot of what's going on in fashion into question. His preoccupation with Chanel continues, and he showed a classic navy-and-white cardigan suit made out of crocheted pot holders; skirts with trompe-l'oeil double-strand chain belts embroidered in gold thread and dangling "medallions" that say "CARTOON COUTURE"; and a white blouse on top of which is worn a pearl-and-gold chain halter (this last, alas, so close to the mark that it could pass for something Karl Lagerfeld had done for the house of Chanel itself). Other Moschino targets this season were fashion junkies (printed in red in the lining of a red jacket was the message, in Italian, "I discovered that the most important thing in my life is my wardrobe"), visible panty lines (a navy skirt with the outline of a pair of underpants traced in gold-embroidered letters repeating the word "MUTANDINE"), and the haute-couture hippie revival (cocktail dresses with gold sequin halters in the shape of peace signs at the back). For evening he showed a simple black floor-length sheath with three huge gold sequin letters running down the front: V(bordering the neckline), I, P.

Sitting at the Krizia show and reading the big gold hoop earrings of the woman in front of me ("CHANEL 29, rue Cambon 42.61.83.35"), I imagined a world in which a fashion enthusiast, suffering from amnesia and wandering the streets or stranded in an airport after her purse has been stolen, is extradited on the basis of her earrings to the local Chanel boutique, where, thanks to sales records, her identity is discovered and she is reunited with her family. As if to put the woman sitting in front of me to shame, another member of the fashion audience in Milan wore a houndstooth blazer from Moschino's fall collection with "EXPENSIVE JACKET" embroidered in gold thread across the back. The eighties, that decade of flagrant self-advertisement, are finally over.

On the runway at Krizia were short polka-dot slip dresses with matching platform sandals—a rehash of a look from the seventies which was itself a rehash of a look from the thirties. The retro treadmill has run its course. The most compelling clothes shown this season were the ones that seemed in a hurry to get on with things. As for the recent free-floating nostalgia for the golden days of the haute couture, when fashion had no doubts about its own importance and women changed clothes five times a day, Moschino understands it but doesn't subscribe to it. "I don't want you to think that I'm a futuristic person," he says.

> I like the past. But to think about the forties and the fifties today is too easy, because past things always look better than they were. It's true that if we go back and look at special things in fashion, the special things are from the couture. And I can see that in the thirties and the forties and the fifties the couture was symbolizing more than a style of dress—it was making people hope and dream about having a beautiful dress that they didn't have. The human being is like that. So it makes sense in this way. But we are 1990, and we have to put it on the calendar now.

When people congratulate Moschino, telling him how beautiful his spring collection is, he says, "My reaction is 'Too bad you missed the things we did before.' The concepts are the same, but now they're filtered through the manufacturing process." This collection is more successful "because we know more how to present it, how to introduce ourselves to people," he concedes.

> And this season I realized that I'm less powerful in fashion, because fashion has given me success. The more fashion gives me success, the less I will be able to move it a little bit, the more involved I will be with the business. I'm using fashion to give me fame, and I use this fame to sing my songs and to continue saying my revolutionary things.

For a good ten years, the clothes that qualified as fashion—that gave us hope and gave expression to our daydreams—and the clothes that were just clothes were one and the same; our fantasy of a better future was a world in which people dressed year in and year out in "real clothes," clothes that were "classic" and (understood but never stated) safe and, above all, "modern." This season, for the first time in a long while, the distinction between fashion and clothes was clear, as if fashion, in eclipse since the late seventies, were finally moving out from behind the racks of navy blue blazers and khaki trenchcoats.

There was fashion at Dolce & Gabbana, where the two designers have parlayed their ongoing fascination with fifties longline bras into black elasticized cat suits and minidresses, with bra bodices and hook-and-eye closings, and at Zuccoli, where a group of cotton jackets, dresses, tunics, pants, and skirts scrambled black and white stripes with a print featuring the façade of the church of Santa Maria Novella, in Florence. Karl Lagerfeld's collection for Fendi, with its opening passage of putty-and-black knits, was unmistakably fashion. So was Gianfranco Ferré's collection, with its caramel-colored leather jackets perforated with big brass grommets, its leather pants embossed to look like anaconda, and its open-weave burlap suit.

At Basile, Genny, Complice, Erreuno, Krizia, and Emporio Armani, there were, for the most part, just clothes: sundresses and jackets and halter tops and shorts that were eminently wearable but empty somehow, lacking the sort of ideas—research into the science of dressmaking, or notions of dress-up and make-believe—that transcend but don't necessarily override practical considerations.

There was also fashion where you would least expect to find it. At Ferragamo, for instance, a white denim miniskirt and jacket with white grosgrain-ribbon edging and lined in silk printed with some of the house's most famous designs for shoes over the years and a short skirt paved in navy matte sequins accompanied by a navy sweater with a big white organza shawl collar proved that clothes that are conservative, steeped in their own tradition, need not be vapid.

But it was at Sybilla that fashion began to seem as if it were off and running again, in clothes that invoked such unlikely bedfellows as Claire McCardell and Balenciaga. The show, which one member of the audience described as "sweet, almost amateurish," was presented by an assortment of models so disparate that the only thing they seemed to have in common was their devotion to the designer and her work. The daughter of a Polish mother, who was herself a designer on Seventh Avenue, and an Argentine diplomat father posted to Egypt, Sybilla was born in New York and raised in Franco's Spain. She was, by her own description, "an ugly, nasty, spoiled little girl who wanted to be an oceanographer," but after Franco died, she says, night life in Madrid "exploded," and for a girl who was extremely shy ("I almost didn't speak") clothes suddenly took on a new importance; they became her social lifeline—a means of expressing herself and communicating with other people. At eighteen, she went to Paris and found work as a seamstress at Yves Saint Laurent. The clothes Sybilla now designs (in Madrid, though they are manufactured in Italy) are often intricately constructed, even when they fall into the most deceptively simple categories—like the tank bathing suits with darts at right angles, or the grass-green cotton shirtwaist dress with the bodice sewn in triangles, or the shorts that, seen from the back, look like a skirt, or even the handbags, sewn in leather sections, in the shape of gourds.

Sybilla says that she, too, is feeling the constraints imposed by success and by the necessity of supporting a business that keeps getting bigger. Now there are people telling her to listen to them—telling her that they have years of experience, that she can't do this that, that that's the way things are. These days, she says, she thinks often of a Spanish saying that goes: "You had better change the world quickly, before the world changes you."

What constitutes modernism in fashion has been a subject of debate for the better part of this century. Chanel defined it as freedom of movement. Other designers, over the years, have understood it to mean synthetic, low-maintenance fabrics, or disposable paper dresses, or neon colors, or black, streamlined shapes, or lack of construction, or one-size-fits-all, or the absence of zippers and buttons and hooks, or men's clothing for women, or space suits, or the elimination of bras and girdles—or even going bare-breasted, as if the whole of fashion history had been a long, slow march toward that day when we would at last cast off our inhibitions and go naked. Mostly, it seems, modernism has been whatever we've wanted it to be at the time. What all these approaches had in common was a certain pragmatism—an insistence on function at the expense of ornament, on "real life" at the expense of fantasy.

In retrospect, the course of modernism in fashion seems to have run parallel to the course of modernism in the arts and architecture, which have already moved on past postmodernism, whatever that was, to its sequel, whatever that is. In fashion, as in art, modernism abolished the extraneous, isolated the elements of composition, and explored their possibilities—a process that led inexorably to minimalism. In painting, the image was freed from what had been its function, the obligation to represent something; in fashion, the article of clothing was freed from decoration, from its obligation to ingratiate. What began as liberating eventually ran its course and in the end revealed its limitations: art in time dwindled into sheer decoration, with people selecting, say, a Kenneth Noland painting because its colors looked good with the living-room rug, and clothes degenerated into uniforms, functional and generic—with men, women, and children living, day in and day out, in bluejeans.

Though the ideas modernism defined in art and in architecture now strike us as dated, and figures like Picasso and Mies van der Rohe seem more and more remote, situated somewhere just this side of the nineteenth century, "modern" is still a buzzword in the world of fashion, still applied for lack of a better word to clothes that are stripped down and serviceable. Designers—particularly American designers—still talk about wanting to make clothes that are, above all, "modern"; when the fashion reviewers write that something is "modern," they mean it as a seal of approval, indicating that the clothes have passed the tests (suitcases, taxi cabs) of everyday life as we now live it. In this, its vaguest sense, modernism in fashion is assumed to be not a movement but an era, stretching from here into the horizon of the twenty-first century and beyond—an endless future, already under way, from which there will be no turning back, nor any reason anyone would ever want to. All fashion, according to this plan, divides into the modern and the pre-modern.

People who tend to read history in dialectical terms can interpret the story of fashion in this century as a few mere swings of the pendulum between modernism (or reason) and nostalgia (or sentimentality). Others, intent on progress, will see modernism as a movement whose rise has been continuous, despite an occasional setback. (On witnessing the helplessness of a woman dressed in Dior's New Look who dropped her purse and couldn't bend over to pick it up, because her corset was too tight, Chanel remarked to a companion that in the space of a few seasons Dior had managed to undo all that she had worked a lifetime to achieve.) Those who believe that in history every movement runs its course will find in the recent appetite for the clothes of a designer like Romeo Gigli plenty of support for the theory that modernism in fashion is in its dying days.

Taken all together, Gigli's museum-quality flocked velvets and antique gilt brocades and iridescent organzas, his Fortuny pleating and chandelier earrings and Venetian-glass hair ornaments add up to a look that is highly particular—what David Livingstone, of the Toronto *Globe and Mail,* called in conversation "a very bookish kind of decadence." Apart from the stretch fabrics—stretch wool gabardines, stretch linens, stretch velvets—and apart from the streamlined cut of the pants, Gigli's clothes are not "modern" by almost anyone's definition. They do not for the most part afford the freedom of movement that Chanel considered so important. In skirts and dresses hobbled at the knees, Gigli's models walk in slow shuffling steps, like geisha girls, wearing shoes that look like fabric bound around the feet. "Never have women in flat shoes looked so helpless," a friend remarked after a recent Gigli show. In fact, their presentation suggests that Gigli's clothes weren't *meant* for moving in: that they were, intended to be seen stock-still, frozen in a moment of repose—to be admired the way a fresco is admired. The models never lift their arms or spin or dance; they move along like icons on wheels.

This fall, for the second season in a row, Gigli chose to present his collection in Paris, and his absence from the schedule in Milan was the more conspicuous in that his influence was everywhere. If five years ago someone had drawn up a blueprint for the very antithesis of the swaggering, hard-edged, broad-shouldered, smart-tailored, slim-hipped woman who dominated the runways and the streets—a woman first and best visualized by Saint Laurent—it would surely have been Gigli's woman: the narrow, sloping shoulders, the body swathed in fabric, the pear-shaped silhouette that echoes the images of madonnas in fifteenth-century Florentine paintings. Not since the beginning of the seventies, when Saint Laurent put a woman in a blazer and pants, with a fur boa and high heels, has a single designer transformed fashion so drastically—and so rapidly.

"Here's the Romeo Gigli group," the woman sitting next to me at Versace said at the start of a passage of gilt-embroidered kimono jackets. "There's one in every collection." At Prada, the raw-silk pants suits were cut high-waisted, close to the body, with the jackets fastened by a single button—like Gigli's this fall. At Jil Sander, the silhouette followed the same lines as Gigli's—the pants so narrow that they fastened with zippers or snaps at the ankle, the jacket long and fitted through the torso. "I guess this is the look of the nineties," one department store executive remarked. Even Giorgio Armani seemed to go out of his way to justify kilim jackets, ethnic-inspired drop earrings, pearl-encrusted organdie scarves, and a silhouette that bore a striking resemblance to Gigli's when he projected Bakst's painting of Nijinsky in "Les Orientales" on the backdrop—as if to say that he hadn't taken his cue from Gigli but had gone straight to the source for his inspiration, and that, besides, this stuff is all in the public domain.

A few weeks later, at the collections in New York, random fragments of the look Gigli pioneered kept cropping up all over the place—Ralph Lauren's Fortuny-pleated silk bandeau here, Norma Kamali's jersey togas in earth colors there, shiny fabrics and long pendant earrings and beaded scarves everywhere. Carolyne Roehm sent out a blush-colored rendition of a one shoulder ballerina dress that Gigli did in black last year. At Donna Karan, a strapless matte-gold tunic with a fringe of beads dripping down over a short skirt, and a full-cut, stole-collared cocoon coat with drooping shoulders, called Gigli to mind; at Charlotte Neuville, it was cuffed pants, cropped a few inches above the ankle; at Yeohlee, narrow Indian silk Capri pants with charms around the ankle. In many cases, in both Milan and New York, the similarity to what Gigli has been doing was confined to a single passage or a single outfit, or even a single detail, which was the more striking because it looked so unlike the style in which these other designers usually work.

If fashion can be said to have a subject, or subjects, surely one is time—how we feel about the past and the future at any given moment. The balance we strike in the clothes we wear—between nostalgia and curiosity, between boredom and apprehension—indicates the speed at which we're moving forward. Lately, it has seemed as if many designers—particularly the younger ones, with the shadows of Chanel, Madeleine Vionnet, Dior, Balenciaga, Charles James, Claire McCardell, and others falling across their worktables—had felt the past to be too much with them. Sybilla claims to feel no such pressure, and says, "I get very insulted when people say that everything in fashion is already invented, that you can't do anything new."

For most of us, the height of high fashion is the photographs of the fifties and early sixties—stark black-and-white images of long, willowy women in Dior suits or Balenciaga coats or Jacques Fath cocktail dresses, as seen by Richard Avedon and Irving Penn. These clothes contain something—let's call it glamour—that is missing from the clothes we've been wearing. Is this irretrievable? Does it exist only in retrospect? Why over the past ten years have so many designers turned to Audrey Hepburn's old movies for inspiration? "I know that women want glamour," Sybilla says. "But I think there is another kind of glamour—intelligent glamour, I would call it. A kind of glamour that mixes very well with a woman's way of being, and doesn't impose too much."

Moschino says,

You can call it glamour or chic or class, whatever you want, but all these words don't mean anything, because they have always been defined visually. They all stand for the same never-never land, and we will never get there. There's a paradox here, because a lot of the people who have glamour don't need it, and the others, who do need it, who are all the time reaching for it, will never have it.

Gigli's detractors predictably claim that his clothes are unwearable and impractical, a throwback to the days when fashion was the common faith and women were there to be venerated rather than known and loved. Maybe. But it strikes me as more likely that Gigli's sudden popularity, like Christian Lacroix's a few years ago, when the pouf skirt swept the market, is a sign of something deeper and more chronic.

Fashion is essentially an optimistic undertaking, the means by which we sustain our hopes and persuade ourselves that tomorrow is not only another day but a different day. Without this foothold for our imaginations, we would find ourselves mired in an interminable present, in which the clothes for next spring—however well cut, however wearable—would look no different from the clothes we had worn last spring, or, for that matter, from the clothes we were wearing now. Modernism in fashion, as in art, is founded on certain inarguable principles, and even now that we're disillusioned with where they have taken us there's no refuting them. We have reached an impasse: as far as fashion's concerned, we still adhere to the principles of modernism intellectually, and no one is prepared to say that clothes shouldn't be practical and enduring and uncomplicated, but the fact is that we now realize just how useful fantasy can be—more useful, at times, than the earnest jacket that goes with everything.

There have always been the fashion enthusiasts and the people who just aren't interested—the people whose imaginations think in terms of clothes and the people whose imaginations turn elsewhere. But thirty years ago, when most women made some sort of effort to conform to a certain standard, it was harder to tell the two camps apart, and the women who weren't interested nevertheless played along. Since then, some of these women have discovered that they don't need fashion at all, that in fact they've never needed it. Fashion has lost them—perhaps not for good but for the time being. They're content to wear jogging suits to the grocery store, oblivious of the spring collections, and invest their money in real estate rather than satin jodhpurs. Fashion has become specialized, with a tradition of its own, to be followed the way one follows the theatre or the opera, and Gigli and the designers under his influence are preaching to the converted.

20

Haute Coiffure de Gel

Elizabeth Wilson

The New Statesman and Society, December 22, 1989

The eighties was the *style* decade. We glammed our way through Japanese shrouds and skin-tight leather, taffeta mini-crinis and lycra leotards. The eighties have been *smart*.

Visit Rumours cocktail bar in Covent Garden any night of the week and you'll find more candidates for *Blind Date* in every square foot than there are sequins on a *Come Dancing* outfit.

The women—white and Afro-Caribbean—wear their hair very long, often in tangled curls, tight, thigh-length dresses in dark knits, and the ubiquitous red lipstick. The men still have the gelled post-*Bride Revisited* hair flopping over the forehead or combed back à la *Wall Street,* and they still wear their suits a size too large. I am not sure whether they have read *Today's* recent article on how not to look naff. Style is larded thickly on, yet, like the Flying Tigers and Brandy Alexanders that everyone's knocking back, it's style in quantity rather than quality.

Or maybe it's reproduction chic—clones of Kylie, Sade and other, even more recent, pop stars. In the smart restaurant a few yards away there's a more up-market version of the same style: more short skirts and black tights and ragamuffin curls. These young men and women have created a look that spells money in some impossible-to-pin down way. There's little sense of creating your own appearance, it's more a question of buying it.

Down in Knightsbridge and Brompton Square you can still see that otherwise endangered species, the natural brown or "black glama" mink coat. Full length, it's worn with loose, well-tailored trousers and sometimes a headscarf. The men wear crombies so smooth and fudge coloured they could be coated in toffee. Soft, delectable. The rich seem to have retreated into the comfort of a style that's dreary yet comforting—furs, Burberry cashmeres, hand-stitched boots. It's all in the fabrics, oozing with wealth, the style's degree zero. In Hampstead it's different again; Italian leather or West German raincoats made of svelte synthetics and lined with real fur.

In 1980s Britain it was once again chic to look rich. The problem was that *haute couture* had forgotten how to be haute. Accustomed now to borrow from street fashions, the couture houses took some time to adjust to the new money snobbery. The marquees at Wimbledon, Ascot and

Henley were being taken over by big business; models and budding actresses were invited along to add to the glamour and they had to look smart.

And then there was a new generation of career women: ex-feminists in the law and the media who felt they could no longer wear second-hand frocks, little "forties" jackets and jeans. For a while, the Italo-Japanese solution seemed to be the thing: a bulky, straight tuxedo and a long shapeless skirt, both in black or charcoal grey, worn with flat shoes and a post-punk haircut. A sort of sartorial Brezhnevism.

Style aimed to respond to the fragmentation of class and to more minutely differentiated social groups of shoppers. The curious thing, though, about market segmentation, boutique niching and all the rest of the jargon, was that it did the opposite of what it claimed to do.

The result was not more choice, but just a Next, a British Home Stores, a Laura Ashley and a Marks and Spencer in every shopping precinct in the land (and in some cases all over the world). The theory of the market-nichers was also extremely crude. They thought there were just three types of people—aspirers, achievers and those who were neither. But wasn't this just a re-packaging of what we used to call class, upper, middle and lower? Nothing very new or subtle about that.

The operation remained a mass market one; and all the talk about design concealed the fact that, in fashion at least, a few huge firms have cornered most of the market. Marks and Spencer account for about one third of retail spending on clothing in Britain.

The result has been conservatism of style, although there has been technical innovation in fabrics and fibres, so that we now have cotton mix tights and silk mix sweaters. Even Warehouse, a chain which sells innovative high fashion at relatively low prices, is itself part of the huge conglomerate, Sears.

The popular discussion in the media of fashion, style and design has conflated or confused at least two separate trends. There was the Next/Laura Ashley operation; there were also the street styles, disco styles and music styles. In the 1970s these had a political dimension. With punk, confrontation dressing was taken as far as it could go.

In the 1980s there were new cult styles but the politics faded. It was less and less clear what the rebellion was about, or whether there even was one. Punk had originally been a totally radical assault on every received notion of fashionability and beauty, yet in the 1980s punk motifs were taken up into what passed for mainstream fashion (the black, the haircuts, the double earrings, the harsh makeup).

Its fate was to be consumerised into a hard-edged urban style, suitable indeed for the eighties, but no longer radical.

This was decay, not decadence. At the *fin de siècle* decadence meant, paradoxically, the search for authenticity, for some new mode of being for new times, for truth to feeling, even the farthest reaches of feeling, and above all sexual desire. Sexual politics and aesthetic politics strove for expression in "decadence"—extreme experimentation in style as a fit vehicle for ideas and beliefs. Sometimes politics was displaced into art and personal relations, but the search was always the opposite of decay: it was the search for the "new life."

In pre-1990s Britain the special kind of Thatcherite decay is already at work, and before it's born "New Age" fashion has become little more than a style cliche. Ecology consciousness now dictates that soon we'll all be wearing calico sacks decorated with our own ingenuity and the help of a few dead leaves and twigs from the nearest park.

Personally I preferred consumerised punk to that. At least the take-up of punk created a credible urban style. At least it had a brutal, porno defiance, appropriate for the times. The worst style nightmare of the 1990s, so far as I'm concerned, is of Britain becoming the Albania of the western world, with all of us dressed up as Druids—a dying society pretending that it has been born again.

When style is reduced to market relations it can never say anything at all. Yet don't despair— at this very moment someone in some art school, cavern, squat or sink estate is creating what will be the real 1990s style: let's hope it's deeply decadent, worthy of this very special *fin de siècle*.

21

Hippie Heaven

Eve Babitz

Vogue, October 1992

The sixties were a dance that began because everyone was so sick of the uptight fifties, they just went hog wild, and then wilder and wilder. One English boyfriend of mine in those days told me about a party in Washington, DC, where a young girl dressed as a mime/princess went around blessing all the guests with a lily as she was about to leave. When she got to the last man in the room, a large executive filled with Scotch, and was about to touch him with her flower, his eyes began to bulge and his throat grew taut, and he snarled: "You don't scare me!"

But she did. That was the point.
He knew exactly what a girl like her meant.

Maybe the reason some of us so long for the sixties to come back is because the world has gone so seriously dismal, it makes the sixties look like they had character—flaky or not. After the eighties, if you begin wearing long fringe, suede hip-hugger bell-bottoms, and boots, you're no longer some "material girl," but someone intent on more important, higher, spiritual things—the rain forest, jobs with heart, recycling.

Of course, we know that the minute you throw away a long-treasured costume because it'll never come back, it comes back. Knowing this, I never did throw my sixties things away because for one thing I still wore them anyway, even when they were grossly out of style, and for another, to me they were art. Especially the red rayon forties dress, cut on the bias, that I'd worn the nights I waited in the Troubadour bar in West Hollywood, looking for trouble like Jim Morrison. Or my navy wide-leg sailor pants with the thirteen-button front (giving sailors thirteen chances to change their minds, was the idea—not that I ever did). These were the original bell-bottoms and not the Cher cut that came later, when the waistbands hit the hips and looking like a hula dancer became of the essence. I still have those pants, and I've worn them since 1967 when I bought them in an army surplus store. I look elegant in them and people have asked me if they're Chanel, they're so classic and well cut.

I showed a guy I know photos of the latest Perry Ellis, Betsey Johnson, and especially Anna Sui designs and asked him what he thought. He said, "It's 1968, right?"

In the actual sixties, there were no designers; there were girls who made clothes for their friends or small shops selling one-of-a-kind things. In Los Angeles it started with a store on the Strip called Belinda's, and with people like Trina Robbins who made Renaissancey clothes to wear. People wanted to look like storybook characters, to wear clothes that meant something. One of the things our clothes meant was "We don't believe a thing they say."

My sister began by making a maroon suede dress. Her boyfriend had learned about leather from a sandal maker in Chicago. He knew what tools you needed to work with leather, and together they made this dress, in 1967. "I wore this dress into this shop on the Strip, Belinda's, and the girl took one look and asked if I could make four more, and I said yes."

A month later, she'd followed her boyfriend to London and the next thing she knew, her boyfriend had designed a line of suede and leather hunting shirts they took to Blades on Savile Row, one of London's oldest tailors, who loved this line so much, my sister told me, "they said, 'we'll take lots, but you don't know how to cut, we'll show you.'"

So, it being the sixties when anything went, my sister, a twenty-one-year-old American with a talent for sewing, was taken down to the basement of a Savile Row tailor and taught how to make real patterns, because, before then, all leather clothes had been boxy and depended on fringe or people not caring if things really fit or not, and these old men taught her, in three weeks, how to cut patterns that really fit—and from then on, she was in business in a very big way.

Eight months later, they returned to Los Angeles and opened a shop on the Sunset Strip named for my sister, Mirandi (she'd changed her name from Miriam, another thing you could do in the sixties without being thought too weird), and there, in 1968, with rock and roll coming into full bloom—next door to a place called the Psychedelic Conspiracy, everyone's favorite paraphernalia store—she had her own store.

"Our first customer was a guy in the Mafia who had rolls of hundred-dollar bills in his boots, and he put in a thousand-dollar order and we were off ... " She made clothes for Steppenwolf, David Crosby, Stephen Stills, and Graham Nash, Cream, the Jefferson Airplane, Sharon Tate, "and this black suede tuxedo for this drug king to get married in."

She also made clothes for Jim Morrison: "Two suits, leather, with extra pants and a laced crotch, like sailor pants. And snakeskin lapels. With a stash pocket concealed in the lining." Mica Ertegun wanted a black glove-suede calf-length coat with snakeskin lapels, double-breasted with a fitted bodice and flared at the bottom—like a Russian princess, lined with green brocade silk. This was the year she was named to the ten best-dressed list. She sounds awfully well dressed to me now—"glove suede" sounds divine.

Eventually, my sister got divorced, quit making clothes, and began a career as a rock-concert promoter. But then she realized rock and roll was too hard. Today she's a therapist, seeing young girls in their early twenties with major crushes on very bad boys—which is recycled revenge, if you ask me.

I myself, in those days, was nothing if not in love with very bad boys, the worse the better, I realize now, although in the sixties the boys were very sweet and the only flaw you could find in them was that they were dealers or else rock stars, which made faithfulness impossible. Except that it didn't matter then because the worst things you got were social diseases that were only embarrassing—they didn't kill you.

In the sixties, nobody wore padded shoulders; they wore tiny fitted jackets and shirts. Men weren't supposed to look "buff," they looked scrawny and poetic. Guys on the streets, tan, dressed like pirates with long blond curly hair flowing past their shoulders, and eyes of periwinkle blue, and high cheekbones would look at me as I passed and say *I* was beautiful. I couldn't believe it. "You're the beautiful one," I would say, "look at you!"

"Hey, I live over there in that house with the blue door, if you want to come hangout," they'd say.

In those days I learned to tell people they were beautiful, and indeed, everyone seemed to be.

On Hollywood Boulevard yesterday I saw two young men, in their early twenties or late teens, both with long flowing hair—the high cheekbones, the tans, etcetera. I was in a shoe store, looking at these great purple shoes that reminded me of the old days, when these boys came in and one said, "Hi, we're both vegetarians and don't like animal products, do you have any boots not made of leather?"

They were both in jeans, T-shirts, and sneakers (no leather), and the girl managing the store said, "No, we don't."

Later, on the street, I came upon these boys again and said, "Are you from San Francisco?"

"Yes," they said, "how did you know?"

"Something about you," I said, "reminded me."

In San Francisco, of course, there are still hippies and in Berkeley, lots of them. And they have "raves" where two or three thousand people stay up all night, outdoors, and dance. If that isn't hippieness, I don't know what is.

In Miami Beach there's a renaissance of recycling old buildings, those gorgeous art deco two-story hotels and bungalow-court places that we still have in L.A., except not as well tended, and there I met a beautiful guy with a yin-yang tattoo on his shoulder and that laid back intensity kids used to have in the sixties, and it seemed to me that Miami Beach right now, with all its thrift stores, very cheap rents, and nonstop nightlife, might be a perfect place for the sixties to be recycled too.

The weirdest thing in the world is seeing a style return that only a year ago was considered ugly by everyone who was anyone, i.e., bell-bottoms—in fact, a friend of my sister's just flew into L.A. from London and said, "I'm so happy to be here so I can buy some pants that aren't bell-bottoms."

A friend of mine, Caroline Thompson, who wrote the screenplay for *Edward Scissorhands*, told me that in London, where she went recently, "the kids are all in platform shoes with bell-bottoms, the guys have long hair and wear John Lennon glasses. And they were hanging out in Leicester Square singing 'Hey Jude.'"

According to a girl in her twenties I know in L.A., what really galled everyone enough to not mind the sixties coming back in a major way was the Gulf War. "That really made everyone mad," she said. "I was at UCLA and the kids were just furious. And Rio. And Clarence Thomas."

It's no wonder that kids have taken to wearing old clothes and hanging out in beatniky coffeehouses and talking about psychedelics.

Near my neighborhood in Hollywood, hippieness has sort of sprung up overnight. There's a block on Franklin Avenue where a coffee shop called the Bourgeois Pig is right next to an alternative-magazine store called the Daily Planet, which sells wild tracts from Berkeley and tattoo and piercing quarterlies. Not too far away is Big & Tall Books, which is also a café and is open until 2 a.m., jammed with aspiring hippies eager to talk all night and all day. On Vermont Avenue in East Hollywood, there are almost three blocks of hippieness, beginning with Chatterton's, which was always on the beatnik side; the Onyx coffee shop, which is cappuccino city; the Los Feliz theater, which runs great movies from far and wide; a men's store called X-Large, partly owned by Michael "Mike D" Diamond of the Beastie Boys, which has such great clothes that artists I know in San Francisco drive down just to shop there; and other little places, like the Amok bookstore, which has this great catalog entitled *Fourth Dispatch: Source Book of Extremes of Information in Print*. And the Dresden Room, where old people living in Los Feliz Hills used to eat prime rib but which is now jammed with just plain weirdos from around the neighborhood in their twenties, thirties, and forties, eager for a dark place to hang out and drink beers. The Dresden Room is the kind of place hippies would never have enjoyed because they had no ironic detachment, but nowadays the innocence of the sixties has been cut by extremes of information, and ironic detachment is all the rage. It adds balance.

It occurred to me that when things on the outside get too disgusting and wretched or boring, kids will turn to things on the inside to see beauty. A friend of mine who manages rock groups said, "In London right now they're drinking Ecstasy punch as we speak. It's like mescaline, acid without the side effects. It makes everyone happy and stay up all night. Things are so bad there." Psychedelics are everywhere—mushrooms, DMT, Ecstasy. I hear that LSD is having a comeback—and I'll tell you, it can be a refreshing spiritual experience akin to selling your house and moving to Tibet. Even the rumor of LSD could make people rethink their idea of what to wear.

When I was a hippie, the main social rule was under no circumstances was anyone to be a bummer—you had to have a personality so full of sweetness and light that someone completely wrecked on LSD could run into you and think you were holy. We used to think that if only we hung on with enough of a vengeance, things would have to get better—kinder and gentler and certainly more colorful. Every time we saw the remotest evidence of this, we'd sigh, "It's happening, it's happening."

By which we meant "they" were getting it, that pretty soon the war would end, police would blend into the scenery, and Latin American dictators would divest themselves of their worldly goods and even Richard Nixon would show up wearing flowers. We thought beauty was power.

Of course, we were wrong.

In the sixties going to thrift shops and dressing up in the styles of another era became de rigueur: we began recycling the past and using it to bring romance, drama, and "it's happening" into the room with us. For very little money, girls could wear great clothes of days gone by and, because we were young and beautiful, get away with it. "Their" wives wore stuff from Paris, the couture creations that could make entrances at charity balls and opening nights at the opera, and things to wear shopping while buying other things to wear shopping.

The fact that the things in Paris now look like things you can get in the thrift stores, is, to me, amazing.

If today the women who lunch in New York are going to begin having dinner parties wearing long fringe, platform shoes, low-slung bell-bottoms, and headbands, or cut-velvet vests, brocaded-satin jacket lapels, tons of colors, tons of bracelets, and Cher-type short-skirted dresses with full sleeves and a renaissance flavor (Cher *avec* Bob Mackie), if thirties-style dresses by Marc Jacobs for Perry Ellis cut on the bias with tons of sequins and transparent blouses, if faux-fur vests and crushed velvet from Betsey Johnson and turquoise blue gloves, if Janis Joplin—type floppy hats with ridiculous feathers return, then it's happening, it's happening.

But what, really, is happening?

In the early sixties, before the big buildup in Vietnam had begun and the Beatles hadn't even left Liverpool, the polls showed that nearly 80 percent of the American public trusted the government in Washington " ... to do the right thing." In the summer of 1992, only 20 percent feel that way. The numbers are completely reversed. It's hard to believe that everything we tried to free up in the sixties—the heavy-handed police dealing with "people of color," the small minds who championed backwater values and regarded women as a "splinter group," the ones who hated sex (or said they did, from pulpits, before they were photographed sneaking out of motels), the ones who didn't want anyone to have fun except them, the ones who savaged the coastline with oil rigs and polluted—is still with us; it's hard to believe that the sixties ever happened. It's enough to make you throw out your clothes from those days, but I never did. I suffered the eighties in silence, partly because it took me a whole decade to get sober and partly because I couldn't believe that such ugliness was so merrily multiplying. That people would forget about each other and settle for BMWs instead.

Perhaps people are just so tired of how awful everything is, they've given up and decided to just have fun in a cheap and simple way. We're afraid of the environment and extinction, we're afraid of the future, we're afraid of "urban unrest," and perhaps this a way to stave off the stares of the homeless, because hippies had a great way of making being homeless seem a sensible idea. They had crash pads, and as my sister remembers, "In the sixties, panhandling meant you refused to be part of the system."

Since today you can't get in the system even if you're dying to compromise your politics, recycling seems our only hope. If we can recycle the spirit of "it's happening, it's happening" along with those expensive clothes from Paris, maybe having fun will come back into fashion. And fun isn't to be sneezed at. The sixties were fun. The trouble was, we thought fun was enough. But if we don't watch out, the only people having fun are going to be the three people who own everything.

Of course, this sixties surge of Anna Sui, Perry Ellis, and even Christian Lacroix could be a "trend." But if these platform shoes, hip-hugger bell-bottoms, and long fringe are just another "trend," I'll eat my Italian red straw hat.

Because one of the things one learned from the sixties is that the price of freedom is eternal vigilance and, though thinking about running things wrecks your peace of mind, even MTV is airing "Choose or Lose" ads to get kids to vote.

When an entire generation gets dazzled by a drug with the density, force, and newness of LSD, we can't really blame ourselves for hip-hugger bell-bottoms—we couldn't get our pants all the way up. And when through our marijuana-clouded living rooms we saw the non-war on TV or the napalm photographs on the pages of *Ramparts* in 1968, and when suddenly an entire generation became As One waiting for the next Beatles album to come out, and it does, and it's *Sgt. Pepper,* and when Jim Morrison calls himself an "erotic politician," and when an entire generation laces itself into high boots and long, flowing street clothes, giving each other flowers and beads, and sets out to prove we didn't "need" war, alcohol, or families because we were each other's family, and when the new star is Jack Nicholson, then not just a girl dressed like a psychedelic princess, blessing an old man from the old school, but an entire generation was met with the words, "You don't scare me!"

But she did. We did. That was the point.

22

Calvinism Unclothed

Valerie Steele

Design Quarterly, Autumn 1992

He's Mr. Clean when it comes to style—sleek, minimalist lines and pale, neutral colors. But he's Mr. Dirty when it comes to advertising—naked bodies and simulated sex. The combination of modernist design and erotically charged publicity has made Calvin Klein one of America's best-known fashion designers. Like Ralph Lauren, who was also born in the Bronx, Klein has capitalized on the crucial importance of fantasy to the fashion industry. Whereas Lauren's dream world is nostalgic, Klein's emphasizes sexual liberation. But is Klein's image getting old? The designer turns fifty on November 19, and though he is being feted by the fashion press, the financial papers have struck a sour note. Reports that Calvin Klein Sport lost more than $14 million in 1990 resulted in *Wall Street Journal* headlines declaring Klein's "Magic Touch Appears to Be Slipping," as his "Core Sportswear Lines Fail to Excite Young Buyers." Yet new advertising campaigns are emerging from Klein's in-house ad agency, heating up the Calvin Klein image once again.

When Klein graduated from the Fashion Institute of Technology in 1962, New York City's Seventh Avenue garment manufacturers were mostly producing knockoffs of Paris couture and London youthquake styles. There was, however, a genuine American tradition that looked back to such pioneering women designers of the 1940s as Claire McCardell, and even farther back to the work clothes made by long-established companies such as Levi-Strauss. In the 1970s, as women entered the labor force in greater numbers and at higher levels, they demanded comfortable, stylish separates, comparable to menswear classics, but with a sexually liberated undercurrent. At the same time, changing demographics made the youth subculture a powerful force and blue jeans a potent symbol of freedom. Klein would exploit the potential of both movements to become one of the leading exponents of the new American look. Denouncing "gimmicky, overdesigned clothes," and extolling "simple clothes" that looked and felt "easy" and "free," Klein combined basic shapes like the tank top and the sports jacket with sophisticated fabrics in neutral colors. It was a monochromatic and minimal look, but it also had a discreet erotic edge. "I like clothes that slide when the body moves," Klein said (Waltz and Morris, 1978, 145). The effect was "sexy in a refined way," he insisted, "not trashy" (Moor, 1979, 4).

From the outset, luxurious fabrics were important to Klein's vision, but they were not the stereotypically sexy satins. He used fine wools like cashmere, cavalry twill, camel hair, and crepe gabardine, in weaves like Prince of Wales, glen plaid, and houndstooth tweeds. Soft leather and suede were also important, as were "all-natural cotton," linen, and silk—what his company called "couture fabrics." Klein's use of color, too, was subtle and sophisticated. Preferred hues included alabaster, bone, parchment, ivory, cream, blond, bisque, buff, stone, pale taupe, dove gray, platinum, pewter, wheat, maize, khaki, caramel, olive, navy, and black. Occasionally he veered toward brighter colors—a chrome-yellow suit or a shocking-pink skirt. But neutrals such as beige avoided the negative connotations of traditional feminine colors, such as pink, which may look cheerful but run the risk of seeming loud or frivolous. Within the context of contemporary fashion, these (mostly pale) non-colors read as feminine—since men's business suits tend to be made in dark colors such as charcoal gray and navy. Neutrals can look mousy, however, unless the wearer is extremely well-dressed and well-groomed, so the Klein ideal implied both money and self-discipline.

This was not "luxury or extravagance for its own sake," Klein insisted in his promotional literature; he simply "refuse[d] to compromise" on quality. His ideal style was "the look and feel of cashmere with crocodile," the "quiet look of luxury," à la Katharine Hepburn. "Like the woman who wears it, real luxury defines a state of being. Self-assured. In control. And definitely modern," a Klein brochure stated. By implication the Parisian style of luxury was ostentatious, superficially decorative, and old-fashioned. For a quarter of a century Klein has built a following among modern working women. "Klein's style of pure American minimalism appeals to the successful, self-confident woman," says Jennifer Whitbeck, a former senior vice-president and creative director at Klein's company. "You wear it, it doesn't wear you."

Klein was not the only designer to sense the new zeitgeist, of course. Halston's minimalist clothes of the 1970s influenced many New York designers, and *Women's Wear Daily* once explicitly compared a 1989 ensemble by Klein (pants, tunic top, and long scarf) to a similar 1977 outfit by Halston. Like Halston, who was a friend of his, Klein designed interrelated separates, often featuring trousers for both day and evening. Meanwhile, in Milan, Giorgio Armani was experimenting with softer; sexier, "unconstructed" tailoring. Successful working women in search of a powerful yet seductive business style soon adopted Armani's loose jackets and man-tailored suits. It is sometimes suggested that Klein's work is derivative of Armani's. Certainly, there seems to be a correlation, but it is also true that Klein had evolved the basis of his style by the mid-1970s—before Armani began designing women's wear.

Klein has never been revolutionary in his clothing designs, preferring to refine rather than to innovate. Perhaps the quintessential Klein garment is a beige pantsuit that has not changed significantly over the course of his career. But in one respect he has been profoundly radical, becoming "America's undisputed pacesetter in turning out erotic ads and commercials," (Castro, 1985, 69). Not many people can afford a cashmere coat from the Collection (the designer's prestige line). But many people can buy a pair of Calvin Klein jeans or underpants, or a bottle of perfume, which collectively make up some eighty percent of his business. The sexy way in which he has promoted these products is already part of fashion history. *Women's Wear Daily* in 1990 described Klein as "the man who virtually invented designer jeans." Dungarees were originally proletarian work clothes, but by the 1960s many young people wore them as an antifashion statement. In the 1970s, clever marketing made customers willing to pay double or triple the price of ordinary jeans for more highly styled designer versions. In 1980 Klein launched six television commercials directed by Richard Avedon and featuring Brooke Shields, a fifteen-year-old model and actress, who had played a child prostitute in the 1978

Louis Malle film *Pretty Baby*. In the most famous of these Klein ads she asked, "Want to know what comes between me and my Calvins? Nothing." After television censors objected to the nymphet's suggestive poses and risqué lines, CBS killed four of the commercials. Another was banned by NBC; it featured Shields laughing and saying, "Help! I'm going to split my Calvins." Cynical observers wondered, though, if the controversy had been engineered by Klein himself. He denied it, but when he appeared on a TV talk show, he stressed how sexy his jeans were: "The tighter they are, the better they sell." Within a few years the very word *Calvins* was used in his commercials as a synonym for sex organs: "All she has to do is wiggle her Calvins to make my Calvins crazy."

More profoundly revolutionary than the Brooke Shields commercials were Bruce Weber's epoch-making advertising photographs of sexy men clad only in their underwear. Provocative images of women in lingerie have long been a staple of both erotic art and advertising, but the puritanism of American society has made it seem shocking to emphasize male sexual beauty. This changed in 1982, when Weber and Klein collaborated to produce the first openly erotic men's underwear advertisements. Soon gigantic billboards towered over the American cityscape, depicting naked muscular male torsos above the waistbands of pure white underpants that bulged provocatively. More than any other contemporary photographer, Weber has fostered the contemporary image of the male sex symbol. Many observers thought they perceived a homoerotic message in Weber's photographs of men, but Weber himself insisted that "any kind of sexuality in a photograph is really determined by the person looking at the photograph .... I felt the Calvin Klein underwear pictures were really photographs these guys could show their grandchildren when they are in their eighties and say, 'Look at the way I looked. Wasn't I really special?'" (Weber, 1992, 8–9).

Female sexuality, too, was redefined in the 1980s, and again, Klein and Weber were among the first to sense the new mood. In 1983 Klein launched man-style cotton underwear for women. *Women's Wear Daily* called it "the hottest look in women's lingerie since the bikini brief," but *Time* magazine reported nervously on "Calvin's New Gender Benders," noting that the bikini looked like an athletic supporter, while the boxer shorts still had a "controversial "fly opening. "It's sexier with the fly," Klein said. "These things are seriously thought out," ("Calvin's New Gender Benders, 1983, 56"). Androgyny was in style, and so was athleticism. Sex appeared to have been recast—as a contact sport. Weber's photographs treated men and women alike as magnificent physical specimens. Illuminated by a clear, bright light, the models were often shot from below to add to their godlike auras.

Group sex was the implied theme in other advertisements—at least, that's the way many viewers interpreted the ménage à trois of two muscular men lounging with the beautiful but androgynous-looking female model, Josie Borain, all dressed only in genital-hugging underpants. When Klein launched his perfume Obsession in 1985, the body beautiful was stripped of clothes altogether and put into a blue-movie ambience. Launched with a $15 million advertising budget, Obsession immediately caused a sensation and was quickly followed by Obsession for Men. One advertisement showed a couple in bed— whether the man or the woman was on top depended on which perfume was being advertised. Another featured three men and a woman, naked and amorously entangled. The sexual ambiguity of this image raised a few eyebrows, largely because it was unclear exactly what the men were doing. Taboos were again flouted in an Obsession television commercial that showed an adolescent boy apparently lusting after a thirty-something woman. "Ah," he moaned, "the smell of it!"

"In Calvin's world, polymorphic perversity is par for the course," wrote the fashion journalist Michael Gross. "Quaint morality is banished." (Gross, 1985, 49). The models in Klein's advertisements, with their young faces and hard bodies, look as though they "don't just have sex. They are sex." And not the ordinary variety but the raw, orgiastic, and forbidden. "Between love and madness lies Obsession," warned the advertising copy. Obsession "was about insanity," Klein said, implying that in the 1980s people had been obsessive about sex, drugs, and sensation (Stanley, 1991, 232). But by the end of that decade, the popular mood had changed, and in 1988 Klein launched a new perfume, Eternity. As he told *Women's Wear Daily*, "spirituality … love … marriage … commitment. I think that's a feeling that is happening all across the country." A response, perhaps to the "new morality" that had developed in the era of AIDS, the perfume also reflected Klein's new image as a (re-)married man. But a few journalists were cynical. "Has Klein at last become Calvin Clean?" asked Gross. "It's a perfect image for the 1990s. And it might even play for eternity," (Gross, 1988, 22).

But nothing stands still, least of all in fashion. To stimulate flagging sales, Klein in 1991 repositioned his sportswear collection as a "bridge" line (the retailing niche between mass-market and designer clothes), and provocative new advertising campaigns were launched featuring street-influenced items such as bustiers and leather jackets. "It's the other side," Klein told *Women's Wear Daily*, "the sexy, the outrageous, the crazy, the bitchy." The 1991 jeans campaign was especially sexy. "Jeans are about sex," argues Sam Shahid, an art director who worked with the photographer Bruce Weber on this and other Klein advertising campaigns. Weber photographed a 116-page advertising supplement, which presented rock stars as sex idols and motorcycles as symbols of freedom, eroticism, and power. The outré images included a cute guy standing in front of a urinal, looking back over his shoulder and smiling; a naked male torso in the shower, holding a wet pair of jeans in front of his penis; a naked woman and a man, dressed only in jeans, apparently engaged in sexual intercourse while leaning against a chain-link fence. But "Klein Jeans' Sexy Insert Didn't Spur Sales," reported *The Wall Street Journal*. Shahid insists, however, that the campaign was a success, because "it made black jeans and motorcycle jackets hot." More important, its cutting-edge image made Klein "resurface" and inspired scores of imitators.

Recently, Klein hired Steven Meisel, *Vogue*'s current favorite photographer and the power behind the camera of Madonna's 1992 book, Sex, along with that volume's designer, Fabien Baron, the new art director of *Harper's Bazaar*. Their first underwear campaign (appearing now on billboards everywhere) features the rap singer Marky Mark, who had already worn Calvin Klein underpants as part of his stage act. The most overtly sexual photograph shows the scowling, bare-chested performer wearing a back-to-front Calvin Klein cap and white mid-thigh underpants and grabbing his crotch. Klein has also launched new television commercials, directed by the photographer Herb Ritts, in one of which Marky Mark asks the model Kate Moss, "Do you have Calvin Klein underwear on?" "Calvin's a sexy guy," says Shahid, "not just a marketing genius," who knows that sex sells. He is "always right there," and he acts on his "gut instincts" about contemporary desires and fantasies.

What, then, is the connection between a beige pantsuit and the blue-movie ambience of Klein's advertisements? They are "related by the notion of the body—what he's designing on and for, says Rochelle Udell, another former Klein advertising executive, who, in 1980, was art director for the Brooke Shields television commercials. In real life, she points out, the body is "a little more concealed" by clothes, while it is more blatantly "revealed" in advertising photography. There is much more to Klein's style, however, than what Udell calls his focus on "the archetypal American body," filled with "energy" and "movement." That is a little too wholesome a characterization of the Klein style. But she is on target when she says, "The *body* is Klein's point of departure."

Bibliography

"Calvin's New Gender Benders." *Time*, vol. 122, no. 10 (September 5, 1983): 56.

Castro, Janice. "Calvin Meets the Marlboro Man." *Time*, vol. 126, no. 16 (October 21, 1985): 69.

Gross, Michael. "Calvin Klein." *Adweek Markets and Marketing Special Report* (May 1985): 49.

Gross, Michael. "The Latest Calvin—From the Bronx to Eternity." *New York*, vol. 21, no. 31 (August 8, 1988): 22.

Moor, Jonathan. "Calvin Klein: The Designer as Star." *Daily News Record*. December 10, 1979.

Stanley, Alessandra. "Riding High." *Vogue*, vol. 181, no. 8 (August 1991): 232.

Waltz, Barbra and Bernadine Morris. *The Fashion Makers*. New York: Random House, 1978.

Weber, Bruce. *Hotel Room with a View: Photographs*. Washington, DC and London: Smithsonian Institution Press, 1992.

23

Coming Apart

Amy Spindler

The New York Times, July 25, 1993

The wire hanger was vibrating like a sewing machine in the trembling hand of Hans Schreiber. Dancing joltingly from it was a pearly transparent dress with swatches of fabric sewn to it like so many wads of cotton on shaving cuts.

After four years of studying cut, draping, anatomy, drawing, marketing and design at one of Europe's most prestigious fashion schools, the Royal Academy of Fine Arts in Antwerp, Belgium, Mr. Schreiber was presenting his pieces to a jury last month. The judges included Jean-Paul Gaultier, France's leading avant-garde designer, who is credited with discovering the academy's most notorious graduate, Martin Margiela. Mr. Margiela is the reluctant leader of a revolutionary movement in fashion, deconstructionism, that has permeated everything from haute couture to street dressing.

The jury had not gathered only to see the work of Mr. Schreiber and his classmates. In the same building, there was a retrospective of 30 years of fashion design from graduates of the academy. Archives lie along the log-planked floors of the warehouse chosen for the show, a dank building with stone stairwells and iron pillars.

Fittingly, it looks like a place where fashion might crawl to die.

The academy was the training ground for deconstructionism—the end of fashion as we know it—and three of its graduates, Mr. Margiela, Ann Demeulemeester and Dries van Noten, were the star pupils. Mr. Margiela graduated first, in 1980, followed the next year by Ms. Demeulemeester and Mr. van Noten. Their subsequent successes ruptured the close-knit cabal of the fashion establishment in Paris, shoving Antwerp—and the academy—into the forefront.

Deconstructionist designs, with their unfinished seams and practiced plainness, were initially considered antifashion, a satire of couture values.

They're a bit more complicated than that.

Antwerp's fledgling designers would scurry to Paris during runway seasons, begging, borrowing and copying invitations to get into the shows and see what the future held for them. They witnessed the emergence of Mr. Gaultier and the rise of Rei Kawakubo and Yohji Yamamoto.

And they saw every excess of the '80s played out on runways and in the streets of Paris. The power suits. The gold buttons. The designer logos plastered on everything. The whole haute couture opera, with Brunnhilde trussed up in embroidery, clacking beads and drapery velvet. And the international press, running around with thesauruses to find one more word synonymous with gilt.

A satire would have been redundant. If that was the future of fashion, few of the academy group wanted it.

As a backlash against established 80s excesses—and tempered by the influence of Mr. Gaultier and the Japanese designers—a new style was born. It was one that offered a sort of asbestos suit against the bonfire of the vanities.

Still, it owed much of its success to a decidedly 80s phenomenon: marketing. The Antwerp designers emerged when the Belgium Government wanted to push its fashion industry and helped finance showings of the school's work in places like Brussels, Paris, Tokyo and London.

Without abandoning any of their rigorous training, the three young designers set about creating clothes that would not overwhelm the wearer. Clothes that didn't seem oblivious of the realities of an often unhappy world.

Each of the Belgians pursues that end in a different way: Mr. Margiela with a vengeance, Ms. Demeulemeester with femininity and Mr. van Noten with studied simplicity. And now, right when the civilized world is ready to embrace the Belgians, the founders of the movement have tired of the association. (It's even been parodied in a magazine produced by one of their classmates in which the group is called the Antwerps.) The Belgian movement is dead, its founders say emphatically; they want to be considered as individuals.

Yet, the unspoken question hovered over the jury room in Antwerp: Could the round-spectacled Mr. Schreiber lead another uprising?

The 15 jury members included representatives from three of fashion's most influential stores—Amanda Verdan of Harvey Nichols in London, Maria Luisa Poumaillou of Maria Luisa in Paris and Barbara Weiser of Charivari in New York.

Charivari is selling more Belgian fashion than Italian. "What's important in the movement is that it's a change of consciousness of what is appropriate and what constitutes an outfit," said Ms. Weiser, who has been buying it from the outset. "Maybe it has to do with women no longer having to define themselves in terms of work models. It's not a question of a particular trend, or identifying with a particular social group."

What drew these high-powered retailers to Antwerp is partly a search for the roots of Mr. Margiela's complex movement and partly the hope that if the last revolution started here, the next might as well.

It was a revolution. And a bloody one at that. Mr. Margiela's first show was in a Paris parking garage. Models had blackened eyes, wan faces. They walked through red paint and left gory footprints across white paper. Mr. Margiela used the footprinted paper to make his next collection.

In his anger against what too much money and too little imagination had done to his art form, Mr. Margiela recycled thrown-away clothes, disembowled his perfectly cut jackets and wrapped bright blue garbage bags around the clothes he made.

"Instead of killing fashion, which is what some thought he was doing," Ms. Poumaillou said, "he was making an apology."

Before Mr. Margiela, Ms. Demeulemeester and Mr. van Noten emerged from the Royal Academy, Belgium was for chocolates.

"In every era," Ms. Verdan said,

there is a right look of the moment that comes from a different place. In the 70's, Italy had Missoni, Krizia and Versace. In the 80's, Paris was for the power suit with Chanel, Mugler and Montana. A fashion movement is a mutation. Why Antwerp? Who knows? Like the Cubist movement, which affected all the painters in Paris, was it something in the air?

What was in this air was mostly the demand for discipline from one exceptional teacher, Mary Prijot, the stern Miss Jean Brodie figure who founded, fought for and ruled the academy's fashion program for most of its life. She retired in her prime, the year after her star pupils graduated, in 1982. "I must say that was the best group I ever had," she said. "Sorry for the others, but I'm talking about the group." Her Antwerp apartment, in a sixteenth-century Flemish building, is a private archive of her proteges.

A sketch Mr. Margiela made of Mrs. Prijot is framed on the wall. His rolling script highlights details that are present today: antique Ethiopian ring. Red lipstick. Silver hair. Gold chain. Nail polish.

"Belgium is a great exporter of fabric," Mrs. Prijot said, "and I said, if we make it, we can use it." Her imprint is visible in her students' work, in the meticulous, flawless cuts she demanded. "You've got to know the traditional before you can play with it," she said. "You must know your ABC's. When a costume isn't good, I see the faults. Of course, it begins with talent. You must have a gift, a vision of things. Martin was strong from the beginning. Dries had many qualities you could feel. Ann was a very good drawer. One day she said, "You're always criticizing," and I said, "Yes. It's my job."

Mrs. Prijot's ideal is the work of Coco Chanel. "Chanel invented fashion," she said. "Everything she did was perfect, the lines, the proportions, the equilibrium of the clothes. All is in place."

Mr. van Noten said: "Madame Prijot thought there was only one good designer, and that was Chanel. And only one nice haircut, and that was a chignon." When Ann Deemeulemeester would come to class with her hair down, Mrs. Prijot would send her to put it up. "I think that was a big part of our creativity, later," Mr. van Noten said, "fighting against her strength to do what we believed."

He is the only one of his classmates to serve on the students' jury, and there is a prophet-without-honor-in-his-own-country aspect to the way the boyish designer is treated at home. In Paris, groupies throng his shows. Here, it is Mr. Gaultier who is asked for autographs.

Mr. van Noten's style has been called Amish. Going from Jesuit school to the academy, he has strong personal reasons for that austerity. But he finds a historical one as well. "Fashion 12 years ago had a completely different attitude," he said. "We came out of school in 1981, with Montana and Mugler. Fashion was all about glamour. It was a completely different world, with bigger shoulders."

He considered for a moment, then added: "There was this feeling that it had to stop at some point. Something real had to happen."

When Ann Demeulemeester was 16, she and her small-town sweetheart, Patrick Robyn, a photographer, fell in love with a house in a suburb outside Antwerp and through a magical series of events bought it soon afterward. It was designed by Le Corbusier, and the private, introspective Ms. Demeulemeester loves it in spite of that high-profile image. It is one of the reasons she stays in Antwerp, as does Mr. van Noten. But she fights against being labeled an Antwerp designer.

"Now everyone is trying to develop his own thing," she said. "Our tastes are very different, in fact. I never see the others. I have nothing to do with the academy. I am an individual. My house is here, and I feel protected."

A tree grows in her studio, which was an artist's atelier when it was built. When Ms. Demeulemeester and her husband first moved in, rain leaked through the roof. "I didn't care," she said. "A beautiful design makes a beautiful ruin. It's the same thing for clothing.

"You never get anything for free. Coming from this country, with no fashion tradition, we had to prove a lot. It's really a miracle that we're here. The problem now for the new students may be that after Martin, Dries and I, people expect to find a certain level of design here."

That is an understatement. And it is the sort of association with Antwerp that Mr. Margiela hoped to sever, from the time he got up nerve to contact Jean-Paul Gaultier for work in Paris. Mr. Gaultier had judged a student contest Mr. Margiela had entered.

Mr. Gaultier hired the young designer as a design assistant. "I didn't need a design assistant," Mr. Gaultier said. "And he said, 'I don't care, I'll be your secretarial assistant.' He became in charge of the commercial collection. I could see his strength. And I said, what are you doing here, you could do something incredible."

In his workroom in Paris, surrounded by racks of his clothes covered by white muslin, Mr. Margiela talks quietly over the constant tapping of a sewing machine. This is not the typical designer's lair, papered with pictures of faraway places for inspiration. He does not mine other cultures for inspiration; he mines fashion.

But he does have an archive, a plankboard closet stuffed with clothes: the severed sleeves from his first season, each tiny button at the medieval cuffs unique. The jacket that is now his signature, with its tidy puckered sleeve molded to the shoulder. The first crisp cotton shirt tied with linen laces. His history is stored in boxes of photos, meticulously marked with the year and season. The models, hair parted like drawn drapes, look as if they could pose for tarot card illustrations.

"I'm interested in the entire culture of fashion," he said. "But I'm not interested in taking one moment of history and copying it. Commercial stuff is always in themes. That was one of the details no one could understand in the beginning. There was no theme. And they'd ask, are those long dresses for evening?"

There are those who liken the effect Mr. Margiela will eventually have on cut and shape to that of Chanel's effect in her day.

"Madame Prijot had certain ideas, and I had others about this thing called fashion. I don't know what she said to you about me, but I know she doesn't think much of what I'm doing."

In fact, she had said she thought Mr. Margiela would someday return to the style of Chanel and stop following the "siren song of publicity." But, she added, "He succeeds, because he dares."

Mr. Margiela and his partner, Jenny Meirens, spent a year developing what would be "Margiela," from the blank white labels on the clothes to the urban combat zone locations of the shows.

He met Ms. Meirens when she was organizing shows for Yohji Yamamoto and Comme des Garçons in Brussels. And he leaves no doubt that nothing in his career has been accidental, or luck. "It was very important to come to Paris," he said, "because here, I could feel free. Belgium is a small country. I felt that I needed a bigger space, and distance. Someplace to work alone and express myself without barriers. I wanted to detach from Belgium and all the good and bad things that happened there."

He said that the first show brought strange reactions, or no reactions. "We were working one year, and wanted a concept," he continued. "It's a big word, but if you see what happened afterward, after five years, I think we can call it that."

What Mr. Margiela brings from the academy more than anything is his cutting technique, which is legendary among his teachers. And what has he left behind for the academy? The same thing that Mr. van Noten and Ms. Demeulemeester have left: the intimidating specter of their success.

Back in Antwerp, in the jury room, points are being given to the students. Mr. Schreiber is on the verge of something called Highest Honors. A few points extra, which the jury can award, will win him that.

"What is this high honors?" Mr. Gaultier said to the other jurors. "Look, Martin never had it. Dries never had it. Ann never had it. Should he have what they never had?"

The vote went against Mr. Schreiber; none of the students was granted Highest Honors.

Perhaps no one leaving the academy will be allowed to surpass the level set 12 years ago. And Mr. Margiela, Ms. Demeulemeester and Mr. van Noten have become the new icons to rebel against. They are the Chanel standard, for future graduating classes.

24

The Once and Future Suit

Anne Hollander

Sex and Suits: The Evolution of Modern Dress, 1994

Male costume since the Neoclassic revolution thus shows how the subversive principle operates. At first, the revolutionary new male tailoring proliferated in a thousand ways, both vertically and laterally. Victorian gentlemen became just as good at elaborate clothing as their wives and daughters, owning many different custom-made tailored garments with many accessories for many sorts of social and professional occasion, many of them uncomfortable and demanding, some of them sporting and easier to wear, but all of them equally complicated. Simple lounge suits for the population in the meantime also proliferated in many styles, colors and textures, and naturally in many degrees of quality.

Besides suits for plebeian weddings and Sunday, however, work-clothes were made in the new form. In Realist French and English paintings and illustrations of the nineteenth century, you can see field laborers in trousers of rough wool or corduroy worn with tailored jackets or waistcoats over colored or striped shirts, where breeches and smocks would have appeared two generations before. In the United States, jeans and overalls joined the group.

When every man was in a version of tailored clothes—at the ball, in the office, on the prairie, or down the mineshaft—the system clearly needed an emotional and visual shaking up, especially if the formal principles were to be retained. And so it has gone, with sporting gear, laboring gear, and of course military and criminal gear arriving in the drawing room or at the opera or the restaurant to startle the eye and unsettle the feelings. With the advent of cinema and television, all sorts of outdated, historical, theatrical, and foreign motifs have entered the masculine picture, and the whole society has liberated its male sartorial possibilities so they may often coexist and interpenetrate. A white tuxedo and a purple sweat suit might now be seen at the same occasion without seeming remarkable, just the way truly disparate modes may be seen on women in the same room.

There has nevertheless been a single limiting male principle in all this, the same one women have persistently copied since the beginning. You can see it by noticing what men don't wear, with all their recent variety. First of all they tend not to combine different programs, as women often do; that is, he won't wear the sweatpants *with* the white tuxedo jacket, as women's fashion indicates she might—unless he's in a very self-conscious thrift-shop mode. Most men's dress continues to express a greater sense of visual boundaries than women's, perhaps of esthetic propriety, I would say even a keener sense of modern design, based on the notion that a single costume fulfills a single esthetic purpose, and requires a single idea to unify its visibly separate parts.

Notably, Western men still don't want to wear drapery, gowns and robes or shawls and veils. The body itself must remain articulated, never swathed, and be unified only by the idea, not by loose fabric. Men don't wear skirts either, partly for the same reason—pants may be very baggy, but they are emphatically still trousers. If skirts ever come to be commonly worn by Western men, they might have the character of the kilt or the ancient Roman military skirt, later copied in the Renaissance— something quite short and heavily swinging, to show the legs and allow them full action, and also to carry the right robust Western flavors. The long wrapped sarongs now visible on television as normal male gear in Africa might catch on temporarily, but I believe not generally—old habits, as I have repeatedly said, die very hard. In the West since the Middle Ages, draped and enveloping clothing is emphatically non-masculine, except for priests or monks whose dress carefully plays down the corporeal.

I would claim that the naked male body, coherent and articulated, must still be the ghostly visual image and the underlying formal suggestion made by any ordinary male Western costume, however closely the surface is covered, just as it was made by the suit of plate armor or the first Neoclassic suit. The modern suit survives partly because among all the more showily revealing varieties of current male dress, it has kept its ability to make that nude suggestion.

The classic man's suit continues to evolve without permitting any extreme violations, it keeps its traditional sober beauty and subtle surfaces, and women still normally do not wear it. They have, of course, several times shown that they can; but they usually don't. They wear many approximations and creative versions; but the complete classical suit with shirt and tie is still mostly men's property. And it is partly because of this that some men have begun to feel a bit stuck with it, in the sexually fluid atmosphere that fashion now reflects. The suit remains the uniform of official power, not manifest force or physical labor—it suggests diplomacy, compromise, civility, and physical self-control, none of which are presently in the fashionable ascendant. The Secretary of State ought to wear it, certainly; but nowadays it is obvious that not everyone wants to sport the look of avoiding emotional explosions or open conflict at all costs.

The suit does not itself constrict the body the way armor or Renaissance doublets did; it is an easy-fitting sheath. But it hides the body's whole surface quite thoroughly, and it usually offers its ensemble of lines, colors and shapes with discretion. Consequently the suit now has the reputation of being inexpressive, in an era of trained muscles and near nudity, to say nothing of political protest, sexual revolution and ethnic assertion, besides all the resources of theatrical and cinematic glamor everyone now may draw on.

Suits are obviously not really inexpressive; they express classical *modernity*, in material design, in politics, and in sexuality. In their pure form, they express a confident adult masculinity, unflavored with either violence or passivity. The suit reflects purposeful development, not quixotic inspiration; it has the modern look of carefully simplified dynamic abstraction that has its own strong sexual appeal. In society it began as an apt visual foil for the vivid and variable fanciful inventions worn by women, and it still does—but only if the women's garments match the men's with respect to careful conception, fit, and construction. Today, a modest gathering at which men really obey the "black tie" rule, for example, will often have an embarrassingly unequal look: the women will look dowdy in tired or out-of-date evening dresses, or else insufficiently festive in nice daytime wear, whereas the men will all look marvelous in their dinner jackets, however old their fashion is and whatever their degree of shabbiness.

In the daytime, classic male suits can look less well when juxtaposed to much postmodern feminine clothing, with its throwaway, thrown-together, fragmented character and its deliberately careless, ephemeral look, often unconstructed, unfitted, and essentially unconceived. When juxtaposed to those effects, a man's suit can start to seem stuffy; but it can also, of course, make postmodern women seem sloppy and anarchic and lacking in discrimination, depending on the occasion and the point of view. Suits do have, as I said at the beginning, a way of looking superior.

A man's suit naturally makes a good foil for classic female suits, since those were invented to harmonize with the male version, and for other classic forms of modern female ensemble—dresses in one or two pieces, skirt-and-jacket combinations of all sorts. Such suit-supplementing garments, not all of them suits, are worn by female professionals of all kinds, politicians and television announcers, by women in boardrooms, courtrooms, and in countless offices; and they are lately getting some of the same disparaging rhetorical treatment as male suits, even while they continue as fundamental staples of modern female wardrobes.

Since this mainstream feminine mode is the adult female version of the male suit, its brand of sexuality is similarly adult and essentially self-respecting, rather than exuberant, boastful, infantine or perverse. Its eroticism is unfailingly discreet, and it is therefore inescapably respectable. Consequently this mainstream modern mode for women has lost a certain public éclat, especially in the fashion press, which must uphold the subversive element in fashion, and seek to praise the forms of novelty that seem reliably disruptive and playful. Modern classic simplicity can appear to betray the present spirit of extreme free expression for all, in all contexts; but the tailored, discreet mode for both sexes is visibly holding its own without the need of fanfare. In the Haute Couture it remains a constant challenge for the best creative talent.

Plainly the male suit is no longer universal for men. It nevertheless retains its look of upholding standards, and therefore it retains its prestige, along with its special brand of confident male sexuality. Feminizing variations made upon its basic shapes and textures, invented chiefly for use by women during the last fifty years, along with the new elements brought to it by designers who have worked for both sexes, such as Bill Blass, Gianni Versace, Giorgio Armani and lately Donna Karan, have deeply affected male fashion by demonstrating the possible future development of the suit in a changed cultural climate. But all this invention has gone forward without ever actually killing or dislodging the classic male suit itself.

If suits should prove vulnerable to real corruption, so that pure examples could only eventually be acquired by determined cultists and rabid preservationists, for whom a small number would still be expensively made, then we might admit its day was really over. But so far, no such thing. Excellent ready-to-wear suits are being sold in great numbers in every major city, and exquisite bespoke tailoring is by no means dead. It is in fact still setting the standard for the ready-to-wear business, so that suit merchants will assure you that their product is indistinguishable from custom-made examples except on close inspection.

25

Sexualities

Anne Hollander

Sex and Suits: The Evolution of Modern Dress, 1994

It's clear that modernizing clothes for women has meant copying men's clothes, directly or indirectly, one way or another. To even the balance, however, we can see that many men in the last third of this century have already taken up the formerly female game of finding pleasure in expressive multiple guises. In one man's closet, the new, colorful leisure versions of active gear make sharp contrasts with well-cut business suits and formal sportswear like tweed jackets, classic shirts lie next to extreme sweatshirts, and everything is meant for wear in the same urban milieu. We may now find the curious spectacle of a man privately at ease fifteen stories above the city street, sipping wine and reading Trollope in a warm room furnished with fragile antiques and Persian rugs, dressed in a costume suitable for roping cattle on the plains or sawing up lumber in the North woods. Once, only women and children offered such visual effects.

Apart from such curiosities, however, the new male freedom has produced a pleasing richness of variety similar to the modern female one, though not entirely the same and still not quite so broad. But handbags, necklaces, and earrings have lost their taboo for men, just as all parts of male dress have long since lost their outrageousness for women; they are licensed dress-ups when they aren't practical or elegant. Both sexes play changing games today, because for the first time in centuries men are learning clothing habits from women, instead of the other way around.

Some of what men are taking up, it must be noted, is simply male trappings that have long since gone out of use *except* by women. Purses and earrings, long hair and brilliant scarves, fanciful hats and shoes may be safely regenerated as male habits, since they have been in storage below the surface as very old and vigorous masculine traditions in the West. It does seem unlikely, however, that ancient Western female effects—voluminous skirts, creative décolletage for chest, back, and arms, bonnets or veils for the head—are likely to be taken up very soon by ordinary Western men. Men have relearned from women mainly how to be mutable and multiple, decorative and colorful, and to rediscover their hair; but the most ancient female symbolic material still remains largely taboo.

The female move to male gear, on the other hand, which was always a partial affair in the past and a firm part of the feminine erotic tradition, has lately been fully completed, and society has thoroughly internalized it. Trousers and tailoring and short hair are now wholly female in themselves, and women wearing them no longer look masculine. Women can moreover no longer imitate men specifically to be taken seriously, because male clothes are already female, too. But it follows that current male clothes have less of a uniquely masculine meaning even when men wear them, and therefore they may safely take on new flavors formerly called feminine. It's clear that during the second half of this century, women finally took over the total male scheme of dress, modified it to suit themselves, and have handed it back to men charged with immense new possibilities.

Even conventional men who don't wear long hair or earrings do wear brilliant shirts, sweaters, socks, hats, and scarves in arresting shapes and colors recently seen only on women. Many modish tailored trousers, jackets, and waistcoats for men are abandoning their careful dependence on tradition and branching out into the expressive exaggerations devised for women's use of them. There has recently been a mode for trousers that begin to expose the underpants and appear to fall off the hips, in an unprecedented allusion to the female vocabulary of décolletage. Male street fashion from many sources has at last had an effect on middle-class males, as it once had only on women. The general idea of fantasy and pleasure seems to have re-entered male dress through female influence—that is, through a new acknowledgment and recognition of female reality that has permitted that influence to function.

The qualities of mutability in surface design that were associated with female habits of dress for two centuries no longer need to represent weakness and madness along with attractiveness, and men no longer have to fear them. There are new eyes for the gaudy old devices that once clothed male power before the modern era, in part because bright hues, vivid hair, glitter, and skintight fit are attributes of the great current heroes of sport and entertainment who command vast fees and global attention. The look of male sexual potency in the postmodern world is able to float free of those austere visions of masculinity, solidified in the nineteenth century, that discredited any richness of fantasy in dress by calling it feminine.

Hair has taken on enormous expressive possibilities for men, now that everyone has acknowledged its ancient male authority, and women have naturally given up none of their modern license to play with it in public. Hair has provoked stronger feeling than anything else in the history of clothing, since it's always part of both clothes and body, both intimate and highly visible if the head is left bare. Hair's visual qualities can obviously cause keen anguish and pleasure, both to owners and observers, and it is easy to understand why some traditions have insisted that women keep theirs out of sight. Hair will do for any sort of rebellious expression; cutting it can be aggressive or renunciatory, and so can growing it. Ideas and rules about hair for men and women make constant news, and the visual effects it creates may rely on immediate responses. For men, facial hair has always shared in the general excitement about hair, and there has been constant male play with beards, sideburns, and mustaches; but it should be noted that while women have been carefully painting their faces in this century, most men have been just as carefully maintaining the artificial cosmetic ritual of shaving. Both serve the essentially *pictorial* ideal of the fully dressed body, which must include the face in the composition.

In our present period of exchange, hair may be worn very short by women or very long by men without either looking transsexual, only extreme. Men not only wear long hair, they tie it back with the decorative clips and ribbon-decked elastics formerly used only by women—but it's noticeable that they usually don't wear Alice in Wonderland hairbands, which derive from hoods and veils and so far remain distinctly feminine. Headbands around the brow, by contrast, are unisex. Both sexes shave their heads, dye their hair purple or wear dreadlocks; anyone, in the androgynous infant spirit, may safely imitate the hairdressing associated with otherworldly fantasy, or seize on any headgear from other cultures. One new mode shown on strong and virtuous men in recent films is a classic tailored suit and tie, worn with a ponytail or the long curly hair once the property of girls. Even among the new male freedoms, the suit still goes down well—perhaps because it, too, has become the property of girls.

The intense power of deliberately androgynous looks has lately asserted itself publicly among adored popular performers, visually confirming the ancient idea that pleasure in sexuality may be richer if the two sexes are allowed to acknowledge their erotic affinities and are not kept stringently divided. The world has moreover finally learned that gay men and women are just as various in personal styles of dress as all other free citizens are; and so straight men and women may make new fashions out of old signals once narrowly perceived as homosexual, modes that are now attached to such former associations only by sympathy and irony, as the modern habit of fashion has taught us to use them.

26

The Eastern Bloc

Lynn Yaeger

The Village Voice, October 3, 1995

"Make it cheap, but make it look amazing!" says Richard, of Suspira, a hole-in-the-wall at 201 East 10th Street that, if memory serves, was once the fetid Lower East Side vintage clothes institution known as Bogies. Now it's cheerful and uncluttered and relaxed, like Rick himself. Today, he's swathed in his own creations: a head-to-toe shift with fishnet bodice, a Dr. Seuss hat, and a wool necklace that doubles as a purse. "I've always had luck, but it's backed up by fierce ambition and creativity," he muses, then coins a phrase: "I'm fervorous! Part of the reason I started making clothes is that I don't want to be dependent on the fashion industry—I don't want to make a Prada dress!" There aren't any proto-Pradas for sale here. Instead, there are droopy raiments in interesting fabrics (army coats with chiffon hems, commodious wrap-and-tie jersey dresses) and deliberately rough edges that bring to mind the Belgian deconstructionists. "I consider my things a little more like *re*construction. It's about having a few pieces that throw together: subtle layering and lots of draping. I have to fit two models—one is five-foot-seven and 120 pounds, and the other is four-11 and 150 pounds. When something looks good on both of them, I know it's right."

I love Rick's clothes, but is it just my personal propensity for things baggy and black that's propelling me? For a radical change of pace, I visit Kanae & Onyx, whose double shopfront at 75 East 7th Street is as close to uptown swank as you'll find in these parts. Everything here is tiny and shiny, and though it all looks like Jackie 60 to me, Kanae says, "it's classic–you can wear it to school or to work. It's tasteful!" Actually, she's kind of right—it may be maroon fake snake and cut to the crotch but there is something simple and elegant going on. And certain pieces, like the double-breasted, frankly synthetic belted trench, really could be worn to a job north of 14th. So how did you guys meet? "We both lived in Williamsburg," Onyx explains.

There was a little rickrack fabric store that no one ever went to … all of a sudden, all the cool fabrics were disappearing. I couldn't figure out who was buying them. Finally, I met Kanae. She was wearing a coat that looked so familiar I thought I had designed it, but then she said she designed it! Eventually we teamed up—it's more fun with two people.

The future? To keep going and flourish," says Kanae dreamily. "To secure our market," declares Onyx.

Trooping across East 7th Street, I almost overlook the unobtrusive Marrakech (76)—I think it's an ordinary tailor shop until I notice that the conservative coat in the window is made out of plastic patent pony and looks like the sort of thing Rita Tushingham might have worn in *The Knack*. Inside, Fattah, who's from Morocco, shows me his line of vinyl and leather sportswear. Did you study design? "No. I practice. I can work from any idea. Every time I see a detail on an old coat—like epaulets—I remember to put it in. I admire very much, what's his name, the Egyptian? Alaia. I'd like to be a famous designer someday."

Right next door, at the quirky knitwear store called NOXS, Renee is knitting so ferverously she doesn't even look up. "Oh sorry! I was just making a sweater. I'm distracted—I had a date last night!" The products of her needles—fluffy cocoon coats, bumpy bouclé boudoir jackets—hang in resplendent colors all over the shop. "These are not cookie-cutter sweaters! My specialty is custom orders—is people want cashmere, or anything else, I can do it. I'm different from everyone else in the neighborhood … no one's doing what I'm doing. You can wear my sweaters in five or ten years and not look stupid."

Ah, but who among us doesn't want to look stupid once in a while? With such weighty philosophical problems in mind, I trundle over to St. Marks Place, where looking stupid has been raised to an art form, and visit Christina, the proprietress at Blue (125). Nothing stupid here. Christina is in the midst of trying on samples while a pursed-lipped seamstress stands by. As she slips each simple dress over her head, it takes on an undeniable va-va-voom quality. "I try to make them as sexy as possible, without overexposing," Christina admits. "Most of my designs are realizations of memories: last year, I did mod, a big part of my life when I was a teenager. I have an intuition for what's going on around me and that includes fashion—a designer, like an artist, has to understand what people will want next."

The reverie induced by Christina's wistful remarks is ruptured at my next stop, the frisky Oz (109 St. Marks), where I'm seduced by the hyperkinetic Marilyn Monroe dress in the window. "We carry neighborhood designers, traditional vendors, and our own designs," Mona tells me. "That Marilyn dress is by Xuan—it's pronounced Shawn. He does stuff special, just for this store." Is he a neighborhood designer? "No, I think he lives on the West Side." Oh. "We like very original pieces here: colorful, fun, and very different. And we design ourselves, too." What are you doing for fall? "This!" Mona steps from behind the counter to reveal a hip-hugging hip-hop miniskirt. "I like very futuristic fabrics—a lot of designers are doing animal prints now, so I'm not. I try to stay ahead of the game." Who do you admire? "In the store?" No, in the world! "The one I've been watching is Anna Sui. She does things for my generation."

Right next door at Argentium, Patricia tells me that her store "is like a lab of fashion: Ag, our symbol, is the chemical sign for silver. Clark, my partner, is from Haiti and I'm from Paris. Clark has more of the design background and is perhaps a bit more sophisticated—I am more influenced by the street." I fall in love a lot here, with the bunny-printed blouses made from vintage handkerchiefs and the long, narrow dresses with fake fur tops and the satin evening coats that seem like the products of a bohemian Charles James. "I love to sit on a terrace and just watch people! For me and Clark, it's all about experimentation."

I do a quick pass down 9th Street and pop in on Isabel of Isabel Designs (428), who pleads,

Please write that I'm on the Web! If you can get on the Web you can see everything! I'm Spanish, but don't put that please—although I have a Spanish flair, I'm a designer. My ideas become trends because I sell to the kids who go to the clubs. I have a wholesale line also—for wholesale you need to do lycra and cheetah prints and gold, but even then I try to add some designer stuff.

Isabel's big idea this season is combining semiprecious turquoise stones with dark velvet. The results are admirable—they look like slightly demented Midnight Mass dresses. But wait, what are these burlap smocks? "Everyone made fun of me when I did those—now everyone's asking for them. It's all they want now!"

My last stop is Rebecca Danenberg at 330 East 11th Street (and as soon as I'm done I'm going next door to Veniero's for a cappuccino and the biggest pastry they sell). "*The Village Voice* is here, do you want to talk to them?" Charles shouts down a grate in the mosaic floor, through which I can see a couple of sewing machines and Ms. Danenberg herself. "How can I–I'm finishing this order!" Never mind. "We sell to Salt-N-Pepa, Billy Idol, Stallone, everybody," Charles tells me, waving his hand in the direction of camouflage jackets and quilted nylon evening gowns. "We're cutting edge—it's downtown stuff influenced by cyber-rave but it's still got hints of classic fashion." Suddenly Rebecca yells up from the basement: "Tell her it's sexy futuristic clothing!"

27

Avant Guardians

Lynn Yaeger

The Village Voice, April 7, 1998

Putting on a show during Manhattan's fashion week presents grave challenges to the bohemian designer: how to get store buyers and the Uptown press, not just your cool friends, to attend your show; how to capture attention while still affecting a who-gives-a-fuck air; how to display your creations in a milieu that expresses your artistic convictions without spending a fortune. Some renegades choose to mount conventional runway shows but locate them in bizarre venues (last season, one designer set up a catwalk next to a drained public swimming pool; this year's sites have included a parochial school gymnasium). You can try to build anticipation by keeping the audience waiting, preferably in bad weather, for at least an hour. Or you can just treat the whole affair like performance art.

Downtown-deconstructionist designer Susan Cianciolo was the master of the antishow show: her mannequins would stop mid-runway, disrobe, and declaim original poetry; on other occasions she'd cover the floor with a lattice of ropes and dare the models to traverse it while the audience suffered ear-shattering dentist-drill music. But if one could overlook, or succumb to, the theatrics, Cianciolo offered strangely beautiful clothes.

Cianciolo hasn't shown in New York for the past two seasons, so the crown for Most Transgressive Fashion Show is as yet unbestowed. But so far this fashion week, front-runners for the award are two designers who decided to provoke audiences by literally turning off the lights.

You'd think fashion people, no matter how outré, would want spectators to see their clothes, but no. Christian Blanken, an extremely talented fellow who's been around a while and always seems on the verge of breaking into the big time, illuminated his runway show with seizure-inducing strobe lights. Through the flashes, it was just possible to discern blouson jackets, dangling drawstrings, and stiff denim. Equally frustrating were the two young women who call themselves Bruce—at their presentation, in a loft on Grand Street, the audience was invited to mill about in sepulchral darkness while attempting to identify the six Bruce-clad models loitering somewhere in the crowd. It's hard to say if anyone found all six: two that could be reasonably taken for Bruce girls wore what seemed to be very nice velvet shells with little wing sleeves, backless peasant camisoles, and pants that flopped over shoes.

After a few experiences like these, it's easy to see why everyone at Elena Bajo's fashion-dance-performance event at the Ace Gallery on Hudson Street was having such a good time. Bajo didn't lack for eccentric conceits—her show was entitled "Shadows of Reality," her program carried the epigram "Run away from the noise, fly, breath deeper/put on a dream/kiss me..." and the exhibition itself consisted of five choreographed vignettes symbolizing various stages of life (innocence, maturity, chaos, etc.). But the proceedings were brightly lit, and the models, though frequently heavily pierced, were not overly sullen.

"I think that must be Birth across the hall!" cried a buyer, spotting a completely naked man crouched next to a ululating woman. Well, maybe, but he might also have been the character the handbill referred to as Consciousness. Whoever he was, he was the only one with no clothes on—the rest of the cast wore Baja's gossamer dance-influenced clothing to great effect as they leapt and moaned. There were pale, layered dresses that somehow managed to seem androgynous, fake fur vests that miraculously didn't evoke Sonny Bono or Alley Oop, and even a *tableau vivant* in which the hem of the model's ankle-length sweater turned into an exaggerated train being made ever longer by a furiously clicking knitter.

28

The Only One

Hilton Als

The New Yorker, November 7, 1994

One night last spring, the fashion editor André Leon Talley attended an all-male nude revue at the Gaiety Theatre, on West Forty-sixth Street. He was dressed in a red waist-length military jacket with gold epaulets and black cuffs, black military trousers with a gold stripe down each leg, black patent-leather pumps with grosgrain bows, grey silk socks with black ribbing white gloves, and a faux-fur muff. Accompanying him, rather like another accessory, was the young English designer John Galliano.

As the driver opened the car door in front of the theatre, Talley, characteristically, issued a directive followed by a question: "I shall expect you here upon my return at once! Lord, child, how am I gonna get out of this car in all this drag?" He did not pause for an answer. He stretched out his long left leg, placed his foot on the sidewalk, and, grabbing the back of the driver's seat, hoisted himself up and out—a maneuver whose inelegance he countered by adjusting his muff with a flourish.

Appearances are significant to André Leon Talley, who seeks always to live up to the grand amalgamation of his three names. He has sienna-brown skin and slightly graying close-cropped hair. He is six feet seven and has large hands and large feet and a barrel chest. He has been described as "a big girl." He is gap-toothed and full-mouthed. His speech combines an old-school Negro syntax, French words (for sardonic emphasis), and a posh British accent. Though a wide audience may know him from his periodic television appearances on CNN and VH1, it is in the world of magazines that he has made his name. Currently the creative director of *Vogue,* formerly the creative director of *HG* and a writer, stylist, and photographer for *Women's Wear Daily, Interview,* and the *Times Magazine,* André Leon Talley is, at forty-six, fashion's most voluble arbiter, custodian, and promoter of glamour.

Inside the Gaiety—a small, dark space with a stage, a movie screen, and two tiers of seats—some men sat in various states of undress and arousal while others dozed quietly. Talley and Galliano stood in the middle of the aisle to the left of the stage and waited for the dancers to appear. Talley was hoping for a "moment." He finds moments in other people's impulses ("I can tell you were about to have a moment"), work ("What Mr. Lagerfeld and I were after in those photographs was a moment"), architecture ("This room could use a certain … moment"), social gatherings ("These people are having a moment"). When the dancers entered, one by one, Talley said, "This is a major moment, child." Swaying to loud disco music and against a backdrop of gold lamé, the young men, who were either nude or partly so, offered the men in the front row a thigh to be touched, a bicep to be rubbed.

"Ooh!" Talley exclaimed. "It's *nostalgie, de la boue!* It's 'Déjeuner sur l'Herbe,' no? Manet. The flesh. The young men. The languorous fall and gall of the flesh to dare itself to fall *on* the *herbe.*" André Leon Talley came down hard on the word *herbe* as he caught sight of a lavishly tanned young man onstage who was naked except for cowboy boots and, as his smile revealed, a retainer. "What can one do?" Talley moaned. "What can one do with such piquant insouciance? How can one live without the *vitality* of the cowboy boots and teeth and retainers and so forth?"

Before the end of the performance, Talley led Galliano into a room on one side of the theatre, where several other men were waiting for the dancers. Upon identifying André Leon Tally as "that fashion man off the TV," a black drag queen, who wore jeans, a cream-colored halter top, and a upswept hairdo, and sat on the lap of a bespectacled older white man, said, "That's what I want you to make me feel like, baby, a white woman. A white woman who's getting out of your Mercedes-Benz and going into Gucci to buy me some new drawers because you wrecked them. Just fabulous."

"This is charming," Talley said, calling attention to a makeshift bar with bowls of pretzels and potato chips and fruit punch. "For the guests who have come to pay homage to the breathtaking ability of the personnel." His muff grazed the top of the potato chips.

The room contained framed photographs from Madonna's book "Sex," which depicted scenes of louche S & M violence (Madonna, in an evening dress, being abused; nude dancers, with collars, being ridden by Daniel de La Falaise in a dinner jacket). The scenes had been enacted and photographed at the Gaiety. "*Miss* Ciccone," Talley said, with disdain, barely looking at the photographs. "My dear, we do *not* discuss the vulgar."

In inspecting and appraising his surroundings, André Leon Talley was working—the creative director in pursuit of inspiration. It is the same sort of work he does in the more conventional environs of his working day. At *Vogue*, Talley is many things—art director, stylist, fashion writer, and producer. As a producer, Talley suggests unlikely combinations, hoping for interesting results. Recently, he arranged to have Camilla Nickerson, a young fashion editor at *Vogue* and a proponent of the glamour-misshapen-by-irony look, design a photo spread on Geoffrey Beene, a designer committed to glamour not misshapen by anything. As an art director, Talley from time to time oversees cover shoots, especially those involving celebrities. He tries to ensure that the photographer will produce an image that makes both the clothes and the celebrity look appealing and provides enough clear space in the frame for the magazine's art director to strip in cover lines. At the same time, Talley encourages the celebrity to project the kind of attitude that *Vogue* seeks to promote on its covers; relaxed and elegant but accessible. He does so by acting as both therapist and stylist. He soothes his subjects' anxieties about the cover shoot by exclaiming, as he dresses them, that this or that garment has never looked better.

It is in the production of stories he conceives on his own that Talley employs all his talents simultaneously. Before a season's new designer collections are shown to the press, Talley visits various houses to look for recurring motifs, in order to build a story around them. During a recent season, he discerned that two or three collections featured lace. *Vogue* then devised a story based on the mystery of lace, and had Helmut Newton photograph lace gloves, lace boots, and lace bodices in a way that enhanced the mystery. Talley chose which details of the clothes should be photographed. In conjunction with Newton, he also chose the models, the hair-and-makeup people, and the locations.

Talley will sometimes write the text to accompany the fashion spread he has conceived. At other times, he will act simply as a cultural reporter, writing pieces on new designers and choosing the best examples of their work to be photographed. Talley has written on interiors, too, directing the photographer to capture images that complemented his text. "My dear, an editor must, *must* be there to fluff the pillows!" he says, explaining his presence at these photo shoots.

André Leon Talley's office at *Vogue* in Paris, where he is based, is a high-ceilinged space, painted white, with large windows facing the Boulevard Saint-Germain; it is surprisingly bare, except for two desks and many photographs on the walls, including a large one in color by Karl Lagerfeld of Talley carrying a big fur muff. There Talley will sometimes perform a kind of boss-man theatre—throw papers about, slam telephones down, noisily expel the incompetent. "This is too much. What story do we need to be working on, children? What *story?* Let's get cracking, darlings, on fur. *Fuh, fuh, fuh.* One must set the mood around the *fuh* and the heels, the hair, the skin, the nipples under the *fuh,* the hair around the nipples, the *fuh* clinging to the nipples, sweat, oysters, champagne, *régence!*" He conveys not only dissatisfaction but also the promise that, once he is satisfied, his reflexive endearments ("darling," "child," and so forth) will be heartfelt.

André Leon Talley, in a blue pinstriped suit, walked into his office one day making several demands that could not be met, since his assistant was not there to meet them. That Talley had, hours before, dismissed his assistant for the day was a fact he chose to ignore. He sat at his desk and began upsetting papers on it—papers that had clearly been left in some order. He then complained about the lack of order. He complained about the lack of a witness to the lack of order. He summoned by intercom a young woman named Georgie Newbery, an assistant in the fashion department, to be such a witness.

"Georgie!" Talley exclaimed as she quietly entered the room. Her eyes were focused on Talley, who, as a result of the attention, seemed to grow larger. "I told Sam never, *nevah* to leave my desk in this state of … disorder! I can't find my papers."

"What papers, André?" Newbery asked.

"The papers, darling! The papers! I need a telephone number on the … papers! Can you believe this, child?" Talley asked of no one in particular. "I need the number of the soirée, darling," he said, slumping in a caricature of weariness. He covered his face with his hands and moaned. Newbery picked a piece of paper off his assistant's desk and handed it to him. Talley looked at the paper: on it was a telephone number. There was a silence; Talley seemed dissatisfied at having the phone number, the problem solved, the event over. He paused, as if to consider the next event he would create. Looking up at Newbery, Talley said, "Georgie, I need three thousand fracs! At *once!*"

André Leon Talley has been the creative director of *Vogue* for six years. During that time, he has seen many looks come and go—the grunge look, the schoolgirl look, the sex-kitten look, the New Romantic look, the reconstituted-hippie look, the athletic-wear-meets-the-street look. In the years I have known him, though, Talley's own look has consistently been one of rigorous excess. In his way, he has become the last editorial custodian of unfettered glamour, and the only fashion editor who figures at all in the popular imagination. He is the fashion editor who, seemingly sparing no expense for models, clothes, props, photographers, and airplane tickets to far-flung locations—a farm in Wales, a burlesque house on West Forty-sixth Street—pursues that which the public will perceive, without naming it, as allure.

This pursuit begins in Talley's Paris apartment, which is situated near the Invalides, where Napoleon is entombed. The apartment is small but rich in talismans of allure: scented candles, flower-patterned draperies that puddle on the floor, a large flower-patterned screen, a Regency bed, books artfully arranged on a table in the vestibule. The walls are covered in beige rice paper. There is a small dark room off the vestibule with a VCR attached to an oversized television; on the walls are a number of drawings by Karl Lagerfeld and a poster-size, black-and-white photograph of a black man's torso by Annie Leibovitz.

Talley begins telephoning in the morning, often as early as six o'clock, to suss out what might be "the next thing." When Talley telephones a designer, he may ask, "Darling, have you had a moment?" In an industry notoriously suspicious of language, Talley's grandiloquence transports the designer into the role of artist. It does so by placing the designer's work in the realm of the historic: "This collection is more divine that the last, Monsieur Ferrè, in that it is high moment of Grecian simplicity, of fluted skirts in the material of a high rustling mega-moment, from room to room, à la the essence of King Louis XV, à la the true spirit of couture!"

On the other hand, Talley does not see the work without the frame of commerce around it; in this sense, he is like an art dealer, whose survival is based on an evaluation of the market and of how the work at hand will shape the market, or be shaped by it, in future months. When Chanel, Dior, de la Renta, and other couture and ready-to-wear houses advertise in *Vogue,* they signal the affinity between their aesthetic and the world that André Leon Talley has created. Designers trust him, the moneyed women he brings to the designers trust him, and the women's husbands trust him with their wives. Drawing on this fund of trust, Talley presents, in the pages of *Vogue,* the work of European designers in an atmosphere of guilt-free exuberance that an American audience, standing in line at the supermarket reading *Vogue,* can trust.

"Magazines are not a Diderot moment of œuvreness," Talley says. "They are monthly ventures that should amuse and earn money by showing how *kind* money can be." In the stories that Talley has produced for *Vogue* in recent years—"The Armani Edge," "Feets of Brilliance," "Which Way Couture?" and "The Couture Journals," among others—everything is seduction. Talley's delicate orchestration and manipulation of the designers and buyers and photographers and editorial staff contributing to his vision are never seen, of course. What matters most to André Leon Talley is the image in his head of a woman looking at the page imagining herself on it, unaware of all that André Leon Talley has contributed to her imagination.

André Leon Talley says he owes his desire to uphold what he calls, "the world of opulence! opulence! opulence! maintenance! maintenance! maintenance!" to the late Diana Vreeland, who was the fashion editor for twenty-five years at *Harper's Bazaar,* the editor-in-chief of *Vogue* for eight years, and thereafter a special consultant to the Metropolitan Museum's Costume Institute, where she mounted audacious shows on Balenciaga, the eighteenth-century woman, equestrian fashion, and Yves Saint Laurent. It was during Vreeland's planning and installation of one such show—"Romantic and Glamorous Hollywood Design," in 1974—that Talley and Vreeland first met, through the parents of one of his college classmates. He later came to work for her as an unpaid assistant.

Vreeland was the most recognizable person in the fashion industry—indeed, the very image of the fashion editor—with her heavily rouged cheeks and lips, red fingernails, and sleek black hair; her red environments; her pronouncements (bluejeans "are the most beautiful things since the gondola"; Brigitte Bardot's "lips made Mick Jagger's lips *possible*"); her credos ("Of course, you understand I'm looking for the most *far-fetched* perfection"; "There's nothing more boring than narcissism—the tragedy of being totally … me"); her standards (having her paper money ironed, the soles of her shoes buffed with rhinoceros horn); and her extravagance of vision (photographic emphasis on nudity, drugs, and jewels).

By the time they met, Talley had gradually constructed a self that was recognizably a precursor of the André Leon Talley of today. And its most influential component was the formidable chic of his maternal grandmother. Talley was born in Washington, D.C., and when he was two months old he was sent by his parents to live with his grandmother Bennie Frances Davis, in Durham, North Carolina. "An extraordinary woman with blue hair, like Elsie de Wolfe" is how he describes her. "You know what one fundamental difference between whites and blacks is? If there's trouble at home for white people, they send the child to a psychiatrist. Black folks just send you to live with Grandma."

As a teenager, Talley made regular trips to the white section of Durham to buy *Vogue,* and these forays were another significant influence on his development. "My uncles cried 'Scandal! Scandal!' when I said I wanted to grow up to be a fashion editor," he says.

I discovered so early that the world was *cruel.* My mother didn't like my clothes. Those white people in Durham were so awful. And there I was, just this lone jigaboo … creature. And fashion in *Vogue* seemed so kind. So *opulently* kind. A perfect image of things. I began to think like an editor when I began to imagine presenting the women I knew in the pages of *Vogue:* my grandmother's style of perfection in the clothes she made; her version of couture.

In a snapshot of Talley from his college days, he is sitting with two female friends. What makes him recognizable is not just his physical appearance—the long, thin body; the large, vulnerable mouth jutting out from the long, thin face—but also his clothes. Unlike the other students, who are dressed in T-shirts and jeans, Talley wears a blue sweater with shorts sleeves over a white shirt with long sleeves, a brooch in the shape of a crescent moon, large aviator glasses with yellow lenses, and a blue knit hat. He looks delighted to be wearing these clothes. He looks delighted to be with these women.

Talley earned a B.A. in French literature at North Carolina Central University in 1970. His interest in the world of allure outside his grandmother's closet, away from Durham, coincided with his interest in French. He says of his discovery that couture was a part of French culture, and that his grandmother practiced her version of it,

You could have knocked me over with a feather! And it was stretching all the way back to the ancient regime, darling! Introduced to me by my first French instructor, Miss Cynthia P. Smith, in the fields of Durham, North Carolina! The entire French œuvre of oldness and awfulness flipping one out into the Belle Époque bodice of the music hall, Toulouse-Lautrec, an atmosphere of decadence, leading us to Josephine Baker and … me!

Talley's immersion in French gave him a model to identify with: Baudelaire, on whose work he wrote his master's thesis, at Brown University in the early seventies. And it was while he was at Brown, liberated by the Baudelairean image of the flaneur, that Talley began to exercise fully his penchant for extravagant personal dress. He was known for draping himself in a number of cashmere sweaters. He was known for buying, on his teaching-assistant stipend, Louis Vuitton luggage.

"Obviously, he was not going to teach French," Dr. Yvonne Cormier, a schoolmate of Talley's at Brown, says. "André thought it was just good manners to look wonderful. It was a *moral* issue. And his language reflected that. André could never just go to his room and study. He had to *exclaim,* "They've sent me to this prison! Now I have to go to my chambers and have a moment."

After Talley left Brown and completed his stint as a volunteer with Diana Vreeland at the Met, he became known in New York fashion circles for these things: insisting, at his local post office, on the most *beautiful* current stamps and holding up the line until they materialized; serving as a personal shopper for Miles Davis at the request of Davis's companion, Cicely Tyson; answering the telephone at Andy Warhol's *Interview,* in his capacity as a receptionist, with a jaunty *"Bonjour!"* and taking down messages in purple ink (for bad news) and gold (good news); wearing a pith helmet and kneesocks in the summer; being referred to by the envious as Queen Kong; becoming friends with the heiress Doris Duke and attending, at her invitation, many of her appearances as a singer with a black gospel choir; overspending on clothes and furnishings and running up personal debts in his habitual effort to live up to the grand amalgamation of his three names.

The late seventies, when André Leon Talley came into his own, is the period when designers like Yves Saint Laurent and Halston produced the clothes that Talley covered at the beginning of his career as a fashion editor at *WWD,* clothes often described as glamorous. It is the period referred to in the clothes being produced now by designers like Marc Jacobs and Anna Sui. "It was a time when I could take Mrs. Vreeland and Lee Radziwill to a LaBelle concert at the Beacon and it wouldn't look like I was about to mug them," Tally says.

Daniela Morera, a correspondent for Italian *Vogue,* has a different recollection. "André was privileged because he was a close friend of Mrs. Vreeland's," she says.

Black people were as segregated in the industry then as they are now. They've always been the don't-get-too-close-darling exotic. André enjoyed a lot of attention from whites because he was ambitious and amusing. He says it wasn't bad, because he didn't know how bad it was for other blacks in the business. He was successful because he wasn't a threat. He'll never be an editor-in-chief. How could America have *that* dictating what the women of American will wear? Or representing them? No matter that André's been the greatest crossover act in the industry for quite some time. Like forever.

Talley's fascination stems, in part, from his being the *only one.* In the media or the arts, the only one is usually male, always somewhat "colored," and almost always gay. His career is based, in varying degrees, on talent, race, nonsexual charisma, and an association with people in power. To all appearances, the only one is a person with power, but is not *the* power. He is not just defined but controlled by a professional title, because he believes in the importance of his title and of the power with which it associates him. If he is black, he is a symbol of white anxiety about his presence in the larger world and the guilt such anxiety provokes. Other anxieties preoccupy him: anxieties about salary and prestige and someone else's opinion ultimately being more highly valued than his. He elicits many emotions from his colleagues, friendship and loyalty rarely being among them, since he does not believe in friendship that is innocent of an interest in what his title can do.

Talley is positioned, uniquely, at the intersection of fashion, magazine publishing, television, and high society. He regards his position as a privilege, and he flaunts it. "A large part of his life is *Vogue,*" Candy Pratt Price, the magazine's fashion director, says about him. "Which explains the vulnerable, intense moods he goes through when he thinks someone here is against him. We've all been there with those moods of his, and *there* is pretty intense."

Talley's emotional involvement with women rises in part from nostalgia. He seems to project his grandmother's intentions and concerns for him, and Cynthia P. Smith's and Diana Vreeland's as well, onto his female colleagues at *Vogue,* and he seems to feel spurned when they exercise the independence inherent in a modern-day professional relationship. Often, the results are disastrous. When Talley is in favor, his colleagues adopt him as a totem of editorial success; when he is not, they regard him as a glittering but superfluous accessory.

His interest in romance is nostalgic, too. For him, romance is not about ending his loneliness; rather, it flows from the idea, expounded by Baudelaire, that love is never truly attained, only yearned for. (Talley's contemporary version of this: "No man, child," he might say, telephoning from his apartment in Paris. "No man. Just another video evening alone for the child of culture.") Talley's romantic yearnings are melancholic: he is susceptible to the prolonged, unrequited "crush" but is immune to involvement. He avoids engaging men he is attracted to. Generally, he is attracted to men who avoid him. He avoids the potential rejection and hurt that are invariable aspects of romantic love. Going to a gay bar with Talley, then, is an odd experience. In gay bars, as a rule, all bets are off: everyone is the same as everyone else because everyone is after the same thing. In a sense, the common pursuit divests everyone present of his title. Talley rarely speaks to anyone in this sort of environment. Mostly, he glowers at men he finds appealing and lays the blame for their lack of immediate interest in him on racism, or on the sexually paranoid environment that AIDS has fostered everywhere. Perhaps he just prefers the imagery of love made familiar by fashion magazines: images of the subject exhausted by "feeling," undone by a crush, recuperating in an atmosphere of glamour and allure.

Once, in New York, I had dinner with Talley and his friend the comedian Sandra Bernhard. She asked me how long I had known André. I said, "I fell in love with him in Paris." There was a silence—a silence that André did not fill with being pleased at or made shy by my comment. He grew large in his seat. He grew very dark and angry. And then he exclaimed, with great force, "You did not fall in love with me! You were in love with Paris! It was all the fabulous things I showed you in Paris! Lagerfeld's house! Dior! It wasn't me! It wasn't! It was Paris!"

When I first met Talley, I did not tell him that my interest in him was based in part on what other blacks in the fashion industry had said about him, on the way they had pointed him out as the only one. Blacks in the fashion industry have spoken of Tally with varying degrees of reverence, envy, and mistrust (which is how non-blacks in the fashion industry have spoken of him as well). One black American designer has called André Leon Talley "a fool. He'll only help those kids—designers like Galliano—if they've got social juice, if they're liked by socialites, the women who tell André what to do." Talley complains about people who underestimate the difficulty of his position. "It's exhausting to be the only one with the access, the influence, to prevent the children from looking like jigaboos in the magazine—when they do appear in the magazine. It's lonely."

Talley gave a luncheon in Paris a few years ago to celebrate the couture season's start. The people he welcomed to the luncheon—held in the Café Flore's private dining room, on the second floor—included Kenneth Jay Lane, a jewelry designer; Inès de la Fressange, a former Chanel model and spokesperson; Joe Eula, a fashion illustrator; Roxanne Lowit, a photographer; and Maxime de La Falaise, a fashion doyenne, and her daughter, LouLou, the Yves Saint Laurent muse.

Following shirred eggs and many bottles of wine, Roxanne Lowit, her black hair and black Chinese jacket a blur of organization, invited the guests to assemble in order to be photographed. LouLou de La Falaise removed an ancient huge round compact from her purse and began to powder her nose as her mother sat in readiness. Joe Eula ignored Lowit and continued drinking. Talley got up from his seat to sit near Maxime de La Falaise, who had admired a large turquoise ring he wore.

"Look, LouLou!" Talley shouted. "The color of the ring is divine, no? Just like the stone you gave me!"

"What?" LouLou de La Falaise asked, barely disguising her boredom.

"This ring, child. Just like the stone you gave me, no?"

LouLou de La Falaise did not respond. She nodded towards Roxanne Lowit, and Lowit instructed her to stand behind Maxime de La Falaise and Talley. LouLou de La Falaise said, "I will stand there only if André tries not to look like such a nigger dandy."

Several people laughed, loudly. None laughed louder than André Leon Talley. But it seemed to me that a couple of things happened before he started laughing: he shuttered his eyes, his grin grew larger, ad his back went rigid, as he saw his belief in the durability of glamour and allure shatter before him in a million glistening bits. Talley attempted to pick those pieces up. He sighed, then stood and said, "Come on, children. Let's *see* something. Let's visit the House of Galliano."

29

Buying the Fantasy

Hilton Als

The New Yorker, June 10, 1996

During the early part of my adolescence, nearly twenty years ago, I was drawn to the surreal four-color universe manufactured by fashion magazines. In fashion pictorials I saw something I wanted to be: a woman "captured" by the photographer's gaze and caressed by high production values that made her lips and eyes and hair shine just so. What I meant for those still, gleaming images to give back to me I couldn't say, but I used to pore over them for hours. I remember the feeling of frustration that would come over me during that period of non-exchange, and also a kind of glee: like most romantics, I thrived on rejection. I gradually gained control over the fashion magazines—over the source of so much of my self-conscious "sadness"—by becoming critical of their unreality, and of the women they featured, whom most of us could never know or hope to be.

In the intervening decades, the models I once projected my longings and dreams onto have mostly lost that gleam, and magazine readers have begun to turn to fashion advertising as their source of fashion as fantasy. The most striking of the recent ad campaigns—for Calvin Klein, Hugo, and Jil Sander, shot by Steven Meisel, Juergen Teller, and Craig McDean, respectively—suggest that the most adventurous fashion "journalism" is the ads themselves, and the best fashion "editors" are the photographers and art directors who design the ads. These three campaigns do not vie with editorial fashion for attention; in fact, editorial fashion has taken to emulating its once barely tolerated money-grubbing ugly sister—a reversal of the positions of advertising and editorial "content" which couldn't have been imagined fifteen years ago. The message these ads convey, through the raw, unstudied look of some of the photographs and the raw, dislocated look of the models, is that fashion is dead. It's a message at odds with what editorial fashion, in those four-color features about going "white for summer" or adopting "the strong suit" for fall, still tries desultorily to project—a "finished" woman, made so by fashion. The new fashion advertising has been her undoing.

In Meisel's ads for Calvin Klein's scent cK one, for example ("A shared fragrance for a man or a woman"), it is the casting that makes the campaign so mesmerizing to watch on buses wobbling across the city. Meisel has populated the campaign with ruined faces and bodies that seem to be walking away from his seamless white backdrop, and he singles out the former film star and sex kitten Joey Heatherton, whose battles with anorexia and the law have been well chronicled by the press; she stares out at the viewer like a memento mori with peroxided hair, barely a person. This approach—essentially an attempt to demythologize models as "super"–is more aggressively pursued by the ads that German-born, London-based photographer Juergen Teller shoots. Fingernails with chipped black paint, greasy hair: these are the metaphors Teller uses to explore how trivial beauty seems in relation to depression. In a Teller ad, that depression may be economic or it may be just youthful posturing, but it is always predicated on the subject's failure to relate to the world. In the Hugo campaign, which looks like a series of B-movie stills, a dark-haired youth struggles with a woman wearing a flower-patterned dress. Their exchange is marked by a palpable silence, which has less to do with photography's silence than with the idea of the characters' failure to communicate with each other. Hands grasping, flesh made too pale by the bright light of the flash, these figures pique the viewer because of all that the ad represents: the death of editorial fashion's standard narrative involving couples (woman plus man equals shopping), and the end of an era in advertising. In the new era, ads such as Revlon's look ridiculous and outdated. Poor Melanie Griffith, hair-moussed and lip-glossed, gazes out at the viewer, as though unmindful of the fact that she seems to have been airbrushed to death.

The beginning of the end was in 1990, when the work of a then twenty-five-year-old photographer named Corinne Day started to appear in the British youth-oriented publications *i-D* and *The Face*. Unlike the work of many of her predecessors, which relied on the usual contraptions of fashion photography ("genius" makeup and hair; improbable girls and improbable situations), Day's pictures—of models clothed in the low-budget, mismatched outfits of youth—were about her subjects' unabashed narcissism, and how it sheathed then in the glow or the gloom of self-love. Day's world unfolds in broad expanses of grimy nature, or in dingy council flats that one associated with post-Thatcherite Britain, and the type of girl Day was attracted to was not unlike her: awkward, thin, disconsolate. "That's why I photographed Kate—she was just a schoolgirl then. She reminded me of myself," Day recalls, referring to her great discovery, Kate Moss. In picture after picture, Moss conveyed the qualities that became synonymous with the offhand look of Day's images, which were meant to resemble "snaps" but were artful in their design and controlled in their execution. Her vision—of a young woman who was unaware of the corrosive effects of time as her soul rotted or played at the fringes of boredom, and unaware of anything remotely recognizable to us as "glamour"—was, at the time, original and arresting. Day began working for the American and British editions of *Vogue,* but in 1993, when her startling images of Moss in underwear appeared in British *Vogue,* "the commercial aspects of fashion photography began to frighten me," Day recalls. "Kate came to me and said that her agent told her that it wasn't good for her to be seen in my pictures anymore."

The pictures in question were in some ways Day's apotheosis as a photographer. Besides being intensely moving—Day had managed to capture on film Moss's transition from young chum to commodity—the photographs are a first testament to the fashion industry's now pervasive flirtation with death. The naked, bruised look in Moss's eyes was an apt expression of the brutality that Day was beginning to experience in the fashion world. "Corinne can't compromise, not one bit," Edward Enninful, *i-D*'s current fashion editor, says. Day's increasingly challenging suggestion that fashion was not strong enough to contain anyone's fantasies made her alienation from the industry inevitable; it also accounts for the beautiful minimalism of her Barneys ad campaign from 1993. The models—slouching, walking, or sitting—were objectified totems of indifference or cool.

Ironically, just as one began seeing Day's poetic indifference influencing—indeed, defining—many ad campaigns and magazine pictorials, Day herself began to drop out of sight. The industry had pigeonholed her as the photographer of grunge, which was on the way to extinction; it took what it needed from her and moved on. Photographers like Meisel, Teller, David Sims, and Mario Sorrenti have all benefited, in my view, by imitating aspects of Day's groundbreaking work, while she has pursued other interest—including directing short films for MTV. "Fashion's become an all-boy world," she says.

Perhaps the most interesting of the recent fashion-ad campaigns are those produced for the German designer Jil Sander by Craig McDean, which evoke glass-encased wax figures. Born in 1964, in Cheshire, England, McDean, like Day, published his first photographs in *The Face* and *i-D*. The rough, unfinished look favored by those magazines was something he had explored initially as a teenager photographing his passion: motorbikes and motorcyclists. After a stint at the Blackpool School of Art, in the late eighties, McDean rejected the academicism of photo training, "which wasn't training at all," he says. "It's just teaching you how to tidy up after a photography class." He moved to London and apprenticed himself to the photographer Nick Knight. In addition to the Jil Sander campaign, McDean has received commissions from *Harper's Bazaar* and, just recently, Calvin Klein, for whom he has shot Kate Moss in sleepwear.

But in his rich Paul Outerbridge-like printing McDean deviates from the watered-down, Day-derived raw look that most of the new fashion advertising has adopted. He luxuriates in alchemy—in revealing on the page his interest in how lighting defines a photograph. His lighting often acts—in the Jil Sander campaign, especially—as a strange kind of fluorescent accessory for the skin and hair. His highly finished veneer is probably what has made his work more commercial than Day's; he makes the "down" feel "up." But his women don't seem much affected by the concentration of light on their faces. Their dark interior selves cast it off, like a repellent; the universe that revolves around them consists only of McDean's lights and camera. The attitudes they strike seem the outgrowth of some silent distress, and one wishes, somehow, that they would stop looking in and look out.

McDean's style has just begun to be reflected in the work of photographers like Meisel, who is a survivor precisely because he knows how to imitate trends. McDean himself disavows his trendiness. "Don't call me a fashion photographer," he says, with a laugh, echoing the sentiment expressed by many photographers before him: that fashion photography is the glittering stepchild of "art" photography. "What I try to show in my work is detail." And it's true that the photographic effect of his work is naturalistic—as though he were conveying the impression of a bird by focussing on the feathers of its wing. But the ennui that has infiltrated the fashion industry is reflected in this kind of highly aesthetic advertising—and in the way its photographers want women to appear either oblivious of fashion or exhausted by it.

30

Fashion's Military Fascination: Unsettling, Romantic Esthetic

Suzy Menkes

The International Herald Tribune, March 10, 1996

There is something unsettling about the forward march of military style on designer runways in the opening weeks of the international fashion season. Uniforms, battle fatigues, camouflage patterns and Eisenhower jackets have all made appearances.

At Gucci in Milan, Italy, epaulets appeared on crisp tailoring and shiny belts with metallic buckles cinched the waist. Gianni Versace, in his Istante line, made four-pocket military jackets the focus of his collection—even if he presented them in sleek satin or reduced the battle blouse to strategically placed pockets on a wisp of lace dress.

At the London shows, the military look was popular for the fall season, with khaki or darker browns favored colors and army shirts and jackets key items. In an ironic take on street style, where army surplus coats are cold-weather gear, Red or Dead mined the cold war zone. The line was shown in a barrack-like building where army-clad dummies were stood on a balcony like Red Square comrades and ugly industrial prints were described as "Gdansk colliery."

At Alexander McQueen's show, the theme was more subtle and more somber. Looking at war through the ages, the edgy British designer presented sharp military tailoring, buttoned pants and denim outfits photo-printed with the stereotypes of aggressors on the front and of victims on the back: Biafran soldiers and innocent children, American soldiers in jungle camouflage and an elderly Vietnamese man.

"It is about war and peace," Mr. McQueen said of his show. "But I am not the sort of person who is going to stand up and say this—either you see it in my collection or you don't."

However sincere the designer, the linkage of fashion with war is problematical; fashion tends to be perceived as trivial, and its raiding of blood-soaked references might therefore seem crassly exploitative.

Military looks on the runway are often badly received. Recently, Prada's trench coats, with their whiff of Fascist rigor, drew unfavorable comment, as did Comme des Garçons's showing of recycled khaki clothing, although the designer Rei Kawakubo said that it was an exercise in deconstruction unrelated to war.

Valentino's use of camouflage prints in his 1994 couture collection—just when the United Nations peacekeeping force was in Rwanda—was rejected by clients. Yves Saint Laurent's safari suits and military accessories were reviled by the press and clients in the late 1960s at the height of the antiwar demonstrations.

If fashion's war images are so badly received, why do designers persist with such references? Often, they are simply responding to the romance in the uniform from a long-gone era. Mr. Versace described his concept this season as "romantic military," and other designers have frequently found inspiration in the picturesque uniforms of toytown soldiers and gay hussars.

A 1995 exhibition at the Costume Institute of the Metropolitan Museum of Art was called "Swords Into Ploughshares" and showed the origins of military looks turned fashionable: the safari suit was developed by the need for camouflage in the heat and dust of Britain's far-flung empire; gilt braiding was designed to protect the chest, before its use became merely ceremonial.

Wartime images tend to be absorbed into fashion when the clothing no longer serves its original function. Either practical things turn decorative—like the silver-ball buttons that were once designed as backup ammunition. Or in a postwar period, practical army gear is absorbed into civilian life, as with the blouson jacket or trench coat.

But war fashion also appears suddenly, apparently from nowhere. The most likely reason for the current vogue is the flood of secondhand or surplus army clothing that came from Eastern Europe after the fall of Communism. The clothes were practical and affordable for a young generation not necessarily making any statement about dressing aggressively.

Another explanation is that designers absorbed the imagery of the military that appeared on television screens and magazines last year as Europe celebrated the end of World War II fifty years before. Articles about the twentieth anniversary of the Vietnam War may also have pricked the visual consciousness.

Retro fashions have also thrown up army looks, like the Eisenhower combat jacket from the 1940s as part of neo-conservative male dressing, or safari suits revived from the hippie era. Some garments, like the military blouson or the pilot's flying jacket, have just evolved into design classics.

One designer may act as a catalyst. Prada has stirred a general influence in uniforms, which have been developed as a fashionable look. Gucci's Tom Ford deliberately described the theme of his new collection as "uniforms, not military."

In a period when relatively few young people in Western societies do active military service, there is an esthetic attraction for trim clothes that are the antithesis of sloppy sportswear. Fashion follows its own logic, and any apparent connection between what goes on the runways and what appears in the headlines and on the nightly news programs is likely to be specious.

PART III

Twenty-first Century

Introduction to PART III

The third and final part of the anthology surveys criticism produced in the new millennium when barriers between digital and print unraveled. It is during this period that the phenomenon of fashion blogs and the move toward hypertextuality took hold (Rocamora, 2012). This shift opened up the linearity of the text and accelerated the times of production and consumption of fashion media. However, in the fast-changing media landscape, many independent fashion blogs soon became supplanted by social media—particularly Instagram. This period also saw the proliferation of "niche fashion magazines": small circulation independent magazines "that merge high fashion with art and style cultures" and which provide a forum for slower forms of fashion criticism (Lynge-Jorlén, 2012).

The section opens with the work of fashion critic Cathy Horyn. Currently a critic-at-large for *New York Magazine*'s "The Cut," Horyn spent a long part of her career at *The New York Times,* where she became fashion critic in 1998 (succeeding Amy Spindler) and worked until 2014. Horyn is also notable for having started an early fashion blog while at *The New York Times:* "On the Runway," around which grew a vibrant community of readers and commentators. Horyn is known for her uncompromising critical voice. In interviews, she commented on how being free of influence is central to criticism (Wingfield, 2015). The anthology includes her 2004 review of menswear collections in Paris that initiated a long-term spat with Hedi Slimane. The article is a detailed and well-argued assessment of that season's menswear collection in Paris, which discussed in positive terms Raf Simons's collection, while giving a tepid review of work by Hedi Slimane, then designing menswear for Dior. The fact that Slimane banned Horyn eight years later when he started designing womenswear for YSL can be read as a testament to her influence—to say nothing of the volatility of some designers.

Caroline Evans's article on Hussein Chalayan in *032c,* the Berlin-based style magazine, is a beautifully written example of the overlap between academic and journalistic modes of writing, which occurs within the pages of niche fashion magazines. In her signature lyrical style, Evans, an established fashion historian and theorist, analyzes the work of Cypriot-born, London-based designer Hussein Chalayan through the lenses of nostalgia.

Judith Thurman's "The Misfit," on the Japanese designer Rei Kawakubo of Comme des Garçons, is an outstanding example of a designer profile, a closely researched type of biographical article for which the *New Yorker* is known (Rothman, 2012). A cultural critic who is a recipient of a National Book Award, Thurman began writing on fashion toward the middle of her career, when she returned to the *New Yorker* as a staff writer in 2000. Thurman claims to write about fashion "as an important element of culture and itself a culture [...] a form of expression, a kind of language dealing with identities," which is evident in her detailed and intimate account of Kawakubo. (Thurman as interviewed by Granata, 2013, 34). Also included in this section is Thurman's review of the watershed exhibition "Alexander McQueen: Savage Beauty" at the Metropolitan Museum of Art, Costume Institute. This is an exquisite example of a fashion exhibition review—a genre that proliferated in the new millennium; alongside the fashion exhibitions themselves, it reached a turning point with the famous McQueen exhibition, which proved unprecedently popular with the public and critics alike both at the Met in New York and, in a subsequent iteration, at the Victoria and Albert Museum in London.

In "Why I Hate Abercrombie and Fitch," Dwight A. McBride, scholar of race and literary study, examines the politics of race and sexuality that are articulated by the American casual clothing brand Abercrombie & Fitch through its advertising campaigns (at the time by Bruce Weber) and the looks embodied by its "brand ambassadors" (the retail staff). The essay argues that the company, with its history steeped in the life of the American leisure class, upholds young, white, upper-class bodies as equivalent to desirability and furthers a narrative of Americaness being equated with whiteness.

The established British fashion critic Sarah Mower has had a long career in the field of fashion criticism working as a fashion editor for the *Guardian* and, later, writing for several fashion magazines. "The Mystery Man: Margiela, Be Mine," originally published in American *Vogue,* is a witty and precise first-person assessment of the author's relation to Maison Margiela's clothes written in advance of the designer's twenty-year retrospective at the ModeMuseum in Antwerp, which punctuated his retirement.

"All Hail the Leader of the Fashionable World" is an article on Michelle Obama's 2009 inauguration-day wardrobe by Robin Givhan. Writing for the *Washington Post,* Givhan has an unusual vantage point on American fashion (recalling an earlier Washington-based fashion writer Eleni Epstein, whose mid-century work is included in the anthology's second section). Being based in Washington, away from the capitals of fashion and glamour—thus an ostensible hindrance to a fashion critic—was what attracted Givhan. "I was more intrigued by how it [fashion] functioned in a city that was so quick to deny its interest in public appearance and at the same time be so completely obsessed by it" (Givhan as interviewed by Labrague, 2013, 10). Her writings on fashion, for which she won a Pulitzer Prize in 2006, are imbued by "the importance that our culture places on public presentation and the way that is woven into our economics, politics, religion, social hierarchy" (Givhan as interviewed by Labrague, 2013, 10). This approach is exemplified in the article included in the anthology, in which Givhan, reflecting on the power of fashion in politics, comments on how Michelle Obama's choice of a gown by Isabel Toledo for the inauguration is rich with meanings: "As her husband's administration promises more jobs and help for small-business owners, and emphasizes creativity as one of this country's greatest assets, Obama's choice of an iconoclastic, immigrant female designer with a modest business sends a profound message of intent" (Givhan, 2009, A1).

The following two articles are by Anja Aronowsky Cronberg, founding editor of *Vestoj*—one of the most interesting fashion publications to develop in the new millennium. A hybrid between an academic journal and a fashion magazine, *Vestoj,* covers "fashion in a manner that opens up for dialogue between theory and practice in order to raise awareness for fashion as a cultural phenomena and field of research" (Cronberg, 2009). The two articles both dissect the fashion industry and its mechanism: "The Revolution Will Be Branded Vetements" analyzes the press reception of the brand Vetements, while "Will I Still Get a Ticket?" is an interview with Lucinda Chambers, which addresses Chambers's sudden firing from British *Vogue,* where she had worked for thirty-six years. The latter article was highly controversial, as it laid bare some of fashion's unkind power dynamics (Paton, 2017).

"Trump vs. the Disappearing Tie," by Vanessa Friedman, was published in *The New York Times* before Trump's election in 2016. It offers a dissection of the way mediatization has shaped politics and has increasingly placed image and fashion at the forefront. Friedman became the fashion director and chief fashion critic at *The New York Times* after working as a fashion critic for the global financial newspaper *The Financial Times*—a position that sharpened her attention to the ways politics and economics intertwined with fashion. The article discusses the move toward a tieless look among male politicians in the West, in the context of Trump's insistence on wearing Brioni wide-style ties. Friedman interprets this somewhat unorthodox choice in an increasingly less formal political landscape as an attempt to channel the 1980s—"the boom years of the American economy, when it was 'morning in America' and Gordon Gekko preached the 'greed is good' gospel." She concludes that, through his sartorial choices, Trump positions himself as "emphatically and consciously not the new-look candidate. He is the old-look candidate" (Friedman, 2016, D1).

"Suket Dhir, Men's Wear Designer, from Delhi to the World" covers the work of an emerging Indian fashion designer, whose transnational minimalism caught the attention of the Woolmark Prize jury. The article, written by *New York Times*'s style writer Guy Trebay, places Dhir's work in its socio-cultural context, as is customary for the Trebay. The journalist's career has an unusual arch. After a stint at Andy Warhol's *Interview*, Trebay wrote a column about New York City life for the *Village Voice* in the 1980s and 1990s (anthologized in the book *In The Place to Be: Guy Trebay's New York*) before writing about fashion for *The New York Times*. And while the move from covering the Bronx in the 1980s—including the burgeoning hip-hop scene and the crack epidemic—to fashion might seem unlikely to some, in Trebay's mind, it followed the thread of a certain approach to fashion as urban anthropology (Trebay as interviewed by Ruttenberg, 2013, 26).

Bringing the book back to the entanglements of media, fashion, and politics, Rhonda Garelick writes about Melania Trump's controversial outfit (including Manolo Blahnik stiletto heels) to board Air Force One en route to visiting victims of Hurricane Harvey in Houston. Garelick—a scholar of performance, fashion, literature, visual arts, and cultural politics—contributes a weekly column to *New York Magazines*'s "The Cut," which has been described as advancing a kind of "criticism of aesthetics"(Spellings, 2018). In the article in this anthology, she dissects the ways in which Melania Trump's appearances take on the unreality of a fashion spread:

> When you see Melania headed to Marine One, or dining with world leaders, or standing on a White House balcony, the entire scene looks like a magazine spread in which 'real' people, equipment, and buildings are being used merely as dramatic backdrops for a fashion layout. On Tuesday, this meant that instead of being a supporting presence in the president's trip to survey flood damage, Melania became the star and the trip morphed into a simulacrum. (Garelick, 2017).

The book's final article is by Connie Wang, who developed an incisive new voice in fashion criticism in "the blogging explosion of the mid aughts" (Idacavage, 2018). Wang is the Executive Editor at *Refinery29*, a digital media company aimed at young women. Her criticism distinguished her for taking on difficult and complex topics (both for *Refinery29* and in other publications including *The New York Times*), as Wang uses fashion as an entryway "to talk about more inaccessible issues like race, class, and politics" (Wang as interviewed by Idacavage,

2018). In her 2008 article "Is Wokeness in Fashion Just Another Illusion?" she unpacks the controversy surrounding the use of a racial slur by a designer and questions whether inclusivity in fashion is simply skin-deep or if it will lead to permanent structural changes in the industry.

Bibliography and Further Readings

Cronberg Aronowsky, Anja. "About Us." *Vestoj*. Accessed September 2, 2019. vestoj.com.

Evans, Caroline. *Fashion at the Edge: Spectacle, Modernity and Deathliness*. London and New Haven: Yale University Press, 2003.

Garelick, Rhonda. *Mademoiselle: Coco Chanel and the Pulse of History*. New York: Penguin Random House, 2014.

Granata, Francesca. "'Woman's Work: An Interview with Judith Thurman.'" *Fashion Projects*, no. 5 (2013): 7–18.

Idacavage, Sara. "Connie Wang." *The Fashion Studies Journal*, 2018. Accessed September 2, 2018 fashionstudiesjournal.org.

Labrague, Michelle. "Fashion Criticism—A Critical View: An Interview with Robin Givhan." *Fashion Projects*, no. 5 (2013): 7–18.

Lynge-Jorlén Ane. "Between Frivolity and Art: Contemporary Niche Fashion Magazines." *Fashion Theory*, vol. 16, no. 1 (2012): 7–28.

Paton, Elizabeth. "Lucinda Chambers, Fired Vogue Director, Gives Fashion Industry a Kicking." *The New York Times*, July 4, 2017.

Rocamora, Agnès. "Hypertextuality and Remediation in the Fashion Media." *Journalism Practice*, vol. 6, no.1 (2012): 92–106.

Rothman, Joshua. "The New Yorker's Profiles." *newyorker.com*, November 20, 2012.

Ruttenberg, Jay. "This Is Not a Fashion Critic: An Interview with Guy Trebay." *Fashion Projects*, no. 5 (2013): 7–18.

Spellings, Sarah. "Meet Rhonda Garelick, the Cut's Critic of Fashion, Aesthetics, and Politics." *New York Magazine, The CUT*, February 1, 2018.

Thurman, Judith. *Cleopatra's Nose: 39 Varieties of Desire*. New York: Picador, 2008.

Trebay, Guy. *In the Place to Be: Guy Trebay's New York*. Philadelphia: Temple University Press, 1994.

Wingfield, Jonathan. "You Just Have to Say What You Think." *System*, no. 5 (2017).

31

Future, Take Note: Raf Simons Was Here

Cathy Horyn

The New York Times, July 6, 2004

Few journalists were more aware of the danger of observation than Joseph Roth. "The 'good observer,'" he wrote in 1925, soon after arriving here from Berlin, "is the sorriest reporter. He meets everything with open but inflexible eyes." In his reports in the Frankfurter Zeitung and in his novels, Roth, who died of alcohol poisoning in May 1939, at age forty-four, perceived that the world was continually changing: "In the space of a single second, everything can be transformed a thousand times over, disfigured, rendered unrecognizable." At most, he argued, a journalist can say how an experience felt to him. Because by the time he has set down his impressions, "the realities have grown out of the tight clothes we've put them in."

Roth's feelings sometimes overwhelmed his reporting. But wherever people strive to do more than what is expected of them (and very often we are content with less), don't they deserve our strongest emotions?

On Saturday, I almost skipped Raf Simons's show. It was far away and very late. And I had already begun to put my ducks in a row: Louis Vuitton (English flannels, cricket sweaters, silk pajamas—or "Brideshead Revisited" on a commercial level); Dries van Noten (Prince Harry on a pub and country-house crawl, with fab kilts); Junya Watanabe (potential potheads in Alpine hats and plaids lurking amid the edelweiss).

What Mr. Simons did in an instant was to render the day, and most of the previous one of the spring men's collections, obsolete. In eighteen years of reporting on fashion, the last five at this post, I have stood up from only a handful of shows with a conviction that everything had been transformed. And I don't know why it is that out of a generation of so-called visionaries, only a few have Mr. Simons's capacity to deal with the future in a believable way. I don't want to see any more flabby impressions of the 1970s or hear them described as "ironic." And I don't want to go to "another country," because that country doesn't exist anymore.

Beginning with the skinny suits that made his reputation nearly a decade ago and made a Hedi Slimane possible, Mr. Simons gave a real glimpse of the future—heightened by the solemn descent of the models on an escalator and the music of Vangelis. To silky sport shirts he added trousers in a glacier-white leather that looked otherworldly, while chunky white sneakers were an ingenious blend of N.E.R.D. and NASA. In the fabrics, in the modern proportions—in the way a slim leather tunic resembled a T-shirt or a white nylon raincoat floated over a suit—it was evident that Mr. Simons was trying to work out fashion's next passage. In the past, Mr. Simons, who is thirty-six, used his clothes as social commentary, and he was startlingly prescient on the fear of terrorism. But he is no longer the reactionary. On his invitation was a random list of people and things that changed the world: sign language, Rosa Parks, the drinking straw, Taliesin West, Alan Turing, who cracked the Enigma code and hastened the end of World War II. Can a fashion designer make such a difference? Mr. Simons is bold to think so.

"I've always focused on my own history, my own evolution," he said as he was greeted with cheers backstage. "But now I want to think about the future." Last year, the Swiss Textile Federation awarded Mr. Simons a $120,000 prize. He should have a Swiss bank.

The other cornerstones of the Paris season were Helmut Lang, Mr. Slimane and Rei Kawakubo of Comme des Garçons. On Sunday, Mr. Lang moved away from the dangling straps and erotic gestures that had punctuated his collections, though the fit of his jackets, now in seersucker, had a seductive pull. These appeared with white trousers, swagged with an ambiguous hank of maritime rope, and white clogs, some covered in glossy fur. Very cool, and funny. Shirt sleeves were crunched just above the biceps. But except for a riotous Hamptons flower print on white jeans, the message was tough, impeccable tailoring.

By contrast, Mr. Slimane's Dior show on Monday was marked by sullenness, restlessness and, in a way, the rootlessness of the young lives that influence him. "I wanted everything to look natural, like the boys dressed themselves," he said.

Few designers are as concentrated on the continually changing world. The moment is his medium, and Mr. Slimane interprets it in all its banality and sweetness—with shrunken jackets, beautiful pin-tucked voile shirts in pale shades of green and pink and the tightest, lowest-riding jeans in the business. You can see the influence of the West Coast skate and rock world, which has caught his interest. He has published a book of his photographs of rock concerts, called *Stage*. And like his clothes, its view of Bowie, Beck and the Stones is gauzy, reverent and curiously abstract.

The Pink Panther, hardly a cat you would expect to pop up at Comme des Garçons, grinned its naughty grin on T-shirts, though Ms. Kawakubo insisted after her show on Saturday that she wasn't thinking of the old pouncer. "Rose-colored glasses," she said in her enigmatic way. Nonetheless, it was kind of wonderful to see so much pink on a man, even if her models seemed to be striving for the nerdy prize. Her jackets had that shrunken, hopeless look, but in the soda-pink brightness, there was no lament. Ms. Kawakubo was just suggesting that it is sometimes better to see the world through rose glass. Judy Blame, a London jewelry maker who has been on the scene for twenty years, supplied the gold chains dangling with pink toy soldiers.

Jean Paul Gaultier skimmed the headlines for his show, based loosely on the politics of gay marriage. But except for the wedding theme, he rejected the heavy sexual gestures and focused on washed silk layers and muddy-colored knits that most men will comprehend.

This leaves John Galliano free to roam the barricades. His show on Friday night, complete with pirate galleon, amounted to a manifesto of sexual swagger. But underneath the top hats and medicine man feathers were great clothes, especially football-style pants inset with ruching and others that unzipped to show off Mr. Galliano's signature newsprint.

What do young Japanese guys, without Mr. Slimane's resources, dream of? They dream of the same thing—the grainy rose-colored light of a stage, moppy hair, the eternal wish of "Stairway to Heaven." Takahiro Miyashita's Number Nine show had models in broken-down leather, tight pants and kilts, their faces cast downward in a thirteen-year-old boy's favorite bathroom pose. Some things just never change.

32

Hussein Chalayan: Nostalgia for the Future

Caroline Evans

032c, Summer 2005

We claim that the nostalgic man, in his attachment to the past, searches for his lost childhood from where he is henceforth exiled. Yes, no question. But I think that his homesickness has another source. It's not the past that he idealizes; it isn't the present on which he turns his back, but on what is dying. His wish: that anywhere—whether he changes continents, cities, jobs, loves—he could find his native land, the one where life is born, is reborn. Nostalgia carries the desire, less for an unchanging eternity than for always fresh beginnings. Thus time that passes and destroys tries to take away the ideal figure of a place that remains. The homeland is one of the metaphors of life. (Pontalis, 2003, 27)

With this quotation from the psychoanalyst J.B. Pontalis, the curator Judith Clark opened the "Nostalgia" section of her exhibition *Spectres: When Fashion Turns Back*, at London's Victoria & Albert Museum (January–May 2005, shown in 2004 under the title *Malign Muses* at MoMu in Antwerp). Following Pontalis's suggestion that nostalgia may be for fresh beginnings as much as for a lost past, Clark's "Nostalgia" installation was the only part of the exhibition not to feature real clothing. Instead, fleeting moments in fashion were idealised into giant 2-dimensional wooden figures that loomed above the visitor, saw-cut from flimsy plywood with frayed edges, taken from the fashion illustrator Ruben Toledo's catalogue drawing The Avenue of Silhouettes.

Were the silhouettes historical dresses or designs for the future? They were festooned with giant iron locks and keys that suggested the figures could be understood as doors opening into other routes and ideas. The exhibition was concerned with genealogy and "fashion memory" in contemporary dress; it showed the hidden, yet haunting, connections between recent fashion and its past. For the curator, this was much more than a question of mere fashion history, or the recycling of past styles. By using a psychoanalytical quotation in the nostalgia section, she unequivocally inserted the idea of psychic longing into fashion and design history. Susan Stewart describes nostalgia as a form of sadness without object, a yearning for a past as unreal as its future is unobtainable. "Hostile to history and its invisible origins ... nostalgia wears a distinctly utopian face, a face that turns towards a future past, a past that has only ideological reality" (Stewart, 1993, x and 23). Our sense of what it is to be modern today is haunted by the ghosts of modernity, and for Judith Clark, too, "nostalgia and a sense of impossibility go together" (Clark, 2004, 25).

Clark presciently put her finger on a very modern problematic: in the absence of any meaningful utopian ideas today, how can a designer access moments from the past that carry that meaning yet avoid naive optimism? How to articulate a new design language that does not resort to excessive historicism or nostalgia for the past? Many contemporary fashion and textile designers are fired by the exciting possibilities of new technological processes, and this recalls the way early twentieth-century modernist designers experimented with utopian ideas, speculatively mapping the future through imagined technological Utopias, resolutely turning their backs on the past. By the early twenty-first century, however, for a designer to fetishise technological progress and novelty suggests a double ghosting: a return to heroic modernism that refuses the sedimentation of history, seeking to expunge the insistent past-in-the-present of modernity.

Clark's *Spectres* questioned whether nostalgia consists of hoping for a forgotten past, or longing for an impossible future. These elusive ghosts were raised in another fashion display without fashion, Hussein Chalayan's short film from 2003, *Place to Passage*. It follows an androgynously styled woman travelling in a self-piloted pod in a state of perfect self-sufficiency. Setting out from an underground car park across London, as night turns to day the white pod flies smoothly and swiftly about a meter above the ground, its jet thrusts pulsing regularly. While its inhabitant eats, sleeps and dreams, troubled by only the occasional faint turbulence, the pod glides on across Europe through anonymous post-industrial wastelands and over indeterminate icy wastes, Russia perhaps, that leave one wondering if this is a real landscape or a fantasy of a post-Chernobyl nuclear winter. Approaching Istanbul via the Black Sea, it skims up the Bosphorus and comes to rest in an underground car park identical to the one it left in London. The film suggests that travel itself is a kind of no-place or no-man's-land that takes us out of culture and history. Chalayan's itinerant model is like Pontalis's nostalgic man, cited at the beginning of this article, who changes continents, cities, jobs, loves, searching for his native homeland. Paradoxically, the more the quest for origins remains unfulfilled, the more it produces new beginnings, through restless searching and endless journeying.

Travelling light, the pod's gnomic inhabitant eats and sleeps as she travels in seamless symbiosis with her vehicle. The design of the pod borrows the utopian design language of 1960s' architectural groups such as Archigram. Constructed with 3-D modelling techniques inspired by a visit to the Formula One car factory (the film was sponsored by Formula One racing team BAR Honda), the pod is something between a car, a plane and a platonic ideal. A sensitive membrane bordering on a home, the pod-vessel of *Place to Passage* begs the redefinition of comfort, familiarity and nostalgia. Chalayan speculates on the possibilities:

Our lives are in a constant state of mobility and ... in some ways that could affect memory, could affect our attachment to domestic things. What would new comfort zones be in those kinds of situations? You know it's this whole idea of creating a refuge wherever you are. It's quite abstract, in a way it's like meditating on solitude, maybe a bit about nostalgia, how we reminisce, creating a place within a cavity, all those kinds of ideas. (Fairs, 1993)

The pod's inhabitant wears her home like a shell. She finishes her meal of fresh food served from an automated white plastic compartmentalised tray that seamlessly glides back into the fittings, her leftovers having been hoovered into the refuse slit in her arm-rest, before watching comfort images—memories? projections?—on the panel ahead of her of traditional domestic food preparation and dish-washing. Clad in pale, minimal vest and knickers, she tears large sections of pre-cut cloth from a dispenser to her left when she needs it for warmth or comfort, and discards it to her right afterwards, where it disappears by suction down the elongated slit set in the right-hand arm rest. At one stage the pod's concave, moulded interior fills with water, perhaps for washing or perhaps—since the model remains immersed for some time—as a heating and cooling system, a kind of automated amniotic fluid for embryonic adults.

Yoking together domesticity, refuge and the cavity, Chalayan's comment on *Place to Passage* evokes Gaston Bachelard's images of rootedness, such as "the house, the stomach, the cave" (Bachelard, as quoted in Vidler, 1992, 46). Bachelard relates these images to the overall theme of the return to the mother, the idea articulated by Sigmund Freud in the saying "love is homesickness" (Freud, [1919] 1955, 245). In his 1919 essay on the uncanny, Freud argued that whenever we dream of a place which we think we have visited before, we are in fact dreaming of the maternal body, the place from which we all came and to which we cannot return. The first home, which is lost to us, except as a form of congealed longing, is the womb, and there is something of this nostalgia for the maternal space in Chalayan's pod.

The pod thus embodies a contradiction. It is, on the one hand, a version of the modernist ideal first formulated in 1923 by Le Corbusier in his rational "House-Machine" of the future, "healthy … and beautiful" (Le Corbusier, 1946, 227). On the other hand, traces of history and the past produce their own ghosts. Set against any utopian fantasy of self-sufficiency are the claims of nostalgia and home, even if only of an imagined home (Vidler, 1992, 64), such as the domestic images watched by the model on the viewing panel in front of her. The idea of home thus becomes an object of generalised nostalgia and, precisely because it is an imagined home, we cannot get back to it: "You can't go home again. Why? Because you are home … " (Garber, 1987, 159).

For Pontalis's nostalgic man, the invisible companion to Chalayan's migratory model, the homeland is one of the metaphors of life. Homesickness without an object produces the deracinated longing encapsulated in Susan Stewart's idea that "nostalgia is sadness without an object" (Stewart, 1993, x), which is part of the alienation that attaches to fashion. *Place to Passage*, a film made by a fashion designer and reprising many of his previous themes, suggests that in fashion we are all migrants, and there is no such place as home. The fashionable being is constantly in the process of re-imagining and re-creating him or herself in a rootless world, and this process of self-fashioning may be simultaneously pleasurable and alienating, nowhere more so than in the metaphor of the journey that has patterned Chalayan's work from the beginning.

An early Hussein Chalayan jacket in paper fabric stamped on the revers with the par avion postmark was redesigned as an envelope sent through the post that unfolded into a wearable dress. *Absence and Presence* (Spring/Summer 2003), his first menswear collection, contained T-shirts that could transform into A3 envelopes and be posted. Several other collections have featured a range of travel motifs. *Along False Equator* (Autumn/Winter 1995) included dresses printed with the flight paths of aeroplanes and paper suits embedded with fiber-optics that flashed like aeroplane lights at night, tracing flight-path patterns on the paper. *Geotropics* (Spring/Summer 1999) explored the idea of an itinerant existence through the idea of carrying a chair with you, so that you can sit down wherever you are. This concept carried the germ of a later idea, that travel can be a permanent state of being as much as a functional way of arriving at a destination.

In the following collection, *Echoform* (Autumn/Winter 1999), Chalayan looked at the body's natural capacity for speed and the way it can be enhanced by technology, focusing on ergonomics and the interior design of cars in a black leather dress with a padded collar like a car head rest. In these two collections and the subsequent *Before Minus Now* (Spring/Summer 2000), Chalayan also developed a single concept in three monumental dresses that used technology from the aircraft industry. Made out of a composite of glass fibre and resin, they were cast in specially created moulds. The second, the white aeroplane dress from Autumn/Winter 1999 which Chalayan would subsequently develop into a film and installation project with Marcus Tomlinson, *Echoform*, was fastened with chrome automobile catches. It contained a concealed battery and gears and wheels activated through an internal switch by the model on the runway, so that sections slid down and flapped out like the moving parts of aeroplanes. For Spring/Summer 2000, the third dress, in pale pink, was operated by a small boy using a remote control on the runway.

Marcus Tomlinson's film for *Echoform* made explicit the link between woman and aeroplane, that emblem of modernist progress and mobility. When Chalayan repeated this design motif in three rigid dresses across three collections, like a series of musical variations, he posited a series of experiments in constructing the self. The plane technology is about engineering and suggests that perhaps it is not only the dress but also the self that can be engineered, fine-tuned, technologically adjusted and played with. As Susan Sontag wrote: "the self is a text ... a project, something to be built" (Sontag, 1985, 14). Gilles Lipovetsky has proposed an optimistic analysis of the connection between fashion and psychological flexibility, arguing that modern fashion has produced a new individual, "the fashion person, who has no deep attachments, a mobile individual with a fluctuating personality and tastes." Thus the fashionable person is an avatar of modernity. Such social agents who are open to change, constitute "a new type of kinetic, open personality" that societies undergoing rapid transition depend on (Lipovetsky, 1994, 149).

For Lipovetsky's argument that fashion trains the modern subject to be flexible, mobile and psychologically adaptable, Chalayan provided the physical cladding and the metaphysical speculation about identity in the twenty-first century. In *Afterwords* (Autumn/Winter 2000), a table becomes a skirt and chair covers turn into dresses, while the chair frames fold up into suitcases. The blurring of the boundaries between the traditional functions of clothing and dress brought to mind furniture designers who have thought of furniture as a flexible membrane, possibly an intelligent one, that mediates between the body and the built environment. For many designers from the late 1990s, thinking about how to live in the modern world involved thinking about how to live flexibly, imagining new forms of urban nomadism, in which the differences between dress and architecture diminished and cladding and clothing became— equally—flexible membranes that responded to their environment.

When, in *Afterwords*, Chalayan replaced the tailor with the furniture maker, or made pockets the same shape as possessions, he rethought fashion as a kind of portable architecture. Yet the show was about travelling light, about having to leave one's home in time of war and to take all one's possessions with one. The dislocation and rootlessness of enforced migrancy were evoked through the opening scene of a refugee family of five that shuffled offstage, converting pinafores into cloaks as they went. The idea was reiterated in the sparse set design of the living room, the transformation of its furniture into portable possessions as the show unfolded, and the existential bleakness of the harsh, Bulgarian singing that accompanied it. It could not, therefore, by any stretch of the imagination, be understood solely as a paean to the infinite flexibility of the modern subject.

The theme of travel so prevalent in Chalayan's work can be understood, both literally and figuratively, as a journey of alienation and loss, as much as it is one of self-discovery and self-fashioning. Although Chalayan's design motifs in many of his collections were the modernist ones of technological progress (flight, engineering, travel and mobility), they were shadowed by the darker motifs of dislocation, migrancy and exile. For all the modernity and refusal of obvious nostalgia and historicism in his designs, there is a melancholy edge to them.

As guest editor of the Belgian magazine *No.C* (September 2002), Chalayan included in the magazine an elongated horizontal fold-out of a shabby, abandoned aeroplane at Nicosia International Airport. The aeroplane was once a great icon of modernist design. Nowadays, as budget airlines proliferate and more people than ever take regular flight from reality on cheap holidays, the plane is part of the everyday technology that enables consumer desire and escapist fantasy. This loss of glamour is perhaps inevitable. Design that is lead solely by technological innovation fetishises the new and invokes redundant myths of progress that are no longer viable in the early twenty-first century, following the dark history of the twentieth.

In work in which, however, the ghosts of modernity are permitted to trouble the present, although without falling back into pastiche, its complexity and nuances can be acknowledged. This dialectic underpinned Chalayan's melancholic modernity. For, as Susan Stewart writes, nostalgia is a social disease, and longing is always a "future-past, a deferment of experience" (Stewart, 1993, x). Whereas early twentieth-century modernism effaced history in its revolutionary pursuit of the new, at the end of the century it was possible to glimpse the ghosts of modernity in Chalayan's thoughtful and poetical modernism. If we overlay his experimental forms with shadows from an earlier moment of commodity culture we can see traces of earlier reified, technologised and fetishised bodies. Chalayan takes the tropes of modernist progress (travel, technology, aerodynamics) and inflects them with modernist trauma (alienation, reification and the uncanny). His model in the aeroplane dress is generic, robotic, and mechanical in her gestures. His eloquent technological modernity is haunted by the ghosts of commodity fetishism and modernist alienation. At the same time, he makes modernist design complex, by patterning it with echoes and whispers: of soft dresses mimicking hard ones, of morphs in time and space, of correspondences between virtual and real environments. Thus while his work is abstract and pure in formal terms, it is also complex and nuanced in terms of its suggestive possibilities, shadowed by history and time. It raises the bigger question of how a late twentieth-century designer might draw on the aesthetic and language of early twentieth-century modernism, even though the historical conditions that gave rise to the early optimism and utopianism of modernism are long gone, without falling back on a contemporary sense of cynicism and ennui, or on millenarian visions of apocalypse.

Bibliography

Bachelard, Gaston. *La Terre et les reveries du repos*. Paris: Librairie José Corti, 1948. Quoted in Anthony Vidler. *The Architectural Uncanny*. Cambridge, MA and London: MIT Press, 1992, page 64.
Clark, Judith. *Spectres: When Fashion Looks Back*. London: Victoria & Albert Publications, 2004.
Fairs, Marcus. *Icon*. December 1993.

Freud, Sigmund. "The Uncanny." In *Works: the Standard Edition of the Complete Psychological Works of Sigmund Freud*, vol. XVII. Edited by James Strachey, 545. London: Hogarth Press, 1955.

Garber, Margery. *Shakespeare's Ghost Writers*. London: Methuen, 1987.

Le Corbusier. *Towards a New Architecture*. London: The Architectural Press, 1946.

Lipovetsky, Gilles. *The Empire of Fashion: Dressing Modern Democracy*. Princeton, NJ: Princeton University Press, 1994.

Pontalis, J-B. *Windows*. Lincoln, NE: University of Nebraska Press, 2003.

Sontag, Susan. "Introduction." In *One Way Street and other Writings*. Edited by Walter Benjamin, 14. London: Verso, 1985.

Stewart, Susan. *On Longing*. Durham, NC: Duke University Press, 1993.

Vidler, Anthony. *The Architectural Uncanny*. Cambridge, MA and London: MIT Press, 1992.

33

The Misfit

Judith Thurman

The New Yorker, July 4, 2005

Does it really matter what one wears? I sometimes think my life might have been different if I had chosen the other wedding dress. I was getting married for the second time, and until the overcast morning of the ceremony I dithered between a bland écru frock appropriate to my age and station, which I wore that once and never again, and a spooky neo-Gothic masterpiece with a swagged bustle and unravelling seams in inky crêpe de laine, which I still possess: hope and experience.

The black dress—and other strange clothes in which I feel most like myself—was designed by Rei Kawakubo. In 1981, when she brought her first collection to Paris, Kawakubo was nearly forty and preëminent in Japan but largely unknown in the West. Mugler and Versace were the harbingers of a new moment: of a giddy, truculent materialism embodied, in different guises, by Margaret Thatcher, Madonna, Princess Di, Alexis Carrington, and Jane Fonda, and by legions of newly minted executives who wore block-and-tackle power suits to the office and spandex stirrup pants to the gym. These women were tough and glitzy and on the make without apologies, and so was fashion. Then, the following year, a collection that Kawakubo called "Destroy" hit the runway. It was modelled by a cadre of dishevelled vestals in livid war paint who stomped down the catwalk to the beating of a drum, wearing the bleak and ragged uniforms of a new order. Few if any spectators were left blasé, and some went home dumbstruck with rapture, while others lobbed back at the invader what they perceived as a blast of barbarity, tagging the look "Hiroshima's revenge." Kawakubo has never quite lived down (she has at times played up) that show of audacity, whose fallout is still being absorbed by fashion's young, yet which was much more Parisian than it seemed—a piece of shock theatre in the venerable tradition of "Ubu Roi" and "The Rite of Spring."

Kawakubo works under the label Comme des Garçons ("like some boys"), though she has never wanted to be like anyone. There are few women who have exerted more influence on the history of modern fashion, and the most obvious, Chanel, is in some respects her perfect foil: the racy courtesan who invented a uniform of irreproachable chic and the gnomic shaman whose anarchic chic is a reproach to uniformity. They both started from an egalitarian premise: that a woman should derive from her clothes the ease and confidence that a man does. But Chanel formulated a few simple and lucrative principles, from which she never wavered, that changed the way women wanted to dress, while Kawakubo, who reinvents the wheel—or tries to—every season, changed the way one thinks about what dress is.

Early Comme, as devotees winsomely call it, gave comfort to the wearer and discomfort to the beholder, particularly if he was an Average Joe with a fondness for spandex stirrup pants. Kawakubo's silhouette had nothing to do with packaging a woman's body for seduction. Nearly any biped with sufficient aplomb, one thought, might have modelled the clothes, though especially, perhaps, a self-possessed kangaroo, whose narrow shoulders and well-planted, large feet are a Comme des Garçons signature. The palette was monochrome, with a little ash mixed into the soot, and one hears it said that Kawakubo "invented" black—it is one of the "objective achievements" cited by the Harvard school of design when it gave her an Excellence in Design Award, in 2000. What she objectively achieved was the revival of black's cachet as the color of refusal.

The French Old Guard, needless to say, reviled Comme des Garçons, but it immediately became popular among women of the downtown persuasion. In Kawakubo's voluminous clothes one felt provocative yet mysterious and protected. They weren't sized, and they weren't conceived on a svelte fitting model, then inflated to a sixteen. Their cut had the rigor, if not the logic, of modernist architecture, but loose flaps, queer trains, and other sometimes perplexing extrusions encouraged a client of the house to improvise her own style of wearing them. Shop assistants showed one the ropes—literally. A friend of mine who included Kawakubo in a course on critical theory suggested that these "multiple open endings" were a tactic for liberating female dress from an "omniscient male narrator."

Conventional fashion, and particularly its advertising, is a narrative genre—historical romance at one end of the spectrum and science-fiction at the other, with chick lit in between—and Kawakubo doesn't have a story line, insisting, not always plausibly, that she works in a vacuum of influence and a tradition of her own creation. "I never intended to start a revolution," she told me last winter. "I only came to Paris with the intention of showing what I thought was strong and beautiful. It just so happened that my notion was different from everybody else's." Yet so many entitlements were challenged by the black regime of Comme des Garçons that it is hard not to see its commandant as a Red. The hegemony of the thin was one target, and the class system that governed fabrication was another. Kawakubo ennobled poor materials and humbled rich ones, which were sent off to be reëducated in the same work camp with elasticated synthetics and bonded polyester. She crumpled her silks like paper and baked them in the sun; boiled her woollens so that they looked nappy; faded and scrubbed her cottons; bled her dyes; and picked at her threadwork. One of the most mocked pieces from 1982 was a sublimely sorry-looking sweater cratered with holes that she called (one assumes with irony, though one can't be sure) "Comme des Garçons lace."

Kawakubo's most radical challenge to the canons of Western tailoring lay in her cutting. Couturiers before her had experimented with asymmetry in the one-shouldered gown or the diagonal lapel, though they were still working from a balanced pattern with a central axis—the spine. She warped her garments like the sheet of rubber that my high school physics teacher used to illustrate the curvature of space, and she skewed their seams or closures so that the sides no longer matched. Just because a torso has two arms, she didn't see any reason that a jacket couldn't have none or three, of uneven length—amputated and reattached elsewhere on its body. Among the many mutants that she has engineered are a pair of trousers spliced to a skirt; the upper half of a morning coat with a tail of sleazy pink nylon edged in black lace; and her notorious "Dress Meets Body, Body Meets Dress" collection, of 1997—"Quasimodo" to its detractors—which proposed a series of fetching, body-hugging pieces in stretch gingham that were deformed in unsettling places (the back, belly, and shoulders) with bulbous tumors of down. The historian and curator Valerie Steele sees "a kind of violence—even a brutalism—to Rei's work that made most fashion of the time look innocuous and bourgeois, and from that moment an avant-garde split from the mainstream and hurtled off in its own direction." Steele was, she adds, "an instant convert."

Yet if Kawakubo consents to call her style "rebellious" and "aggressive" it is also intensely feminine in a bittersweet way. Her clothes suggest a kinship with a long line of fictional holy terrors: Pippi Longstocking, Cathy Earnshaw, Claudine—motherless tomboys who refused to master drawing-room manners and who, when forced into a dress, hiked up their petticoats and climbed a tree. Crushed frills are a leitmotif at Comme des Garçons, as are fraying ruffles; droopy ruffs; distressed pompoms; drab roses of wilted tulle, eyelet, crinoline, and broderie anglaise; and the round collars and polka dots that Kawakubo wore as a fauvish girl. In March, she showed a Fall-Winter collection whose theme was the "The Broken Bride," which was almost universally admired. (I doubt that she was entirely happy with the reviews—when everyone understands her, she seems to get depressed.) The models wore whiteface and antique veils anchored by floral crowns. The ensembles, despite their sovereign refinement, had an eerily familiar air of desperate, last-minute indecision. They were trimmed with passementerie that might have been salvaged from a Victorian steamer trunk in which the finery of an old-fashioned maidenhood had been abandoned along with its illusions. The show, in its melancholy romance, captured the tension between vigor and fragility which dominates most modern women's lives, including Kawakubo's.

Tokyo was enjoying an unseasonable warm spell when I arrived at the beginning of February, and the famous allées of cherry trees in the Aoyama cemetery had been lured into bud. In the labyrinth of paths that fret the verdant tract of incalculably expensive real estate, which is sacred to Buddhists, Shintoists, Christians, and fashion photographers, I kept running into an old man and his two whippets, all three in Hermès coats. The dogs upset the great flocks of crows—*karasu*—that nest in the foliage or perch insolently on the tombs and whose bitter cawing fractures the peace. A *karasu* was said to be the messenger of the sun goddess, Amaterasu, Japan's mythical progenitress, from whom the imperial family claimed descent. Through the millennia, this brazen and potent female deity hasn't been much of a model to her countrywomen, particularly once they marry. Of the numerous characters for "wife," the most common, *okusan*, means "a figure of the inner realm."

Japanese girls still tend to sow their wild fashion oats before they settle down with a mate and disappear, if not into the shadows, into a Chanel suit. But Kawakubo started out making clothes, in the seventies, she said, for a woman "who is not swayed by what her husband thinks." (She was then deep into her black period, and her devotees were known in Tokyo as "the crows.") Two decades later, and shortly after her own wedding, to Adrian Joffe—a South African-born student of Asian culture ten years her junior, who is the president of Comme des Garçons International—she told an interviewer from *Elle* that "one's lifestyle should not be affected by the formality of marriage."

Kawakubo owns an apartment near the cemetery, in one of the modern towers on its perimeter, not far from her headquarters and the three stores she has in the smart Aoyama shopping district. The apartment's precise location is a secret (very few friends and none of the longtime employees whom I met had ever crossed its threshold), and she lives alone there with her twenty-year-old cat, the last of five. Joffe, who is based in Paris, sees her, he says, at least once a month, and between collections they take a week to travel—generally choosing somewhere off the fashion radar screen, like Yemen or Romania. He is a slight, intense man who speaks five languages, including fluent Japanese, and he acts as his wife's interpreter. Small talk—indeed any talk—is not Kawakubo's forte. She doesn't take invisibility to theological extremes, like Martin Margiela, fashion's Pynchon, who is, with some of his fellow-alumni of the Antwerp School (Ann Demeulemeester, Walter van Beirendonck, Olivier Theyskens, and Raf Simons), one of her acolytes, though she rarely poses for a photograph or gives an interview anymore, and, several years ago, she stopped taking a bow after her shows. From the beginning of her career, she has insisted that the only way to know her is "through my clothes." Her employees, including Joffe, treat her with a gingerly deference that seems to be a mixture of awe for her talent and forbearance with her moods.

Kawakubo is now sixty-two. She is the sole owner of a company with a dozen boutiques and some two hundred franchises on four continents, which manufactures twelve lines of clothing, and grosses about a hundred and fifty million dollars annually. But, despite her wealth, her only apparent major indulgence is a vintage car, a monster Mitsubishi from the nineteen-seventies, which attracts the kind of stares in Tokyo that her clothes attract in Houston. The recreations common to designers of her prestige, such as collecting villas or art and socializing with celebrities, don't appeal to her, and the atmosphere of her office "is more monastic than commercial," as the journalist Deyan Sudjic puts it in a monograph on her career that was published in 1990. But she recently learned to swim, and on her way to work she sometimes takes a detour through the Aoyama cemetery to feed the stray cats.

Before I met Kawakubo in Paris, Joffe and I spent a day in Berlin at a Comme des Garçons "guerrilla store," which then occupied the former bookshop of the Brecht Museum, on a seedy block in the eastern sector of the city. It is part of an experiment in alternative retailing (inconspicuous consumption) which the company launched in 2004. There are now seven such outposts, most in Northern Europe, in cities like Helsinki and Ljubljana. Each of the stores is an ephemeral installation that opens without fanfare and closes after a year. Their decorating budgets are less than the price of some handbags at Gucci and Prada, and original fixtures, including raw cinder block and peeling wallpaper, are left as they are found. Brecht might have approved the poetic clothes and the proletarian mise en scène, if not the insurrectionary conceit. "But the word 'guerrilla' as Rei understands it isn't political," Joffe says. "It refers to a small group of like-minded spirits at odds with the majority. She's fascinated by the Amish, for example, and the Orthodox Jews."

Part of Joffe's role is to help make his wife intelligible whether or not she is present, and an unease sometimes creeps into his tone: the anxiety of a parent who resents the injustice yet accepts the inevitability of having to subject an antisocial prodigy to a school interview. "Are you scared of her?" I asked him bluntly over a Wiener schnitzel at the Café Einstein. "No," he said, "but she can be dictatorial, and I'm sometimes scared of the way she might treat people." Kawakubo treated me with a courtly if reticent politesse, and our conversations weren't unlike a tea ceremony: exquisitely strained. She is a tiny woman with taut cheekbones, a graying pageboy, and an aura of severity. When we were introduced in her showroom, last January, she was wearing a pair of trousers most easily described as a hybrid of a dhoti and a jodhpur, with a trim cardigan and a corsage of safety pins. Though she cultivates a reputation for being both timid and intimidating, some of her friends—among them Carla Sozzani, the Milanese retailer and gallerist, and Azzedine Alaïa, the couturier—assured me that, in private, Kawakubo can be a charming pal, congenial and even "hysterically funny." (I duly asked her what she laughs at, and she answered deadpan, "People falling down.") She patiently entertained the speculations with which I tried to prime her, and allowed that some of them "might be true." "But I'm very grateful that you haven't asked me about my 'creative process,'" she said, as I was leaving one afternoon. "I couldn't explain it to you. And, even if I could, why would I want to? Are there people who really wish to explain themselves?"

Kawakubo was born in Tokyo in 1942. She was the oldest of her parents' three children and their only daughter. (One of her brothers works as a director in the commercial department of Comme des Garçons, and the staff refers to him as Mister, to differentiate the two siblings in conversation, because there can be only one Kawakubo-san.) Their father was an administrator at Keio University, a prestigious institution founded by the great Meiji educator and reformer Fukuzawa Yukichi, a champion of Western culture and, according to Kawakubo, of women's rights. She admires Yukichi as an "enlightened man," but she has never belonged to a movement, followed a religion, subscribed to an ideology, or worshipped a hero, "because for me belief means that you have to depend on somebody."

Sudjic relates a few anodyne details about Kawakubo's girlhood (that she bunched her socks down as a revolt against the conformity of her school uniform, for example). Her home was "comfortable," he writes, and her family "a close one," and she told me that her mother made all the clothes. The trauma of war and the privations that Japan suffered in its aftermath didn't, she thought, have an appreciable effect on her. Yet however ordinary she felt her upbringing to be ("You think I'm not normal because you're looking at the clothes," she said to me somewhat plaintively when we met in Tokyo. "But I am. Can't rational people create mad work?"), her biography neglects to mention that she grew up with divorced parents. Her mother was trained as an English teacher—Kawakubo understands and speaks the language better than she lets on—and when the children were of a certain age she wanted to work. Her husband disapproved, and for almost all Japanese wives of that class and era his word would have been law. Kawakubo's mother left him, however, and got a job in a high school. "She was unlike other mothers," Kawakubo says. "I always felt like an outsider." But she also had a model of defiance and autonomy.

In 1960, Kawakubo enrolled in her father's university and took a degree in "the history of aesthetics," a major that included the study of Asian and Western art. In 1964, the year she graduated, Japan hosted the Olympics. "The postwar period of poverty, humiliation, and, until 1952, Allied occupation was finally over, and the boom years of the economic miracle had begun," Ian Buruma writes in "Inventing Japan." Kawakubo's generation discovered—and in varying degrees embraced—the counterculture of the sixties. At twenty-two, with a nod toward her mother's act of lèse-majesté, she left home "without telling my parents where I was going or what I was doing," and moved into a shared apartment in Harajuku, which was Tokyo's East Village and is still a mildly louche neighborhood of clubs and boutiques where pierced teens (most of them home by dinnertime) hang out wearing outré street fashions and trying to look ghetto. Kawakubo was never a druggie or a rebel, she says, "though in my head I liked the bohemian life style." On the other hand, she went to college with "a lot of rich people—that's who goes to élite institutions, and they are generally conservative." She found the solidity of their lives appealing, and she considers herself to have a dual character: the right half "likes tradition and history," the left "wants to break the rules." Nearly every statement Kawakubo makes about herself is hedged or negated by a contradiction, and she resists being defined even by her own words. The desire to be unique and the sense of isolation that the feeling generates are a predicament common to artistic people. What makes Kawakubo's clothes so attractive to them is precisely her genius for wrapping up the paradoxes of being a misfit and a cipher in something to wear that is magically misfitting.

Tokyo in the sixties was not yet the world's capital of luxury consumerism. Many women still made their own clothes or patronized a local tailor, and the best-known Japanese couturier, Hanae Mori, worked in a decorous Parisian mode. Kawakubo wasn't thinking of a fashion career: her only vocation was for a life of self- sufficiency. She found a job "at the bottom of the ladder" in the advertising department of Asahi Kasei, a textile manufacturer. Her boss was sympathetic to her ambitions. He accepted her unusual refusal to wear the standard uniform of an office girl, and he allowed her some modest creative freedom in helping to scout props and costumes for photo shoots. After three years, one of her older colleagues, Atsuko Kozasu, who later became an influential fashion journalist and an early booster of Comme des Garçons, encouraged Kawakubo to go freelance as a stylist. When she couldn't find clothes suitable for her assignments, she began to design them, and she often says that she's grateful to have skipped fashion school or an apprenticeship because, in the end, even if she can't sew or cut a pattern, she had no preconceptions to unlearn, and no master to outgrow.

By 1969, Kawakubo's work as a stylist had become a sideline that helped finance the production of the youthful sportswear that she sold through trend-setting shops like Belle Boudoir, in the Ginza, whose communal fitting room—"just like a London boutique"— impressed her. She rented office space in a graphic-arts studio and hired a few assistants. Tsubomi Tanaka, who is Comme des Garçons' chief of production, has been with her almost from the beginning. Tanaka was then a country girl who had left home to work in a Harajuku shop and, she says, "do my own thing," and she first noticed Kawakubo on the street. "Even in those days, she had an aura," Tanaka says, "and I asked a friend if she knew her name, because I wanted to meet her."

Sudjic writes, "Kawakubo's experiences as a stylist had taught her the importance of creating a coherent identity"—a philosophy of design that is followed as strictly in the company's Christmas cards as it is in the flagship stores. But the styling of that signature is a collaborative effort that demands an almost cultish attunement among the participants, and it is one of the paradoxes of Comme des Garçons that a designer obsessed with singularity and an entrepreneur allergic to beholdenness have spun such an elaborate web of dependence. In the workplace, Kawakubo's laconic detachment—the refusal to explain herself—forces her employees, particularly the pattern cutters, to look inward, rather than to her, for a revelation of the all-important "something new." Tanaka says, "The work is very hard, and I have to delve deep into my own understanding because her words are so few. But there's always some give to the tautness. And I'm still moved by the collections. That's why I've been here for so long."

Comme des Garçons' chief patterner, Yoneko Kikuchi, a thirty-year veteran of the firm, describes the arduous, if not mildly perverse, esoteric groping in the dark through which a collection comes into focus. It begins with a vision, or perhaps just an intuition, about a key garment that Kawakubo hints at with a sort of koan. She gives the patterners a set of clues that might take the form of a scribble, a crumpled piece of paper, or an enigmatic phrase such as "inside-out pillowcase," which they translate, as best they can, into a muslin—the three-dimensional blueprint of a garment. Their first drafts are inevitably too concrete. "She always asks us to break down the literalness," Kikuchi says. The quest proceeds behind closed doors, like a papal election, and successive meditations on the koan produce more or less adequate results. The staff calls the process by a deceptively playful English word, "catchball," though as the deadline for a collection approaches, and Kawakubo is still dissatisfied, the "anguish and anger" mount in the cutting room. "We all want to please her," Kikuchi explains, "and it's sometimes hard for patterners who have come from other companies, because they just want you to tell them how wide the collar is supposed to be. But you can't teach people to let go, and some end up leaving." ("They make it sound more interesting than it is," Kawakubo says, dryly. "The ideas aren't as abstract as they used to be.")

The business flourished, and was incorporated in 1973. By 1980, Comme des Garçons had a hundred and fifty franchised shops across Japan, eighty employees, and annual revenues of thirty million dollars. Fans of the house had none of the designer's scruples about hero worship: they went on camping weekends together organized by the franchisees, and there was talk of a Comme des Garçons restaurant where the faithful could meet. The clothes they loved were inspired by the loose and rustic garb of Japanese fishermen and peasants. When I asked Kawakubo what those early designs looked like (she hasn't kept many pictures in her archives), she answered after a long, perhaps embarrassed, pause, "Denim apron skirt. Very popular. I made different versions of it." Their chicest detail may have been the Comme des Garçons label, typeset in a font created by Kawakubo, with a star for the cedilla, which hasn't changed. It isn't obvious how she made her evolutionary leap, but it occurred in the early eighties, when she abandoned representational fashion and introduced the notion of clothing as wearable abstraction.

Most people naturally assume that Comme des Garçons is not just a logo but a slogan, and when Kawakubo was still giving interviews she compared her work with menswear, in its ideals of comfort and discretion, although she has denied that there was any message to the three words: she had just liked their French lilt. They mean what they mean, however, and there are few women who personify the ideals of seventies feminism with greater fidelity. The phrase comes, with a slight tweak, from the refrain of a pop song, by Françoise Hardy, in which a wistful teen-age girl enviously watches happy couples walking "hand in hand" and wonders if the day will come when—"*comme les garçons et les filles de mon age*"—she will find someone to love her. One may have such yearnings at any age, and Kawakubo was into her thirties when she met the love of her youth, Yohji Yamamoto. There was something pharaonic about their glamour as a couple, that of two regal and feline siblings with a priestly aura, and they shared the regency of a new generation in Japanese design. Both are alumni of Keio University (Yamamoto was two years behind her) and children of enterprising single mothers—his a widow who owned a dress shop. Yet, as the eloquent idiosyncrasy of their work suggests, a match between equals is rarely a balanced pattern whose cuts and edges align.

Like Kawakubo, Yamamoto is an anomaly in the fashion world on a number of counts, his proclivities among them. He married young and fathered two children. A different union produced a third child six years ago. For some years in between, he and Kawakubo were "travelling companions," as Kiyokazu Washida coyly puts it in an essay he contributed to Yamamoto's book, "Talking to Myself," a sumptuous pictorial chronicle of the designer's career which was published in 2002. Malcolm McLaren remembers Kawakubo and Yamamoto as a petite, stylish couple of "excellent customers" (he didn't yet know they were designers) who, in the seventies, turned up at Sex, the mother of all guerrilla shops, an outpost of seditionary music and fashion that he and his partner, Vivienne Westwood, had opened at World's End, in London. (Decades later, Westwood told Kawakubo that she considered her a "punk at heart.") They made their Paris débuts the same year, and were invariably linked, or lumped, together as part of an emerging Tokyo school that was challenging the conventions of Western couture, and of which Issey Miyake was the doyen. Kawakubo bridled at the group portraits. "I'm not very happy to be classified as another Japanese designer," she told *Women's Wear Daily* in 1983. "There is no one characteristic that all Japanese designers have."

Yamamoto was unavailable for an interview, but his friend and associate Irène Silvagni, a former fashion journalist, speaks of "the enormous competition between Rei and Yohji that she, I think, needed and thrived on." As far as Silvagni knows, they never collaborated, but "they both wanted to break the rules, and Yohji likes to say that 'perfection is the devil,' which I think is true for Rei. Japanese temples were always left unfinished for that reason." It is her perception that "they admire each other deeply, but there's a lot of baggage between them." She referred me to the baggage depot at the end of "Talking to Myself," in which Yamamoto sets down some fragmentary aperçus on a variety of existential subjects, including alcohol, gambling, insomnia, and women. "I'm always assuming that if she's my girlfriend she won't create a scandal," he writes of a nameless consort. "I'm sure of this even if it's unfounded."

The relationship ended in the early nineties. When a childless single woman nearing fifty suddenly starts to do her best work, she often has a broken heart. Joffe had joined Comme des Garçons in 1987, and on July 4, 1992, he and Kawakubo were married at the city hall in Paris. The bride wore a black skirt and a plain white shirt. That winter, she showed a hauntingly lovely collection that is still a favorite. It was composed of ethereal chiffon layers yoked to cone-shaped knitted turtlenecks that masked the face from the nose down, worn over flowing shifts with sorcerer's sleeves. Their color was nightshade, and their inspiration the myth of Lilith—a female demon of Jewish folklore, whom God created of "filth and sediment" when Adam, like the girl in the Hardy song, complained that he was the only creature on the planet without a mate. In Robert Graves's version, Adam and his first wife "never found peace together," because she rebelled at "the recumbent posture he demanded." When he "tried to compel her obedience by force, Lilith, in a rage … rose into the air and left him." So much for girlfriends who don't create scandals.

Lilith's heretical divorce was a juncture for Kawakubo, too. She was tiring of black (but she tires of anything once it catches on, and being avant-garde, she said recently, has become a cliché). She began to play with the opulent fabrics she had once disdained: damask, brocade, and velvet; with brilliant, sometimes lurid colors; and even with the staples of drag and bimbohood— sheer lingerie (worn with winkle pickers) and campy bustiers (layered over bulky topcoats). For commercial reasons, she says, she started sizing the clothes and narrowing the gap between dress and body. She edited the guest lists for her shows to a sympathetic coterie of editors and buyers, in part, as Amy Spindler wrote in the *Times*, because "multiplying the attendance figures … only serves to increase the number of people who don't get it." But Spindler also noted that Kawakubo "typically throws a bone to those who still believe clothes are for wearing outside fashion focus groups without being gawked at." Her easier-to-wear subsidiary lines, particularly Robe de Chambre (now called Comme des Garçons Comme des Garçons)—a microcosm of her own wardrobe—streamline the runway concepts to reach a broader public. "I'm not an artist, I'm a businesswoman," Kawakubo says. "Well, maybe an artist/businesswoman."

Despite the relative accessibility of "The Broken Bride," Kawakubo denies vehemently that she has mellowed ("I am still as aggressive as I've always been"), and every few years she reasserts her militance by exploding another bomb on the Paris stage. In 1995, the presentation of her menswear collection, which included a series of baggy striped pajamas reminiscent to some critics of the prison uniforms at Auschwitz, happened to coincide with the fiftieth anniversary of the camp's liberation. Kawakubo apologized for any offense she might, unintentionally, have given, and Jewish organizations who reviewed the videos were satisfied that no sacrilege had been committed. But she was perfectly conscious of the storm she conjured two seasons later with "Dress Meets Body." (Her own staff loved the sexy and salable silhouette, but there were worries about its bulges, and Kawakubo ultimately decided to make the troubling wads removable, though she wore them herself, and adapted them as costumes for a dance by Merce Cunningham. On perfect bodies in motion, they transcend their morbidity.) The collection was inspired, Joffe says, "by Rei's anger at seeing a Gap window filled with banal black clothes." Kawakubo concedes, with an ambiguous grimace that might just be a grin, "I may have been especially angry at the time, but I'm more or less always angry anyway."

Early one morning in Paris, the cobblestones of the Place Vendôme were varnished by a drizzle, and a row of limousines idled in front of the Ritz, waiting for clients in town for the menswear shows. The couture had just finished, and, in the terribly chic restaurants where fashion people eat their tiny portions of mediocre food, they were complaining that the couture *was* finished. Only eight designers had bothered to mount a show, and there was a sense that a once festive, feudal tournament of virtuosity had become a Renaissance fair with demonstrations of spinning and horseshoeing in period costume. But no one had informed Armani, a couture débutant. In *Le Figaro*, he discoursed with a quaint gravity on *les tendances de la mode* and affirmed his belief in "simplified lines that are easy to understand," because "true success means pleasing everyone"—a succinct résumé of everything in fashion that Kawakubo doesn't stand for, in both senses.

Across the square, in a narrow courtyard adjacent to the showroom of Comme des Garçons, the company's Paris staff, joined by a contingent from the Aoyama headquarters, who were groggy with jet lag, assembled for the morning salutation—a monastic ritual of solidarity performed daily in Tokyo. They formed a circle, shivering a little, and waited in silence for Kawakubo. Her protégé Junya Watanabe, who has a wrestler's physique and a cherub's face, squeezed in near Mister, who looked, in his business suit, a little like the hired mourner at a rocker's funeral. Joffe was surprised at his wife's delay ("She's a stickler for punctuality"), but she arrived at her habitual gait—the anxious scuttle of a sparrow with a broken wing—and took her place.

Kawakubo was sporting her favorite accessory: a dour expression. A collection, she says, is never not "an exercise in suffering," and she "starts from zero every time," destitute of confidence. It is ironic to her, she said at our last meeting in Tokyo, that a career she undertook "with one objective: to be free as a woman," has become a Spartan life of self-imposed servitude. But sympathy and compliments both annoy her, perhaps because they rub salt into the incurable and necessary wound of her discontent. The only consolation she can imagine "is an hour to spend with animals."

When she wants to, however, Kawakubo smiles through her clothes. That morning, she had chosen a black sweater strategically appliquéd with two white circles and a triangle that one could read either as a face or two breasts and a pubis, and which was meant as an homage to Rudi Gernreich's bikini and its muse, Peggy Moffitt. On her way to the rehearsal of her menswear defile, Kawakubo threw on one of her cheeky biker jackets from Spring, 2005: a crudely sutured leather blouson bred to an unbroken-in catcher's mitt, then taught some charm by a vintage couture bolero with a standaway collar. "Balenciaga on steroids," as an assistant put it.

Cristobal Balenciaga, who died in 1972, was a chivalric holdout from a courtlier age whose passing he lamented. If anyone "invented" black, he did. The ecclesiastic lines of his sculptural couture liberated women from the tyranny of the wasp-waisted New Look, and later from the ruthlessness of the miniskirt. His clients were the kind of *grandes bourgeoises* at whom Parisian spectacles of shock theatre have always been aimed, but Balenciaga himself might have recognized Kawakubo as a kindred spirit. They are both idealists whose work devoutly affirms that it matters what one wears—something pure in its distinction—and in that sense they have a common ancestor. He was an aging and spindly Spanish samurai who, like Kawakubo in her faintly obscene trompe-l'oeil bikini, was never afraid to cut an absurd yet heroic figure in a cynical world: the ridiculous made sublime.

34

Dressed to Thrill: Alexander McQueen at the Met

Judith Thurman

The New Yorker, May 16, 2011

When Hubert de Givenchy, the aristocrat who had dressed Audrey Hepburn and Jacqueline Kennedy, retired, in 1995, he was replaced at the house he had founded in 1952 by John Galliano, a plumber's son from South London, who left after a year for an even more exalted job, at Christian Dior. (Galliano was fired this March, after a series of anti-Semitic rants.) Another working-class British upstart of prodigious talent and flamboyant showmanship then stepped up to the hallowed plate in his Doc Martens. The new chief designer at Givenchy was a chubby hellion of twenty-seven, with a buzz cut and a baby face, who once boasted, "When I'm dead and gone, people will know that the twenty-first century was started by Alexander McQueen."

McQueen committed suicide, at forty, in London, on February 11, 2010. The housekeeper found his body hanging in his Mayfair flat. He had been under treatment for depression, and a week earlier his mother, Joyce, had died of cancer. (Her funeral had been scheduled for February 12th; the family went ahead with it.) In 2004, Joyce was invited to interview her famous son, by then at his own label, for the arts page of a British newspaper. In the course of an exchange that was fondly pugnacious on both sides (it was obvious where he'd got his scrappiness), she had asked him to name "his most terrifying fear." Without hesitation, he replied, "Dying before you." Normally, it is the parent who dreads losing the child, but the answer makes sense if you take it to mean "killing you with grief." You have to wonder if, for mercy's sake, McQueen hadn't been biding his time.

While McQueen had many anxieties, running dry wasn't among them. He was supremely confident of his instincts and his virtuosity. That ballast freed him to improvise, to take wild chances, and to jettison received ideas about what clothing should be made of (why not seashells or dead birds?), what it should look like (Renaissance court dress, galactic disco wear, the skins of a mutant species), and, above all, how much it could mean. The designer who creates a dress rarely invests it with as much feeling as the woman who wears it, and couture is not an obvious medium for self-revelation, but in McQueen's case it was. His work was a form of confessional poetry.

Last week, a retrospective of McQueen's two decades in fashion, "Savage Beauty," opened at the Metropolitan Museum, in the Iris and B. Gerald Cantor Exhibition Hall. Even if you never bother with fashion shows, go to this one. It has more in common with "Sleep No More," the "immersive" performance of "Macbeth" currently playing in Chelsea, than it does with a conventional display of couture in a gallery, tent, or shop window. Andrew Bolton, the curator of the Met's Costume Institute, has assembled a hundred ensembles and seventy accessories, mostly from the runway, with a few pieces of couture that McQueen designed at Givenchy, and he gives their history and psychology an astute reading. McQueen was an omnivore (literally so; he always struggled with his weight), and the richness of his work reflects a voracious consumption of high and low culture. He felt an affinity with the Flemish masters, Gospel singing, Elizabethan theatre and its cross-dressing heroines (a line from "A Midsummer Night's Dream" was tattooed on his right biceps), contemporary performance art, punk, Surrealism, Japan, the ancient Yoruba, and fin-de-siècle aestheticism. In most particulars, however—including his death—he was an archetypal Romantic.

Bolton has grouped the exhibits according to McQueen's "Romantic" fixations: historicism, primitivism, naturalism, exoticism, the gothic, and Darwinism. (In his last complete collection, "Plato's Atlantis," McQueen envisaged the females of a devolved human species slithering chicly back into the sea in scaly iridescent minidresses.) There is a section on "Romantic Nationalism," which in McQueen's case means Scottish tribalism. His paternal ancestors came from the Hebrides, and he never lost his abiding rage at England's treatment of his clansmen in centuries past. "Fucking haggis, fucking bagpipes," he said. "I hate it when people romanticize Scotland." The idea of its bleakness, though, seems to have warmed him—it resembled the climate of his mind.

McQueen's pride in his ancestry had been ingrained by his mother. (A collection on the theme of witchcraft was dedicated to one of her forebears, who was hanged in Salem.) His father, Ronald, drove a taxi, and Joyce stayed home until her son left school, at sixteen, when she took a teaching job. McQueen was the youngest of their six children—born in 1969—and they christened him Lee Alexander. (He started using his middle name at the outset of his career, because he was on welfare and he didn't want to lose his benefits.) When Lee was a year old, the family moved from South London to Stepney, in the East End. Trino Verkade, who was McQueen's first employee, and was part of the Met's installation team, told me that the area had been a skinhead bastion. "Lee was never a skinhead," she said, "but he loved their hard and angry look."

McQueen had realized very young that he was gay, but it took his family some time to accept him as what he called, with deceptive offhandedness, its "pink sheep." His puberty coincided with the explosion of AIDS, which is to say that he was forced to witness a primal scene that haunted the youth of his generation: sex and death in the same bed. Art, swimming, and ornithology were his primary interests at the tough local comprehensive school. He didn't have the credentials for university, but he always knew, he said, that he would "be someone" in fashion, and when Joyce heard that Savile Row was recruiting apprentices, he applied. At his first job, with Anderson & Sheppard, one of Britain's most venerable bespoke tailors, he learned, painstakingly, to cut jackets. (He later claimed that he had sewn an obscene message—"I am a cunt"—into the lining of one destined for Prince Charles. The firm is said to have recalled every garment for the Prince that McQueen had worked on, but no message was found.) He moved to a competitor, Gieves & Hawkes, then to a theatrical costumer, and on to the atelier of an avant-garde designer, Koji Tatsuno. McQueen ended his adolescence in Milan, working for his idol, Romeo Gigli—the modern Poiret. Gigli, he said, taught him, by example, that a designer can't flourish without a talent for self-promotion.

When McQueen came home to London, about a year later, he thought that he might teach pattern-cutting at the art school that has educated the élite of British fashion, Central Saint Martins. There was no job for him, but the administration invited him to enroll as a postgraduate student, waiving the academic requirements. In 1992, McQueen presented a master's degree collection entitled "Jack the Ripper Stalks His Victims." (At Givenchy, he based a collection on the character of a "mad scientist who cut all these women up and mixed them all back together.") There is a lot of sympathy for the Devil in McQueen's work. Bolton suggests that you consider it as "a meditation on the dynamics of power, particularly the relation between predator and prey."

Isabella Blow, a freelance stylist who later became one of the great "noses" of the fashion world, saw the Ripper show, recognized McQueen's gifts, and bought the collection in its entirety. (A black tuxedo with a bustle and long dagger-shaped lapels lined in blood red is at the Met.) Blow and McQueen were inseparable for a while, then, as his fame increased, less so. She, too, suffered from depression, and killed herself in 2007. Her legendary collection of clothing was saved from dispersal on the auction block by her friend Daphne Guinness.

McQueen's five years in the Givenchy couture ateliers taught him, he said, to use softness, lightness, and draping as foils for the austerity of his tailoring—and of his temperament. Some of his best work is his most ethereal. But Paris didn't teach him docility, and he sometimes took impolitic swipes at his bosses. Givenchy is owned by the French luxury conglomerate LVMH. In 2001, when its chief rival, the Gucci Group, offered to back McQueen's own label, he and Givenchy parted company.

Alienation often accounts for a macabre sense of the marvellous. At the entrance to "Savage Beauty," there is an evening gown conjured entirely from razor-clam shells. Antelope horns sprout from the shoulders of a pony-skin jacket, and vulture skulls serve as epaulettes on a leather dress. There are angel wings made out of balsa wood, and worms encased in a bodice of molded plastic. "I'm inspired by a feather," McQueen said of all the duck, turkey, ostrich, and gull plumage in his clothing—"its graphics, its weightlessness, and its engineering." One of his most demented masterpieces is a glossy black-feathered body cast that transforms its wearer into a hybrid creature—part raptor, part waterfowl, and part woman.

Bolton had full access to the McQueen archives, in London, and the support of McQueen's associates (his house co-sponsored the show). Sarah Burton, who succeeded him, was busy in London with Kate Middleton's wedding dress, but she was interviewed for the catalogue. The Norwegian fashion photographer Sølve Sundsbø took the catalogue pictures. It looks as though he bought the mannequins from a junk dealer, and it is startling to learn that they are live models disguised as dummies. Their bodies were coated with white acrylic makeup, and articulated at the joints by black strings. In the retouching process, they lost their heads. But here and there—on a torso, a thigh, an arm—the makeup has worn away, and a bruiselike patch of pink skin shows through, as if the flesh of a corpse were coming to life. The freshness of the shock is pure McQueen.

"Savage Beauty" is a shamelessly theatrical experience that unfolds in a series of elaborate sets. In the first gallery, examples of McQueen's incomparable tailoring hug the walls of a raw loft. A silk frock coat from the Ripper collection, with a three-point "origami" tail, in a print of thorns (I mistook them for barbed wire), has human hair sewn into the lining. There are several versions of McQueen's signature "bumsters": drop-waisted trousers or skirts that flaunt the cleavage of the buttocks. But his outrages were generally redeemed by an ideal of beauty, and the point of the bumsters, he said, was not just to "show the bum"; they elongated the torso, and drew the eye to what he considered the "most erotic" feature of anyone's body—the base of the spine.

The second gallery is an ornate, spooky hall of mirrors consecrated to McQueen's gothic reveries about bondage and fetishism. One of the loveliest dresses—with a lampshade skirt of swagged jet beading—has a necrotic-looking jabot of lace ivy that reminds you what a fetish mourning was to the Victorians. Leather abounds, masterfully tortured into submission, as in a zippered sheath with fox sleeves latticed by an elaborate harness. "It's like 'The Story of O,'" McQueen said. "I'm not big on women looking naïve. There is a hidden agenda in the fragility of romance."

"The Story of O" proves that a work of art can be distilled from stock pornographic imagery, and McQueen—who has a lot to say, in the wall notes, about the sexual thrill factors of rot, fear, and blood—manages to find beauty, as he put it, "even in the most disgusting of places." Beyond the hall of mirrors is a "Cabinet of Curiosities," where inventive instruments of consensual torture in the form of jewelry, headgear, footwear, and corsets are displayed like talismans. Videos from selected runway shows flicker high on the black walls, and the animal sounds of a cheering crowd and a woman moaning issue from hidden speakers. In a clip from one of McQueen's most radical collections (Spring/Summer 1999), an homage to the German artist Rebecca Horn, the model Shalom Harlow revolves on a turntable, cringing in mock horror as two menacing robots spray her white parachute dress with paint guns. The most striking artifact from this collection is a pair of exquisitely hand-carved high-heeled wooden prostheses that McQueen designed for Aimee Mullins, a bilateral amputee and American Paralympic athlete. She modelled them on the runway with a bridal lace skirt and a centurion's breastplate of molded leather, sutured like Frankenstein's skull.

There were always critics who accused McQueen of misogyny, and he was chastised for "exploiting" Mullins's disability as a publicity stunt. He brazenly courted scandal, revelled in most of it, asserted that "hot sex sells clothes," and certainly subjected his models—like the mannequins in the catalogue—to extreme trials. They were caged in glass boxes or padded cells; half smothered or drowned; masked; tethered; tightly laced; straitjacketed; and forced to walk in perilous "armadillo" booties, with ten-inch heels. In "Highland Rape" (1995), the breakthrough collection that earned McQueen, at twenty-six, his notoriety as a bad-boy wonder, bare-breasted dishevelled girls staggered down the runway in gorgeously ravaged lace, sooty tartan, and distressed leather. According to feminist critics, the show eroticized violation. According to McQueen, it commemorated the "genocide" of his Scottish ancestors. "We're not talking about models' feelings here," he said. "We're talking about mine." In fact, he always was.

Therapists who treat children often use dolls' play as a tool for eliciting their stories and feelings, and one has the sense that the dolls' play of fashion was such a tool for McQueen. He was fascinated by the work of Hans Bellmer, the mid-century German artist who created a life-size, ball-jointed mannequin—the figure of a pubescent girl—and photographed it in disturbing tableaux. "La Poupée," McQueen's Spring/Summer 1997 collection, paid tribute to an artist with whom he shared a kinship in perversity. Yet McQueen felt an even deeper sense of identity with the broken and martyred women who stirred his fantasies, and whom he transfigured. The real agenda of his romance with fragility may have been hiding in plain sight, tattooed on his arm, in the yearning line spoken by Shakespeare's Helena—a scrappy girl who feels that her true beauty is invisible: "Love looks not with the eyes but with the mind."

35

Why I Hate Abercrombie & Fitch (excerpt)

Dwight A. McBride

Why I Hate Abercrombie & Fitch: Essays on Race and Sexuality, 2005

My interest—a polite way of labeling it perhaps—in Abercrombie & Fitch began quite a few years back. It was a rather ordinary weekend night much like countless others where friends and I were out having drinks at a bar (which bar is not important to the story, as will soon become apparent). For the first time, I noticed that easily one-third of the men in the bar were wearing some item of clothing or another that sported the label of "Abercrombie & Fitch," "A&F," or just plain "Abercrombie." I asked one of my friends, "What is Abercrombie & Fitch?" And it was with that—at the time—rather innocent question that my intellectual and political sojourn with Abercrombie began. Once I saw it, I literally could not stop seeing it in any number of the gay spaces that I frequented. Whether I was at home in Chicago or traveling in New York City, Los Angeles, Houston, or Atlanta, in any mainstream gay venue there was sure to be a hefty showing of Abercrombie wear among the men frequenting these establishments. Even at the time of this writing (in the summer of 2003), the trend has only lessened slightly among white men in the U.S. urban gay male scene. Since this label has managed to capture the imagination (to say nothing of the wallets) of young, middle-to-upper-middle-class white gay men (well at least mostly young—there are some men who are far beyond anything resembling Abercrombie's purported target age demographic of eighteen through twenty-two wearing this stuff; and occasionally one does see gay men of color sporting the brand, though not many), I recognized this trend as a phenomenon about which it might be worth finding out more.

What is it about Abercrombie—especially with its particular practice of explicitly branding its products—that seems to have a lock on this particular population? What is it about the "brand" that they identify with so strongly? What kind of statement are the men sporting this brand in this sexually charged, gay marketplace of desire making to their would-be observers or potential … interlocutors? And why is it that the men of color in these same spaces have not taken to this brand with equal fervor? What about the men of color who have? The central question, put somewhat more broadly, might be: what is it that Abercrombie is selling that gay white men seem so desperate to buy in legion?

Let me be extremely clear from the outset that my quarrel with Abercrombie is not of the Corrine Wood variety (she is a former lieutenant governor of Illinois), whose conservative diatribe against the "indecency" of the company's advertising could once be found at her state-sanctioned Web site. Nor is my beef with the company and its marketing strategy to be confused with that of the American Decency Association (ADA). Indeed, I hope never in my life to be associated with anything taking a principled stance on "decency." Quite a lot of that already seems to be going on in the United States these days without much help from the likes of me. If anything, ours is a country that could stand to loosen its puritanical belt a bit and adopt more of a live-and-let-live policy when it comes to human pleasures. Dare I say that we need more of a public discussion about pleasure, a better way of talking without shame in the United States about it—where we seek it out, how it is a great common denominator, how we all (conservatives and liberals alike) want and need it? Such an open dialogue about pleasure might carry us far toward understanding some of the realities of our society, which are currently labeled "vices" and therefore banished from the realm of any "rational" discussion by "decent" people. Upon closer inspection, perhaps some of these so-called vices might be better understood as extensions of our humanity rather than deviations from some idealized form of it. Such a radical approach to conceiving of our humanity, our existence as sexual beings, might go far toward altering the circumstances of those recently much-discussed brothers on the "down low," for example, who have been newly "discovered" in the pages of the *New York Times Magazine* and elsewhere. For I remain convinced that the primary solution to the conditions that lead people to participate in unsafe sexual practices, young gay teens to commit suicide, and cultures of violence to produce and even sanction gay bashings and the like, resides in a loosening of the stranglehold that a puritanical, uncompassionate, intolerant morality (too often masking itself as Christian) has on the neck of our society. So let me set aside the concerns of readers who might lump this critique with those who have cast their lot with the decency police against Abercrombie. My concerns here, I am afraid, go far beyond anything quite so facile or pedestrian.

I begin first with a brief history of the company and the label of Abercrombie & Fitch itself. Second, I want to spend some time discussing the "A&F look," especially as it is exemplified in the *A&F Quarterly*—the sexy quarterly catalog/magazine that has been the source of much controversy among the decency police, the source of great interest among its young target audience and gay men, and the source of capital for serious collectors of the volumes, which sell in some cases for as much as seventy-five dollars on eBay. This last fact my research assistant and I discovered when we began to collect them for the purposes of this book. Third, I consider some aspects of the corporate culture of Abercrombie as it is represented by its stores, managers, and brand reps (as the clerks are called in Abercrombie-speak). This might help provide some insight into the current class action lawsuit that Abercrombie is facing (at the time of this writing) on discrimination charges in their hiring practices. And, finally, I hope to refer back to these points in my analysis of how "Abercrombie" functions as an idea, in order to justify the title claim of this essay in putting forth why it is I hate Abercrombie & Fitch.

The label "Abercrombie & Fitch" dates back to 1892, when David T. Abercrombie opened David T. Abercrombie & Co., a small shop and factory in downtown Manhattan. Abercrombie, born in Baltimore, was himself an engineer, prospector, and committed outdoorsman. His love for the great outdoors was his inspiration for founding Abercrombie & Co., dedicated to producing high-end gear for hunters, fishermen, campers, and explorers. Among his early clientele and devotees was Ezra Fitch, a lawyer who sought adventure hiking in the Adirondacks and fishing in the Catskills. He came to depend upon Abercrombie's goods to outfit him for his excursions. In 1900 Fitch approached Abercrombie about entering into a business partnership with him. By 1904 the shop had relocated to 314 Broadway and was incorporated under the name "Abercrombie & Fitch."

The partnership was uneasy almost from its inception. Both men were headstrong and embraced very different ideas about the company's future. Abercrombie was content to continue to do what they were already doing well—outfitting professional outdoorsmen. Fitch, on the other hand, wanted to expand the business so that they could sell the idea of the outdoors and its delights to the general public. In retrospect, this might have been one of the very earliest cases of big business ideology winning out over small. The result of these feuds was that Abercrombie resigned from the company in 1907.

After his resignation, the company did follow Fitch's vision for its future and expanded into one of the largest purveyors of outdoor gear in the country. Abercrombie & Fitch was no ordinary retail store either. Fitch brought an IKEA-like innovation to the selling and displaying of his goods: stock was displayed as if in use; tents were set up and equipped as if they were in the great outdoors; and the sales staff was made up not of professional salesmen, but of outdoorsmen as well.

By 1913 Abercrombie & Fitch had expanded its inventory once again to include sport clothing. The company maintains that it was the first store in New York to supply such clothing to both women and men. In 1917 Abercrombie & Fitch changed locations once again, this time to a twelve-story building at Madison Avenue and Forty-fifth Street. By this point it had become the largest sporting goods store in the world. At this location, Fitch took the display tactics for which the company was by this time famous to an entirely new level, constructing a log cabin on the roof (which he used as a townhouse), an armored rifle range in the basement, and a golf school in the building. By this time the merchandise the store carried had expanded once again to include such exotic items as hot air balloons, portable trampolines, and yachting pennants, to name but a sampling.

Abercrombie's reputation was so well established by this point that it was known as the outfitter of the rich, famous, and powerful. Abercrombie outfitted Teddy Roosevelt's trips to Africa and the Amazon as well as Robert Peary's famous trip to the North Pole. James Brady recently reminded us in Advertising Age that Hem and Wolfie (i.e., Ernest Hemingway and Winston Frederick Churchill Guest) also shopped there. In an article bearing the title "Abercrombie & Fitch Forgets Its Days of Hem and Wolfie," Brady recounts the "real man" glory days of Abercrombie & Fitch while bemoaning the A&F of our day, when the company takes out a double-truck ad in Rolling Stone featuring half-naked, boxer-wearing white boys on roller skates sporting backwards baseball caps. The masculine anxiety of that writer's article notwithstanding, he does refer us back to a relevant source in Lillian Ross's 1950 *New Yorker* profile of Hemingway, where one of Hem's shopping trips to Abercrombie is recounted. Other famous early A&F clientele included such notables as Amelia Earhart, Presidents William Howard Taft and John F. Kennedy, Katherine Hepburn, Greta Garbo, Clark Gable, and Cole Porter. And apparently during prohibition, A&F was also a place to buy hip flasks.

It is evident that even in its earliest incarnation, Abercrombie was closely allied with white men (and to a lesser extent white women) of means, the life of the leisure classes, and a Norman Rockwell–like image of life in the United States, for which they were famous even then. It is not surprising that the clothier we know today developed from a company with early roots in exploration, adventure, and cultural tourism, which catered to the white upper classes. The advertising from any of its early catalogs even adopts an innocent, idealistic Rockwellian aesthetic in many instances. It was not long after Abercrombie's resignation in 1907 that the company published its first catalog, which was more than 450 pages long. Some 50,000 copies were shipped to prospective customers around the world. So A&F's legacy of an unabashed consumer celebration of whiteness, and of an elite class of whiteness at that, in the face of a nation whose past and present are riddled with racist ideas, politics, and ideology, is not entirely new. Still, I believe the particular form it has taken in our time bears our careful consideration for the harm that it does to our ways of thinking about and imagining our current racial realities in this country, as well as for the seemingly elusive difficulty it poses in our attempts to understand what about it makes many of us so uneasy.

In 1928 Fitch retired from the business. The company continued to grow and expand well into the 1960s, opening stores in the Midwest and on the West Coast. In the late 1960s, however, the store fell on economic hard times—likely due to the rapid changes in American values associated with that era—and filed for bankruptcy in 1977. The company was bought by Houston, Texas-based Oshman's Sporting Goods. The business continued to decline until Abercrombie was acquired by the Limited, Inc., in 1988. The Limited tried to position the brand as a men's clothing line and later added a preppy women's line under the label as well. These efforts, too, failed, until the Abercrombie makeover began to take shape in earnest under the hand of Michael Jeffries, the current CEO of Abercrombie & Fitch, in 1992. Jeffries was no stranger to the retail world before his arrival at Abercrombie. He had done a stint at then-bankrupt retailer Paul Harris, Inc., had a hand at running his own chain (Alcott & Andrews), and a long run at Federated Department Stores, Inc. After assuming his post with Abercrombie, Jeffries hired his own team of fashion designers. He tapped superstar fashion photographer Bruce Weber (widely known for his Calvin Klein, Ralph Lauren, and Karl Lagerfeld ads) for the playful coed shots on the walls of Abercrombie stores. Weber would go on, of course, to become the photographer for the infamous *A&F Quarterly* as well. The *A&F Quarterly* was launched in 1997 to, as one commentator puts it, "glamorize the hedonistic collegiate lifestyle on which the company built its irreverent brand image." Even the words of the commentator here are extraordinary for how "collegiate" and "irreverent" are conflated in the image of Abercrombie. Indeed, it is testimony to part of A&F's genius that it successfully produced a false radicalism by hitching its label to a "collegiate" lifestyle that is inevitably and overwhelming white and upper middle class. Whatever the case, what we do know is that Abercrombie has been a financial success since 1994, only two years after Jeffries took over and reorganized the brand with his own variety of lifestyle marketing, to which they remain thoroughly committed. In 1998, the year following the launching of the A&F Quarterly, Abercrombie spun off from the Limited to become once again an independent, publicly traded company.

Abercrombie & Fitch has devised a very clear marketing and advertising strategy that celebrates whiteness—a particularly privileged and leisure-class whiteness—and makes use of it as a "lifestyle" that it commodifies to sell otherwise extremely dull, uninspiring, and ordinary clothing. I am not, by the way, the first commentator to recognize this fact about the clothes themselves. The danger of such a marketing scheme is that it depends upon the racist thinking of its consumer population in order to thrive. Anyone familiar with the rise of the company and its label in recent years recognizes that it has done precisely that.

Abercrombie has worked hard to produce a brand strongly associated with a young, white, upper-class, leisure lifestyle. Nowhere is this more evident than in the *A&F Quarterly*. Since, however, I could not bring myself to ask for, only to be denied, permission to use photographs from those pages in this book, or to participate in a vicious cycle of perpetuating the lure of those images by repeating them here, I leave it to my reader to seek them out, as they relate to this analysis. They are readily available online and in any number of media venues. Instead, I would like to consider in some detail a document where the A&F look gets perhaps it clearest articulation: the *Abercrombie Look Book: Guidelines for Brand Representatives of Abercrombie & Fitch* (revised August 1996).

Affectionately known in the everyday corporate parlance of Abercrombie as the *Look Book*, this pocket-size (3.5 x 5.5–inch and approximately 30-page-long) book devotes equal time to images and text. The book contains twelve images—all photographs of model brand representatives, save one sketch (which we will come to later). Four of the eleven photos (including the cover) are group shots; the remaining ones feature individual models. Of the group shots, two include the one African American model (or even visible person of color) in these pages, while all of the rest of the photos are of male and female models who appear to be white. All of the models also appear to be solidly within Abercrombie's stated target age group of eighteen through twenty-two, and they all appear in the photographs smiling and often in various states of repose. The book divides neatly into five sections: an introductory section, which addresses the relationship between the brand representative and the A&F look; a section entitled "Our Past," which gives a brief history of the company; a section called "Our Present"; followed by an "Our Future" section; and then finally the longest section (making up more than half the book) on "The A&F Look" (with subsections titled "Discipline," "Personal Appearance," and "Exceptions"). I provide such detail so that the reader will have an image of this book as an object, as well as a sense of its formal content.

The *Look Book* begins thus:

Exhibiting the "A&F Look" is a tremendously important part of the overall experience at the Abercrombie & Fitch Stores. We are selling an experience for our customer; an energized store environment creates an atmosphere that people want to experience again and again. The combination of our Brand Representatives' style and our Stores Visual Presentation has brought brand recognition across the country.

Our people in the store are an inspiration to the customer. The customer sees the natural Abercrombie style and wants to be like the Brand Representative ...

Our Brand is natural, classic and current, with an emphasis on style. This is what a Brand Representative must be; this is what a Brand Representative must represent in order to fulfill the conditions of employment.

[Emphases Appear as they do in the *Look Book*.]

The book continues in much the same vein, touting the virtues of the ideal brand representative. In the approximately seventeen pages of text in the book, the word "natural," for example, appears as a descriptor no fewer than fourteen times. In this regard, it is closely followed by its companion terms "American" and "classic" to account for what the book identifies alternately as the "A&F look" and the "A&F style." Such words in the context not only of Abercrombie, but in the context of U.S. culture more broadly, are often understood for the coded ways of delineating the whiteness that they represent. Indeed, most of us carry in our imagination a very specific image that we readily access when such monikers as "natural, classic, American" are used. That image is not likely of the Native American, who has far more historic claim to such signifiers than those whom we have learned to associate with them. This fact, I think, speaks volumes about the incredible and abiding ideological feat that we encounter in the whiteness of the idea of "America" and of "the American."

Indeed, citizenship in the United States touches upon matters of social identity, including race and gender. While the dominant rhetoric of our national identity presents a color-blind, "united-we-stand," Horatio Alger narrative of upward mobility, in reality, citizenship is raced, gendered, and classed, and the original texts that define citizenship and national identity in the United States reflect this reality. UC Berkeley ethnic studies professor Evelyn Nakano Glenn touches upon one aspect of American ideological citizenship when she discusses the importance of whiteness and autonomy in contrast with non-whiteness, subservience, and dependence:

> Since the earliest days of the nation, the idea of whiteness has been closely tied to notions of independence and self-control necessary for republican government. This conception of whiteness developed in concert with the conquest and colonization of non-Western societies by Europeans. Imagining non-European "others" as dependent and lacking the capacity for self-governance helped rationalize the takeover of their lands, resources and labor. (Glenn, 18)

Glenn goes on to emphasize early in her essay that it is not just whiteness but masculine whiteness that "was being constructed in the discourse on citizenship." Colonization is a key aspect of this ideology of masculine whiteness, according to Glenn:

> Imagining non-European "others" as dependent and lacking the capacity for self-governance helped rationalize the takeover of their lands, resources and labor. In North America, the extermination and forced removal of Indians and the enslavement of blacks by European settlers therefore seemed justified. This formulation was transferred to other racialized groups, such as the Chinese, Japanese and Filipinos, who were brought to the U.S. in the late nineteenth and early twentieth centuries as low wage laborers. Often working under coercive conditions of indenture or contract labor, they were treated as "unfree labor" and denied the right to become naturalized citizens. (Glenn, 18)

A commitment to masculine whiteness, with its emphasis on territoriality, exploitation of resources, and the perception of other non-whites as dependent and lacking in political and mental capacity, is part of the master narrative that formed an important foundation for our ideas of American citizenship. Indeed, we have come to a point in our history where any real variation on what we might mean when we say "American" or "America" is scarcely thinkable. The ideological work of equating American with whites and America with whiteness has been thoroughly achieved. Viewed in this way, Abercrombie's early beginnings as an outfitter of upper-class explorers, adventurers, and outdoorsmen may perhaps be more relevant to our understanding and appreciation of the label's appeal than we first imagined.

The *Look Book* is noteworthy for some of the contradictions it raises as well. For example, the A&F dress code delineates its commitment to whiteness even in terms of what it deems acceptable in the way of appearance. The investment here in whiteness is also an investment in class. Consider the following guidelines:

- For men and women, a neatly combed, attractive, natural, classic hairstyle is acceptable.
- Any type of "fade" cut (more scalp is visible than hair) for men is unacceptable.

- Shaving of the head or any portion of the head or eyebrow for men or women is unacceptable.
- Dreadlocks are unacceptable for men and women.

It is also in this section of the *Look Book* that we are presented with the only sketch that appears in the book. It is a combination sketch of seven heads and faces, which carries the caption "Some Acceptable Hairstyles." Included in these drawings is an African American man with a neatly cut natural (a very short afro cut). There is also among these faces a man who appears much older than the A&F target age group. In fact, this is the only place in the book where an older person is ever pictured. Indeed, it would also be unusual to find older adults working as brand representatives in their stores or being featured as models in the *A&F Quarterly*.

What is interesting to note about the acceptable hairstyles is what is out and what is in. In the mid-90s, when this edition of the *Look Book* was published, the fade was a popular hairstyle for African American men. I confess, somewhat reluctantly, that I had one myself. Also, since shaved heads are excluded, this also would put a mounting segment (at the time) of African American men out of the running along with the odd white skinhead. Finally, dreadlocks, while considered by some to be among the most "natural" of hairstyles available to African Americans, are out. Indeed dreads, as they are often referred to, are even somewhat controversial within African American communities for their association with, among other things, Rastafarianism. So other than as a commitment to a white aesthetic, the exclusion of dreads (even in terms of A&F's own commitment to the "natural" look) seems curious.

On jewelry, the *Look Book* offers the following:

Jewelry must be simple and classic. A ring may be worn on any finger except the thumb. Gold chains are not acceptable for men. Women may wear a thin, short delicate silver necklace. Ankle bracelets are unacceptable. Dressy (e.g., gold-banded or diamond) watches are also unacceptable; watches should be understated and cool (e.g., leather straps or stainless steel). No more than two earrings in each ear can be worn at a time for women. Only one in one ear for men. Earrings should be no larger than a dime, and large dangling or large hoop earrings are unacceptable … No other pierced jewelry is appropriate

(e.g., nose rings, pierced lips, etc.)

Thumb rings signify alternative lifestyles at best and queer at worst. No gold chains for men? Who has been overidentified or even stereotyped with these in the popular imagination more than black men—from Mr. T to any number of rap artists, and "ballers" more generally? In either case, the signifier "gold chain" demarcates potential employees of A&F in coded ways along race and class lines. A similar case can be made with regard to the reference to "large dangling or large hoop earrings." Here, too, Abercrombie codes for race and class without actually having to name it.

Still, of all of the dress code rules, the most amusing one to me has to be the following: "Brand Representatives are required to wear appropriate undergarments at all times." Is Abercrombie afraid that their brand representatives might actually be sexualized? The image of male genitalia flopping about in cargo shorts or, alternatively, of an 18–22-year-old version of the now infamous Sharon Stone leg-crossing scene in the film Basic Instinct (1992) comes to mind. Call me crazy, but there is just something about a company that flies in the face of such propriety in the pages of the *A&F Quarterly*—wherein no one seems to wear underwear or much else for that matter—being concerned about the appropriateness of the undergarments of its employees that strikes me as the height of hilarity and hypocrisy.

If the frequent use of such coded monikers in the *Look Book* were not enough to convince us that the A&F look is styled on a celebration of racial and cultural whiteness, consider that the *A&F Quarterly* is chock full of images of young white men and women (mostly men) with very little in the way of representation of people of color. Consider that criticism of Abercrombie's chosen photographer, Bruce Weber, draws him as (in)famous for his unabashed celebration of the white male nude. Recall the release by A&F in April 2003 of that inflammatory line of "Asian" themed T-shirts, which were hotly protested by the Asian American community among others. One of the shirts featured two stereotypical Chinese men drawn with exaggeratedly slanted eyes, donning pointed hats, and holding a banner between them that read: "Two Wongs Can Make It White." A spokesperson for A&F, when asked to respond to the controversy raised by the T-shirts, said, "We thought it would add humor." The line was pulled by the company soon after they were released. Consider also the variety of social engineering that goes into producing a virtually all-white sales staff in A&F stores. As one former assistant manager of one of Abercrombie's larger stores in the Midwest informed me, all the brand reps in his store were white, and all of the people who worked in the stockroom were black. Stockroom employees (in the larger stores where they employ such staff separately from brand reps) are less visible and are often assigned to work overnight shifts restocking the store.

Many people have asked me while I was working on this project—no doubt many will continue to do so—what's the big deal? Why pick on Abercrombie? They are doing no more or no less than Ralph Lauren or Banana Republic. I have said to those people and continue to say that such a simple equation is not only untrue, but denies the specificity of the particular brand of evil that Abercrombie is involved in capitalizing on. Ralph Lauren does, to be sure, commodify a particular upper-class American lifestyle. Banana Republic has a history of a similar marketing scheme. However, A&F successfully crystallizes a racism that is only rumbling beneath the surface of other stores' advertising. Also, Ralph Lauren attempts to market and sell that lifestyle to everyone equally. That is, the underlying ethos of Ralph Lauren is not unlike the ideology of the American dream itself: you, too, can have this if you work for it.

Ralph Lauren "diversified" its ad campaigns in the 1990s. To demonstrate that fact, among other things, Ralph Lauren in 1993 took on Tyson Beckford, a black model of Jamaican and Chinese parentage, to represent its Polo Sport line exclusively. True, this diversity was of the variety of CNN diversity: news is read by white and Asian reporters, while black reporters do sports and entertainment and occasionally "substitute" for white news reporters. In the same vein, Beckford was engaged to model for Ralph Lauren's "sport" line and not its "blue label" (i.e., blue blood) line of suits, formal wear, and elegant apparel. Still, Beckford's own rags-to-riches story made for good press for a company clearly working its own variety of the diversity angle, which was a popular marketing strategy among hip retailers in the 1990s. Beckford represents perhaps the most notable example of this. He grew up in Jamaica and in Rochester, New York. As a youth he was involved in gangs, drugs, and was on his way down the road toward a life of crime, when an editor of the hip-hop magazine the *Source* discovered him. Not long thereafter, it would be Bruce Weber who would introduce Beckford to Ralph Lauren— whose signing of Beckford sent his modeling career into the stratosphere. Beckford himself has recognized that he would likely be dead or in jail had he not been taken up by that editor from the *Source*. There has been speculation about the veracity of Beckford's narrative of class ascension. Regardless, its construction generated good press for Ralph Lauren.

I should note, too, that neither Banana Republic nor Ralph Lauren participates in the kind of social engineering in terms of their store employees that A&F does. The employees of Banana Republic represent diverse racial backgrounds, while the sales associates at Ralph Lauren tend to represent an older model of the suit-wearing salesman in an upscale shop. The latter, in addition to the Polo stores, also sells its line in fine department stores, where they have no direct control over choosing sales associates to represent the line. An added bit of anecdotal information with regard to Banana Republic also comes in the form of the person of Eduardo Gonzalez—one of the named litigants in the pending class action employment discrimination lawsuit against A&F. The class action complaint notes that Gonzalez, who was not hired as a brand representative at Abercrombie, was offered a job at Banana Republic:

Indeed, immediately following his Abercrombie interview, he crossed the hall within the same mall to apply for a job at Banana Republic, a similar retail clothing store that competes directly with Abercrombie for customers and employees. An employee of Banana Republic asked Mr. Gonzalez if he was interested in applying to work as a manager. He applied to work as a sales associate, and is still employed by Banana Republic in that capacity.

If images tend more often to follow and demonstrate where we are as a society rather than play the role of leading us to new places, then the particular brand of a socially engineered whitewashed world being advertised, branded, and sold to U.S. consumers by Abercrombie should give us pause. Movie lovers may recall the song "Tomorrow Belongs to Me" from the film version of *Cabaret*. The song begins, like the lyrics, in a pastoral mode. The camera is tight on the face of the beautiful, young, blond, boy soprano. The scene is comforting, indeed beautiful. With each successive verse, however, the camera begins to pull back and to show more and more and more of the boy's body … donning a Hitler-youth uniform. His face becomes increasingly emphatic and angry. By the time we get to the fourth verse of the tune, the others in the crowd have joined in the song with a seriousness of purpose that can only be described as frightening:

The sun on the meadow is summery warm
The stag in the forest runs free
But gathered together to greet the storm
Tomorrow belongs to me

The branch on the linden is leafy and green
The Rhine gives its gold to the sea
But somewhere a glory awaits unseen
Tomorrow belongs to me

The babe in his cradle is closing his eyes
The blossom embraces the bee
But soon says the whisper, arise, arise
Tomorrow belongs to me

Now Fatherland, Fatherland, show us the sign
Your children have waited to see
The morning will come
When the world is mine
Tomorrow belongs to me
Tomorrow belongs to me
Tomorrow belongs to me

The number concludes with the final verse above being repeated twice more in a chilling, thunderous unity, as the crowd of townspeople gathered at the picnic joins in.

Some may call a comparison such as the one I am drawing here hyperbole. Others might say that I am overstating Abercrombie's case and undervaluing the realities of the Holocaust. Neither is my intention. I do, however, believe fervently in what Hannah Arendt in *Eichmann in Jerusalem* once called "the banality of evil." I am convinced that a version of it is what is at work in the politics of race in U.S. society today, and that Abercrombie's marketing and branding practices represent only a symptom of that larger concern. Indeed, according to Edward Herman, "Arendt's thesis [in *Eichmann in Jerusalem*] was that people who carry out unspeakable crimes, like Eichmann, a top administrator in the machinery of the Nazi death camps, may not be crazy fanatics at all, but rather ordinary individuals who simply accept the premises of their state and participate in any ongoing enterprise with the energy of good bureaucrats." In the words of another philosopher-commentator on the "banality of evil": "Clichés, stock phrases, adherence to conventional, standardized codes of expression and conduct have the socially recognized function of protecting us against reality." This statement well describes the corporate culture of Abercrombie and the quasi-cultish devotion they seem to inspire.

36

The Mystery Man: Margiela, Be Mine

Sarah Mower

Vogue, September 1, 2008

Few of my friends know this, but I'm conducting a relationship with an invisible man. He's a 57-year-old Belgian recluse who long ago disappeared behind an oblong strip of white tape, a label with nothing on it. His last known appearance was in 1994 in New York at the now-defunct boutique Charivari, where he was seen to be a tall man in a flat cap, quietly driving journalists apoplectic by refusing to grant quotes about his collection.

Since then, not a thing has been seen or heard of Martin Margiela: only robotic written pronouncements issued from a white-painted former industrial-design school occupied by men and women in white couture coats in the Eleventh Arrondissement of Paris. These days, rumors even circulate that this man, whose intelligence I adore and clothes I accumulate, doesn't actually exist. Based on the public face of his work—his exaggerations, twists, puns, and strange appropriations—there are other people who shrug him off as one of the freakiest freak shows in fashion whose clothes could only be worn by avantgarde weirdos. Ha! How wrong can they be?

Because on my side, it's a case of abject Margiela dependency. Without him, my self-image and ability to function in the world would be imperiled. Should some hideous fashion creep burgle my wardrobe tonight and make off with my navy blazer, sharp-shouldered jackets, gorgeous black jersey one-shouldered gown, cap-sleeved day dress, three pairs of man-tailored pants, four shirts, various tube tops, skirts, belts, skinny scarves, Lucite wedges, pumps, bags, innumerable stockpile of T-shirts—oh, and that mad red lamé vest and chiffon cape—I'd wake up tomorrow with a shattered identity. It's that bad.

Given that I fancy myself a strenuous non-belonger to any fan clan, designer or otherwise, this is also quite a funny contradiction. I am a woman who'd be mortified to be caught wearing anything that smacks of recognizable designer trophy, ever—and I'm not one who'd risk any garment that might hang me out on the extreme edge of fashion to be sniggered at. What I require is straight, chic clothes of unidentifiable provenance that are turned just one or two notches up the dial toward UNUSUAL, WITTY, or SEXY (though always at a visual frequency conventional people can't pick up). Martin Margiela is the only designer who does that. Get into him, and you end up with a repertoire that lasts for years because, fabulously, no one can ever guess who made any of it, or when. I've lost count of the people at parties who, after staring a bit, have been forced to ask where I got my matte-black one-shouldered jersey dress. I love it when they have to lean in closer and ask again, "Who?," either because they've never heard of Mr. Nobody (great!) or because they're struggling to align the information with their perception of Margiela as the man who shows clothes made out of party balloons (his latest "artisanal" collection) or sofa covers (fall 2006) or wigs out of recycled fur coats (fall 1997). And call me bad, I can't help enjoying the irritated moue that crosses some women's faces when they hear that this dress is not available any longer: She's wearing an old dress. So how come it looks so damn right now?

Wearing Margiela can bestow a satisfying cleverness upon you like that. Because he's so impersonal, his clothes become personal to you. And because his things are frequently several steps ahead of fashion (or because other designers look to him for a lead), Margiela purchases can end up reflecting glory upon you three, four seasons after you bought them because at some point, the world's caught up, and the stuff looks spot-on. Anyone who bought a jacket from his very first collection in 1988 would be laughing now. It had narrow shoulders with high-set puffed sleeves, in direct opposition to the dominant padded-linebacker silhouette of the power dressing of the time. It proved so long-range influential, you could wear it today, and people would still come up to you and ask where they could buy it.

But Margiela is so secretive, even deliberately obscurantist, he rarely takes the credit for this. When you really analyze it, everything he does is one big dynamic contradiction. He's a so-called deconstructionist who is actually one of the best constructionists in the business (he does excellent tailoring for women and men). He's an arch noncorporate anti-brander (the blank white labels) whose operation is actually branded through and through, from the whitewashed walls and secondhand furniture of his shops to the lab coats of his staff and white canvas shopping bags, right down to the cotton envelopes into which his press communiqués are stitched. An early proponent of alternative street-level fashion politics (he once literally showed on the Paris street, in the Métro, and in an abandoned supermarket), he is now a master of luxury clothes and accessories, and launching a fine-jewelry line and a perfume with L'Oréal next year. And though he's categorized by many as the most high-minded of intellectual designers, the way he converts one thing into another can be quite hilarious. Once, his people solemnly presented a boa to the press in a hushed showroom. It was a fat velveteen studded snake wrapped around a girl's neck. A boa constrictor. I had such a fit of the giggles, I had to leave the room. On the other hand, it's only right to appraise Margiela's method with the seriousness they deserve. In appropriating "found" objects and reassigning them as fashion products, he stands in a direct line from the Surrealists, Dadaists, and Junk artists. One example is the white evening dress in his latest handmade collection. The bottom half is part of a silk mousseline dress; the top is made from two white plastic bags, complete with the handles.

Lots of the things in my personal collection belong to the Replica line he occasionally drops into stores. They're new, but a label inside each garment states its provenance: A BOY'S TAILORED JACKET, FRENCH, 1970s; AN EVENING CAPE, ITALIAN, 1980s; and so on. Is this "designer" creativity? No, just copies, honestly documented and brilliantly selected. Something else, too: While others have made a big noise about vintage, recycled materials, and sustainable sourcing in recent times, Margiela's been practicing them for years.

When I heard that Margiela was opening a twenty-year retrospective exhibition at MoMu in Antwerp (where he attended the Royal Academy of Fine Arts) this month, I had a slight flicker of anxiety that all this—the things that only Margiela's secret appreciation society understands—would now become transparent to everyone. Still, I live in hope. As long and as studiously as I have tried to apply myself to understanding something as apparently methodical and sequential as Margiela's system of numbering his lines, zero to twenty-three, I can't get it. Line zero denotes the "artisanal" handmade pieces and number six the accessibly priced sportswear, but beyond that I'm lost because several of the numbers are skipped over. That's just typical, I feel, of Margiela's meticulous confusing tactics. The exhibition won't be chronological, either: more a mix of personal themes out of which surprising and elucidating juxtapositions my spring. Or then again, I fervently hope, not. Having come this far with the man, I'd really rather prefer to keep him to myself.

37

All Hail the Leader of the Fashionable World

Robin Givhan

The Washington Post, January 21, 2009

Few first ladies have caused as much breathless anticipation for their Inauguration Day wardrobes as Michelle Obama. But soon after she stepped onto the national stage as the candidate's wife, Obama was elevated to a fashion star whose tastes ran from high-end designers to mass marketer H&M. She had the impressive height of a runway model, the figure of a real woman—a size 12 according to one fashion publicist—and took an admitted delight in looking "pretty."

For the historic moment when she became this country's first African American first lady, Obama chose a lemon-grass yellow, metallic sheath with a matching coat by the Cuban-born designer Isabel Toledo. The dress followed her curves—paying special attention to the hips— and announced that the era of first lady-as-rectangle had ended. It signaled a generational shift in what women could be on the national stage. They could boldly embrace color and reveal their power, their femininity and their legs.

Recent first ladies seem to have tried—at least during the first term—to hold on to the idea of normalcy, no matter that they are living in the White House with staff, security and the albatross of history. At their husbands' first inaugurations, Hillary Clinton and Laura Bush wore uninspired clothes that seemed to make a case against the women's being unique.

Obama's mere presence on the Capitol steps yesterday was an anomaly—and her clothes celebrated that. Her coat and dress made her look exceptional—and vaguely regal—as she stood holding Lincoln's cranberry-hued Bible in her gloved hand as her husband took the oath of office. Her daughters, Malia in a grape-colored coat and black tights and Sasha in pale pink and tangerine, were like her little ladies-in-waiting. President Obama, he was the somber one, in his dark overcoat with a tiny flag pin, his white shirt, red tie and his face tilted ever so slightly to the sky.

With Toledo, Michelle Obama reached into the loftiest corners of the fashion industry and chose a small design house where the person whose name is on the label is the same person hunched over the sketchpads, following production and fretting about whether she will be able to get her merchandise to market on time. Obama avoided the expected names, the well-funded houses and the corporate designers. Toledo does not advertise. Her wares are sold in only a handful of stores, from Barneys New York to Chicago's Ikram, the North Rush Street shop where Obama has been a regular customer. She wore the ensemble with olive leather gloves and Jimmy Choo pumps that were a deeper, forest shade of green, refraining from going dreadfully matchy-matchy. The entire picture spoke of womanliness, grandeur and elegance, and it declared Obama's ease with being a woman of modest background thrust into extraordinary circumstances. Shy and retiring personalities do not wear glittering citron under the noon sun.

For her inaugural gown, Obama chose another young New York-based designer, Jason Wu, twenty-six. His custom-made gown, in flowing ivory silk chiffon with a single strap, was embroidered with silver thread and adorned with Swarovski crystal rhinestones. This is the barest gown that a first lady has worn at an inauguration since Nancy Reagan wore a James Galanos gown to usher in Ronald Reagan's first term. Wu's dress bares Obama's arms and shoulders and brings the first lady into the modern era, in which glamour is defined by Hollywood and the red carpet rather than protocol and tradition.

The dress speaks to Wu's signature style: grown-up clothes with a youthful flourish. Wu, who was born in Taipei, Taiwan, and studied in Paris and Vancouver, B.C., as well as at Parsons design school in New York, has been in business only since 2006. Obama wore his clothes and Toledo's during the campaign.

Obama's grace yesterday gave no hint of her ambivalence about the public obsession with her style, which began early in the campaign. Her appearance on "The View" in a $148 sundress proved that she not only could stir interest in fashion but also could move merchandise simply by wearing it. With her Ivy League pedigree, her high-powered job and her soccer-mom credentials, she made the case that any woman could and should embrace fashion. When she casually commented that she never wore pantyhose, the definition of dressing for success changed. When she bounded onto the stage in her sleeveless dresses, with her muscular post-Title IX arms in full view, the definition of a strong woman changed.

Obama has been compared to Jacqueline Kennedy, the last first lady to so thoroughly embrace style as a form of communication. Much is made of the fact that they both wore sleek, sleeveless dresses and had an affection for pearls. But the real similarities may be in the way they used clothes to set a tone for their husbands' administrations.

As her husband's administration promises more jobs and help for small-business owners, and emphasizes creativity as one of this country's greatest assets, Obama's choice of an iconoclastic, immigrant female designer with a modest business sends a profound message of intent. The frantic guessing game of what Obama would wear was fueled by scant information and even fewer rumors. She kept her secret by calling in multiple gowns. A small village of designers created daywear. Her spokeswoman, Katie McCormick Lelyveld, said that in the days before the swearing-in, the first lady had been in no hurry to pick out her wardrobe. Her focus was on her children and getting her family moved, not once but three times, McCormick Lelyveld said.

Obama saved any announcement of her final choices until the last minute. But once the wardrobe began to roll out, beginning with the whistle-stop tour from Philadelphia to the nation's capital, it was clear that she would continue to shift between price points, alternating between fitting in and standing out. For the train trip, she wore a black swing coat—one that she'd been photographed wearing in Chicago this winter—with a purple three-quarter kimono sleeve jacket by Zero Maria Cornejo. Who? Cornejo is another New York-based designer with a dedicated following and virtually no profile outside the fashion industry.

Obama chose a custom-made pale purple Narciso Rodriguez coat when she accompanied her husband to Arlington National Cemetery, where he laid a wreath at the Tomb of the Unknowns. And on Sunday afternoon, she was again wearing custom-made Rodriguez: a camel wool coat and matching skirt with a black silk beaded blouse. She paired it with nude legs and low-heeled pumps. (A quibble: The line of that ensemble might have been better served with a pair of boots rather than those sensible heels.) The look was accessorized with a pair of diamond chandelier earrings by Loree Rodkin that retail for $17,313. They were lent by the Chicago boutique Ikram.

For the Kids' Inaugural concert, she dressed in J.Crew.

The bill for the entire inaugural trousseau was paid by the Obamas, McCormick Lelyveld said. The easy shift between price points has captivated observers accustomed to recent first ladies who have dressed in either pricey designer fashions by Seventh Avenue heavyweight Oscar de la Renta or nondescript blahness. Obama dresses the way contemporary women do, mixing J. Crew with the splurges in their closet. They combine pragmatism with polish. And for this inauguration, despite the dire shape of the economy, they also brought glamour.

At a brunch sponsored by Essence on Sunday afternoon, the room was filled with black women—black women like Michelle Obama with fancy degrees, big jobs and a sense of style. They admired Obama immensely. In fact, the January issue of the magazine with Obama on the cover is on track to surpass the record set by the Tyler Perry cover, which sold 319,000 copies. They admire how she has shifted the perception of how a first lady should look. Perhaps all the attention to her clothes is unfair, too demanding. Perhaps folks should have been breathlessly anticipating what sort of initiatives she will ultimately champion. But where's the fun in that?

"The attention to clothes is always too much, but it's part of the fun. You're curious to know: What style is she going to set for this presidency," said Alexandra Martinez, assistant dean and director of admissions at the Harvard Kennedy School.

Martinez was wearing an aubergine suit by Lafayette 148 and had in her possession no less than three Badgley Mischka gowns, one for each of the balls that she would attend. Who would wear the same dress twice in one inaugural weekend? she asks. And more to the point, why should a successful, smart and fashion-conscious woman have to?

38

The Revolution Will Be Branded Vetements

Anja Aronowsky Cronberg

Vestoj, March 17, 2016

Vogue claims that they have "all the makings of an unforgettable fashion landmark," *The Business of Fashion* has praised their "radical democratic principles" and proclaims that the revolution will be branded in their honour, *W* calls them "truly revolutionary" and *WWD* recently dubbed their designer an "alternative fashion hero." Vetements is the latest brand tasked with saving a staid fashion climate, and fashion critics have been falling over themselves praising the company. In an industry that appears run aground and is rife with discontent due to visual overload and a seemingly stuffy and befuddled producer-to-consumer relationship, it is tempting to long for alternative fashion heroes. For Vetements, being at the right place at the right time has enabled the brand to lead the current *zeitgeist*, and the fashion week cycle that recently concluded in Paris saw the acclaim culminate in another celebrated and celebrity-studded Vetements show and the first collection by designer Demna Gvasalia at the much-venerated fashion house Balenciaga.

The story is an old and familiar one: young, upstart outsiders take on a sedate and conventional system and turn it on its head in the name of authenticity, edginess and cool. Popular culture thrives on this narrative, and in the fashion industry this storyline is a well-worn one. "Real" fashion is thrust, from the street, upon the unsuspecting bourgeoisie, and the bourgeoisie go potty for it. In the case of Vetements, what editors and buyers are waxing lyrical about ranges from oversized hoodies, off-beat dresses and asymmetrical overcoats to elongated knits and jeans ripped and then patched together again. "This is what fashion looks like when you take the L train to Bushwick," according to *Vogue* (Phelps, 2015). The write-up "Vetements: Whiffs From the Underground" in *The Business of Fashion*, was equally quick to proclaim, "It belongs to the street" (Flaccavento, 2015).

Vetements is described as a "collective" helmed by designer Demna Gvasalia and his brother Guram, and their purportedly democratic working methods are an important part of the brand's appeal. Their "no-concept concept" is another element of their allure: Sarah Mower tells us in her review of the brand's most recent catwalk show that "rather than just being subversive for the sake of the gestural politics, Vetements means business" (Mower, 2016). Demna Gvasalia is also quick to point out that his collections are "not trying to push the boundaries of fashion" (Socha, 2015), and that "fashion shouldn't make you dream" (Fury, 2015). This pragmatic approach chimes well with the times, and the Vetements phenomenon no doubt taps into a wider discourse around what we should expect from high fashion: should it be about concepts or about products? Should it sell or make us dream?

The popularity of Vetements, buoyed by hyperbolic articles in the fashion press and brand-affiliated social media accounts prolific in their gritty images of confederates of the "collective" in various states of disarray, speaks to our attraction of kicking against the system. Fashion critics have made a lot of the brand's "outsider status" while at the same time being quick to point out that it has an illustrious pedigree: Demna Gvasalia has worked at both Louis Vuitton and Maison Margiela, and, according to one online retailer of the brand's garments, other "collective members" have previous ties to both Balenciaga and Céline (ssense.com, 2015). The fashion industry seldom takes issue with paradox or rhetoric—in fact most press texts and show reviews seem to revel in it. With the reporting of Vetements, this is particularly obvious—here the ubiquitous and ever anonymous behind-the-scenes staff, a staple of every fashion house, become "a collective" and the insider is transformed into an outsider by virtue of "whiffs from the underground."

Creating myths around a fashion brand is of course an important part of fashion marketing, and the fashion press is the most effective way of perpetuating this type of storytelling. In the case of Vetements, the projected grit on the catwalk makes the conservative and conventional amongst us feel a twinge of excitement: "Just when—by looking at mainstream corporate luxury-goods norms—it seemed that cool was dead and buried and nothing 'alternative' could ever again survive, along came a couple of brothers, Demna and Guram Gvasalia, and their collective of friends, to prove skeptics wrong," (Mower, 2016) as one particularly enthusiastic reviewer would have it.

The semblance of rebellion that Vetements is offering us, comes at a high price: €875 for a stretch-knit jumper, €1025 for a pair of jeans or €9500 for a sequined dress. Any further cost to the wearer is highly circumstantial—the only ones likely to be sporting this garb can afford to observe the grittiness that Vetements is becoming known for from a safe distance. The brand has been hailed for appealing to "a real audience—not just fashionistas" (Flaccavento, 2015) but who this real audience might be is a moot point. Instead, it seems more likely that the reason Vetements currently has the fashion press in a tizz, is that this revolution is one that comes at minimum risk. It may include safari-style visits to gay sex clubs or dingy Chinese restaurants, but the youth culture it glorifies is one that is very happy to accommodate, and buy into, those mainstream corporate luxury-goods norms. The Vetements universe, as it is presented in the press, is one that proffers a romanticised view of lower-class life and of the proverbial "Other." It offers us a bit of rough and the rumble of the L train, while simultaneously fitting very snuggly into the fashion system as we know it. It's curious actually, considering that Demna Gvasalia himself has been quick to point out in interviews that Vetements plays by the same rules as establishment brands (Socha, 2015), that those reporting on (and contributing to) Vetements' ascent have been so insistent about their alternative status.

Linking rebellion and consumption has been a trend since the 1960s, but the band of insiders that make up Vetements are proudly apolitical: they "mean business." The disillusion that many feel with the contemporary fashion system is here being enlisted to keep the wheels of luxury consumption in motion. What might otherwise be described as sales strategy is here elevated to revolution, and the growing discontent with corporate fashion and ever-accelerating consumption is cleverly channeled straight back into the luxury fashion system. We are encouraged to covet the brand's unconventional ugly-beautiful aesthetic in order to feel closer to their collective of social rebels and outsiders, presently coded as cool and desirable. This is not just a look, we are told—this is a way of life. Vetements has the appearance of rejecting mainstream fashion, but their brand of reconstituted seediness, readily consumable through fashion collections and the images published in the fashion press or posted on the social media accounts of the brand's cohorts, is aimed at Western, educated, middle-class fashion insiders hungering for a product with some semblance of "authenticity," without any of the uncouthness that might cling to the underground.

The mystique created around Vetements in the press hovers near one of the most persistent critiques of the fashion industry: that codes of the "underground" are co-opted by the mainstream and sold back at great expense to the fashion elite. The success of the brand is perhaps proof of the weariness many feel for conventional glamour and conglomerate-driven fashion, but the codes Vetements convey are sufficiently familiar for the brand to be slotted straight into the establishment and unthreatening to the degree that the designer has been offered a creative directorship at one of those very conglomerates. There appears to be a fair bit of doublethink going on in the fashion press; one of the major ironies of the reporting around Vetements is that the press is fully aware that the image the brand projects is constructed, yet it still buys into it.

The revolution will, indeed, be branded Vetements.

Bibliography

Flaccavento, Angelo. "Vetements: Whiffs from the Underground." *The Business of Fashion*, October 2, 2015. www.businessoffashion.com/articles/fashion-show-review/vetements-whiffs-from-the-underground

Fury, Alexander. "The Label Vetements Is the Most Radical Thing to Come Out of Paris in over a Decade. So What's the Big Idea?" *The Independent*, October 16, 2015. www.independent.co.uk/life-style/fashion/features/the-label-vetements-is-the-most-radical-thing-to-come-out-of-paris-in-over-a-decade-so-whats-the-big-a6692211.html

Mower, Sarah. "Vetements Fall 2016." *Vogue*, March 3, 2016. www.vogue.com/fashion-shows/fall-2016-ready-to-wear/vetements

Phelps, Nicole. "Vetements Fall 2015." *Vogue*, March 5, 2015. www.vogue.com/fashion-shows/fall-2015-ready-to-wear/vetements

Socha, Miles. 'Demna Gvasalia—His Own Rules." *Women's Wear Daily*, November 18, 2015. www.com/fashion-news/fashion-features/demna-gvasalia-balenciaga-vetements-10279574/

Ssense. "Vetements." March 14, 2015. https://www.ssense.com/fr-fr/femmes/designers/vetements.

39

Will I Get a Ticket?
A Conversation about Life after *Vogue*
with Lucinda Chambers

Anja Aronowsky Cronberg

Vestoj, July 3, 2017

We meet at a cosy private club in West London, the sort of hangout popular with fashion professionals who believe in the semblance of bohemia. For thirty-six years she's been working at British Vogue, twenty-five of those as the magazine's fashion director, but not long before we meet the fashion press has been full of headlines announcing her departure. We order lattes, and I'm struck by how candid she is.

A month and a half ago I was fired from *Vogue*. I phoned my lawyer; she asked me what I wanted to do about it. I told her I wanted to write a letter to my colleagues to tell them that Edward [Enninful] decided to let me go. And to say how proud I am to have worked at *Vogue* for as long as I did, to thank them for being such brilliant colleagues. My lawyer said sure, but don't tell HR. They wouldn't have wanted me to send it.

Later I was having lunch with an old friend who had just been fired from Sotheby's. She said to me, "Lucinda, will you *please* stop telling people that you've been fired." I asked her why—it's nothing I'm ashamed of. She told me, "If you keep talking about it, then *that* becomes the story. The story should be that you've had the most incredible career for over thirty years. The story shouldn't be that you've been fired. Don't muck up the story." But I don't want to be that person. I don't want to be the person who puts on a brave face and tells everyone, "Oh, I *decided* to leave the company," when everyone knows you were really fired. There's too much smoke and mirrors in the industry as it is. And anyway, I didn't leave. I *was* fired.

Fashion can chew you up and spit you out. I worked with a brilliant designer when I was at Marni—Paulo Melim Andersson. I adored him. He was challenging, but highly intelligent. Fragile, like a lot of creative people. We had our ups and downs, but he stayed with us for seven years. Then Chloé came along. The CEO at the time asked my advice about Paulo and I told him, "Paulo is great, but you have to know that he won't turn the brand around for you

in a season or even two. You've got to give him time, and surround him by the right people."
"Absolutely, absolutely," he said. "I'll do that." Three seasons later Paulo was out. They didn't
give him time, and he never got his people. I felt so sad for Paulo. If you want good results, you
have to support people. You don't get the best out of anyone by making them feel insecure or
nervous. Ultimately, that way of treating people is only about control. If you make someone feel
nervous, you've got them. But in my view, you've got them in the wrong way. You've got them
in a state of anxiety. I'm thinking of one fashion editor in particular: it's his modus operandi. He
will wrong-foot you and wrong-foot you, and have everyone going, "Shit, shit, shit, shit, shit."

You're not allowed to fail in fashion—especially in this age of social media, when everything
is about leading a successful, amazing life. Nobody today is allowed to fail, instead the prospect
causes anxiety and terror. But why can't we celebrate failure? After all, it helps us grow and
develop. I'm not ashamed of what happened to me. If my shoots were really crappy … Oh I
know they weren't all good—some *were* crappy. The June cover with Alexa Chung in a stupid
Michael Kors T-shirt *is* crap. He's a big advertiser so I knew why I had to do it. I knew it was
cheesy when I was doing it, and I did it anyway. Ok, whatever. But there were others … There
were others that were great.

In fashion people take you on your own estimation of yourself—that's just a given. You can
walk into a room feeling pumped up and confident, and if you radiate that the industry will
believe in what you project. If, on the other hand, you appear vulnerable you won't be seen as
a winner. I remember a long time ago, when I was on maternity leave, *Vogue* employed a new
fashion editor. When I met with my editor after having had my baby, she told me about her.
She said, "Oh Lucinda, I've employed someone and she looked *fantastic*. She was wearing a red
velvet dress and a pair of Wellington boots to the interview." This was twenty years ago. She
went on, "She's never done a shoot before. But she's absolutely beautiful and *so* confident. I just
fell in love with the way she looked." And I went, "Ok, ok. Let's give her a go." She was a *terrible*
stylist. Just terrible. But in fashion you can go far if you look fantastic and confident—no one
wants to be the one to say " … but they're crap." Honestly Anja, you can go quite far just with
that. Fashion is full of anxious people. No one wants to be the one missing out.

Fashion moves like a shoal of fish; it's cyclical and reactionary. Nobody can stay relevant for
a lifetime—you always have peaks and troughs. The problem is that people are greedy. They
think, "It worked then, we've got to make it work now." But fashion is an alchemy: it's the right
person at the right company at the right time. Creativity is a really hard thing to quantify and
harness. The rise of the high street has put new expectations on big companies like LVMH.
Businessmen are trying to get their creatives to behave in a businesslike way; everyone wants
more and more, faster and faster. Big companies demand so much more from their designers—
we've seen the casualties. It's really hard. Those designers are going to have drink problems,
they're going to have drug problems. They're going to have nervous breakdowns. It's too much
to ask a designer to do eight, or in some cases sixteen, collections a year. The designers do it, but
they do it badly—and then they're out. They fail in a very public way. How do you then get the
confidence to say I will go back in and do it again?

The most authentic company I ever worked for is Marni. We didn't advertise, and what we
showed on the catwalk we always produced. We never wanted to be "in fashion." If you bought
a skirt twenty years ago, you can still wear it today. We never changed the goalposts. Our shows
were about empowering women. We always treated our models beautifully and had incredible
diversity in the company: my team was half boys, half girls, all different nationalities. It was very
transparent, but when the company was sold everything changed. The Castiglionis were naïve.
They sold 60 percent of the company, thinking that the new owner would respect what they

had built. I never understood why they sold it to Renzo Rosso of all people. He is the antithesis of everything Marni stood for. The antithesis. When Consuelo left, I remember thinking why not give the design task to someone from the team? It would have been a reflection of how fashion is created today, and it worked for Gucci—Alessandro Michele had been at the brand forever before becoming the creative director. I talked to Renzo and he agreed, but then at the last minute he changed his mind. He brought Francesco Risso onboard, who had nothing to do with the company. Before Marni, he did celebrity dressing at Prada. He'd never done a show, he'd never run a team. But he knows Anna Wintour. And who is Renzo Rosso enthralled by? Anna Wintour. The last womenswear collection at Marni was a disaster; it had terrible reviews. The show was *appalling*. I heard the cost to produce it was two-and-a-half times what we used to spend, and it sold 50 percent less. A lot of American buyers didn't even bother to turn up. Marni is no more. It saddens me, but then I remind myself that from the ashes something new can emerge.

When Vetements came on the scene, what they were doing felt very new. At that particular time, it wasn't what anyone else was doing. And when I saw the last Balenciaga show … Okay, you could say it's a bit Margiela or a bit this or that, but honestly I was really really really excited. You know what was smart about it? It was the scale—you saw this tiny model emerge and it took forever for her to get close to the audience. It built up expectation. *Everything* was thought through: the casting, the music, the space. Everything. And I loved how we were all seated: so far from each other, it all felt anonymous. Normally at a fashion show, everyone looks at each other—who wears what, who sits where. "Oh, she's got the new Céline shoes." But here you felt as if you were on your own. It was a new feeling.

Fashion shows are all about expectation and anxiety. We're all on display. It's theatre. I'm fifty-seven and I know that when the shows come around in September I will feel vulnerable. Will I still get a ticket? Where will I sit? I haven't had to think about those things for twenty-five years. Most people who leave *Vogue* end up feeling that they're lesser than, and the fact is that you're never bigger than the company you work for. But I have a new idea now, and if it comes off maybe I won't be feeling so vulnerable after all. We'll have to wait and see.

There are very few fashion magazines that make you feel empowered. Most leave you totally anxiety-ridden, for not having the right kind of dinner party, setting the table in the right kind of way or meeting the right kind of people. Truth be told, I haven't read *Vogue* in years. Maybe I was too close to it after working there for so long, but I never felt I led a *Vogue-y* kind of life. The clothes are just irrelevant for most people—so ridiculously expensive. What magazines want today is the latest, the exclusive. It's a shame that magazines have lost the authority they once had. They've stopped being *useful*. In fashion we are always trying to make people buy something they don't need. We don't *need* any more bags, shirts or shoes. So we cajole, bully or encourage people into continue buying. I know glossy magazines are meant to be aspirational, but why not be both useful *and* aspirational? That's the kind of fashion magazine I'd like to see.

40

Trump vs. the Disappearing Tie

Vanessa Friedman

The New York Times, May 11, 2016

Donald Trump, the presumptive Republican presidential nominee, is a political outlier not only when it comes to immigration policy, Twitter and marital history, but also when it comes to image.

This isn't, of course, a coincidence. But it is notable. I am not speaking here of his much discussed hair, or even his somewhat florid skin color. I am speaking of his ties.

And not because, according to CNN, his own-brand ties are made in China and thus seemingly contradict his vow to bring jobs back to America. Or because the ties he actually wears on the stump—the shiny, brightly colored ones with the big knots—are Brioni, made in Italy.

But, rather, because of the sheer fact that he actually wears a tie. Almost all the time. If in the early days of his campaign—while attending, say, the Iowa State Fair—Mr. Trump occasionally lost the neckwear, those days seem increasingly rare.

The pretty much constant presence of the tie has served to highlight another, less discussed but no less pointed gulf between the candidate and those he would call peers: For many politicians, the tie is no longer considered a necessary part of the uniform.

"The president has been wearing a tie less and less," said Tammy Haddad, a Washington media consultant and former political director of MSNBC. "It is an overt expression of the way this White House has been trying to make politics more human."

Indeed, all the way back in 2013, the Business Insider website ran a post entitled, "Is President Obama Killing the Necktie Business?"

The president did not wear a tie to dinner with Princes William and Harry during his recent visit to Britain. (They did not wear ties, either.) He did not wear a tie during his news conference about Justice Antonin Scalia's death in February. (The Internet was not happy.) He did not wear a tie for his opening dinner with President Xi Jinping of China when Mr. Xi arrived in Washington for a state visit last September. (It may have been "informal," but it had photo ops.)

As it happens, neither did Mr. Xi, Vice President Joseph R. Biden Jr., Secretary of State John Kerry, Secretary of the Treasury Jacob J. Lew or Max Baucus, the ambassador to China. Nor did Jeb Bush when he announced his candidacy for president.

And this is not simply an American development. On Saturday, Sadiq Khan took his oath of office as the new mayor of London in Southwark Cathedral—in a navy suit, white shirt and no tie. The previous week, he and his opponent, Zac Goldsmith, were each pictured on the cover of The London Evening Standard going to vote—in blue suits, white shirts and no ties. In an often contentious campaign, it seemed one of the few tactics both men agreed on. Indeed, the campaign itself was labeled by various Britons as "the most informal in memory."

But Mr. Khan's apparent lack of allegiance to the tie does not come close to that of Prime Minister Alexis Tsipras of Greece, who practically made his refusal to wear a tie part of his electoral platform a year ago.

That Mr. Khan and Mr. Tsipras represent left-wing parties may seem significant (Mr. Tsipras being more extreme than Mr. Khan), except that in 2013, Britain's prime minister, David Cameron, who is a Conservative, decreed, as host of the Group of 8 summit, that the dress code would be "informal," which translated as tieless. There is a reason one of his nicknames is "dress-down Dave."

"The tie is an issue that dwells in the minds of candidates, their spouses and their handlers for endless hours," said Bennet Ratcliff, an international political consultant and founder of Thaw Strategies. "I once had a president spend 15 minutes talking to me about his tie when we could have been discussing the language of a peace accord."

If the decision on what tie to wear is so complicated, imagine the conversation about not wearing one at all. Such choices are not made by accident, or without an agenda.

Call it Phase 3 of political dress evolution.

Phase 1 was John F. Kennedy going hatless for his inaugural address in 1961, signaling to all watchers that a new, breezier generation was in charge. Phase 2 was the lose-the-jacket, roll-up-your-sleeves look, adopted by politicians at the end of the twentieth century in multiple in-the-office photo ops, the better to demonstrate their work ethic. And now we are here.

Ties have not disappeared from the political arena, of course. The rules of the House of Representatives demand that men wear a coat and tie on the floor when Congress is in session. (Former Speaker John Boehner was known for rebuking his colleagues if he thought they were showing disrespect to the institution by dressing too casually.) Ditto the Senate. President Obama often wears a tie; so does Mr. Cameron.

World leaders in other hemispheres, of course, have traditionally had a different kind of uniform, one that can involve cultural, often indigenous, garment tropes.

But in the West, there is no question that the tie has become a variable in the political calculation, instead of a constant. Though it is easy to chalk it up to generational change, a more accurate interpretation probably has to do with ideology, opportunism and spin-doctoring. After all, this is a time when social media has meant that the optics of a message—or how it is delivered—are increasingly important. And ubiquitous.

"You can't overestimate it, but you shouldn't underestimate it either," said Steve Hilton, the chief executive of Crowdpac, a site that matches politicians and would-be donors by their priorities, and Mr. Cameron's former director of strategy. "There is a huge interest now in personal character, and how you dress is an immediate access point for that. It's a part of an overall message, and a pretty important one."

This was overtly satirized in a BBC Two show called "The Thick of It" (it inspired the HBO series "Veep"), which ran sporadically in Britain from 2007 to 2012 and featured a communications director called Stewart Pearson. The character was on a mission to update his party, in part by urging elected officials, including his fictional party leader, not to wear ties.

As it happens, Stewart Pearson was inspired by Mr. Hilton, who was widely credited with persuading Mr. Cameron to ditch his tie, the better to sway voters to "take another look at the Conservative party," as Mr. Hilton said in a phone call from California, where he lives now. It wasn't the same old, same old—at least when it came to wardrobe. (You have to start somewhere.)

The decision to play hide-and-seek with the tie is "a reflection of the current cultural environment, and an effort to seem like a part of that," Mr. Ratcliff, the consultant, said, adding: "The leaders are just following the voters. Thank God they haven't all started wearing black turtlenecks like one unnamed entrepreneur, though it will come to that eventually."

The Steve Jobs allusion is a reflection of the new economic power structure, one that celebrates the technical entrepreneurial class and the shadow banking sector, both of whose casual style has had a creeping influence on professional dress code, redefining what future success looks like in the popular imagination.

In part, this is how we find ourselves in this weird, inverted sartorial reality, where Mr. Trump has become the exception to the rule because he follows traditional rules. His tie-wearing harks back to the Wall Street uniform of the 1980s, the boom years of the American economy, when it was "morning in America" and Gordon Gekko preached the "greed is good" gospel. The candidate's mouth says he wants to "make America great again," and his clothes refer back to the last time many Republicans believed that was actually the case. He is emphatically and consciously not the new-look candidate. He is the old-look candidate.

Thus the tie divide, like many others in this particular election, gets ever wider.

41

Suket Dhir, Men's Wear Designer, from Delhi to the World

Guy Trebay

The New York Times, November 4, 2016

New Delhi—In a stifling office on the second floor of an anonymous building along a dusty lane in Lado Sarai—the new hub for young artists in a corner of the southwestern part of this capital city—a 38-year-old men's wear designer Vogue.com has called a "global fashion superstar in the making" sat in semidarkness.

The power had gone out. Somehow the power is always going out in twenty-first-century India, a nation with 1.25 billion people, thousands of years of recorded history and the capacity to deploy nuclear weaponry.

India is a paradoxical country. And Suket Dhir is a paradoxical guy. Born in Banga, India, he is an unshorn and unshaven Punjabi Hindu who styles himself a "wannabe Sikh"; a self-described former "slacker" now blissfully married to a Russian-Indian woman, Svetlana Dhir, who manages the business; a creative talent eager to compete on the global stage, and yet one who shares his small studio office with his elderly father.

He is also an expert craftsman whose subtle tailoring was recognized last January with one of the most prestigious honors in fashion, the International Woolmark Prize, an award that has also gone to Karl Lagerfeld and Yves Saint Laurent.

The judges who selected Mr. Dhir as the latest recipient focused their praise on the romantic and internationalized vision of the designer, whose last foray outside India (before traveling to Florence, Italy, to collect the $75,000 in prize money) was a brief trip to Dubai two decades earlier.

Perhaps most appealing of Mr. Dhir's contradictions is how his restrained tailoring honors and deftly makes use of a range of the varied craft traditions that remain among the wonders of India while simultaneously mining a design vocabulary partly formed by his habit of binge-watching "Seinfeld."

Almost a year after winning the Woolmark prize, he was scrambling to complete and deliver a collection, his first to be sold outside India, to department stores in Tokyo; Sydney, Australia; Seoul, South Korea; and New York. (Saks Fifth Avenue will feature elements from Mr. Dhir's label, called Sukhetdhir, starting in December.)

At the time of my visit, the deadline for the first shipments was just over a week away. Tailors in a back room sat patiently at their silent machines. A cutter scissored through layers of denim methodically in the dimly lit room. A brownout coinciding with crunch time may induce at the very least a tantrum for some designers. Yet with the cool of a sannyasi or a stoner, Mr. Dhir suggested a coffee run.

The spot he chose was Blue Tokai, a hipster joint that is part coffee bar and part industrial grindery. There, amid aclatter of trays and a general conversational din, the soft-spoken chatterbox sketched out the unlikely path he had taken from being an aimless and indifferent student, to "that obnoxious voice" consumers across the world hear when call-center dialers manage to entrap them ("I sold mobile phones for AT&T"), to the great hope for Indian design.

It was at the call center, Mr. Dhir said, that he polished the rough edges off his Punjabi-accented English (a stint at a fancy boarding school probably helped, too). And it was there that he transformed his manner of speaking into a cross between upper-class Indian English and generic American.

"Actually, the great thing about the call center was that you worked all night and slept all day, so you never had a chance to spend any money," Mr. Dhir said over an iced latte. "I saved a lot and started using the money to travel around India: to Goa, the mountains, Pondicherry and Dharamsala."

When he was in his 20s, Mr. Dhir came to the realization that he had no five-year, or even five-minute, plan. "A friend said, 'Do you know what you want to do with your life?'" he said. "And I didn't. And I actually had tears in my eyes."

That same friend then made a canny observation: Perhaps a career cue lay hidden in plain sight. He pointed to Mr. Dhir's habitual doodling, his knack for dressing differently from his friends (in LA Gear tracksuits and Fila sneakers) and his near-obsession with FTV, a fashion-focused satellite video channel.

"He said, 'Have you ever thought of fashion?'" Mr. Dhir said. "To be honest, I never had."

Mr. Dhir applied to the elite National Institute of Fashion Technology in New Delhi, was accepted and quickly gravitated toward men's wear.

"Fashion at this time is about a dream," Haider Ackermann, the Berluti designer who was one of the Woolmark prize judges, said at the ceremony granting the award. "Suket is a person with a dream to tell."

While in design school, Mr. Dhir developed elements of his vision: silhouettes cultivated by his father and grandfather—pocketed Nehru jackets, natty blazers worn over flowing trousers—and a magpie assortment of nostalgic motifs picked up from the Western films and television reruns that first appeared regularly in India with the arrival of satellite TV.

Not every designer cites, with Mr. Dhir's catholicity of taste, inspirations as disparate as Clark Gable's swallowtail coats from *Gone with the Wind* and Paul Hogan's groovy buccaneer drag from *Crocodile Dundee*.

For the panel awarding the Woolmark prize—it included the fashion critic Suzy Menkes; Nick Sullivan, the men's wear director at Esquire; Masafumi Suzuki, the editor of GQ Japan; and Raffaello Napoleone, director of the Pitti Uomo men's wear fair in Florence—the clincher was the way Mr. Dhir's designs update traditional Indian garments while relying on ancient techniques.

"We appreciated the strong creativity but also the work on the fabrics and materials, so the choice of Suket was very natural," Mr. Napoleone wrote by email, referring to tie-and-dyed ikat yarn, hand-block printing, arduous spinning and weaving methods that give a silklike texture to fibrous wool.

"There were two camps," said Eric Jennings, a vice president and men's wear fashion director for Saks Fifth Avenue. "One was looking for something more trend-relevant, and one was more interested in the emotional side of the story."

If emotion won the day, trend relevance did not come off too badly, since one of the first things Saks ordered from Mr. Dhir's new collection was an indigo bomber jacket covered with pin-tucked pleats so minutely hand-stitched that they resemble trompe l'oeil.

It is possible, too, that what the judges detected in Mr. Dhir was something more significant than a single breakout talent. In a sense, his surprise win signaled a generational shift in Indian design. He would not be the first, or even the most gifted, of Indian designers in recent decades to skirt the clichés afflicting Indian fashion.

Abraham & Thakore, Wendell Rodricks and Rajesh Pratap Singh all favor a restrained form of Indian modernism over the more typical turbans and jodhpurs, overembellished tunics or Bollywood bling that leave so much design here, as Mr. Dhir said, looking like costume.

"To say definitively there's a new wave of designers is a bit of a stretch," said Meher Varma, a graduate student in the anthropology department at U.C.L.A. who has conducted a study of Indian fashion in the years since the country's trade policies were first liberalized in the late 1980s and early '90s.

"But there is a general emergence," Ms. Varma added, of designers like Mr. Dhir who, raised on television, the internet, YouTube and social media, view fashion through a global lens.

As often happens, the applied arts followed the lead of the fine arts, with the success of Indian contemporary art stars like Subodh Gupta, Bharti Kher and Dayanita Singh providing an example of how to avoid the curse of provincialism, of Indian-ness as a unitary identity.

"As an emerging market, India was starting to bubble only since 2002 or 2003," said Rikki Kher, a British-born, Delhi-based men's wear designer. "First it was the art world and then designers like Manish Arora getting a name outside the country."

Mr. Dhir chalks up his first few rocky years in business to his commitment to steer clear of both the pitfalls of India-for-export and, equally, a domestic wedding market that drives the bottom line for most of his design compatriots. Even now, his annual sales of roughly $100,000 (mostly from stores in India like the stylish Good Earth chain) amount to little more than what an American designer like Todd Snyder spends on a single runway show.

"I don't do wedding gear, which is where the money is," Mr. Dhir said.

"Of course, there is a certain Indian-ness about me, the humanism, and an ability to approach the business in a holistic manner," he added, although holism may be a euphemistic way of describing the managed chaos entailed in creating a line of men's wear whose elements of traditional crafts are incorporated so subtly that a wearer registers them only slowly. A hand-blocked umbrella print lines a jacket. A band of ikat hides inside a collar. Different colored thread is used to affix each button to a shirt.

"When I'm designing, I'm thinking about the final look of the product, of course, but also about the practical execution," Mr. Dhir said. "How will I get that dyed? How will I reach the weaver's village? Where will I stay? Will there be a toilet there? As a designer, these things become part of your whole everyday life."

Pulling his long hair back into a ponytail, Mr. Dhir said with a laugh that, while he always felt "the need to be a global person," there has never been any question of abandoning his roots. "It's not elephants and camels anymore," he said. "But it's still India."

42

Melania Trump and the Chilling Artifice of Fashion

Rhonda Garelick

New York Magazine's The Cut, August 30, 2017

Yesterday, heated debate over Melania Trump's travel attire nearly overshadowed the very purpose of her trip: to bear witness to the devastation of the Houston hurricane. At stake was whether Melania's look—slim black pants, face-framing blowout, green silk bomber, mirrored aviators, and sky-high snakeskin stilettos—was appropriately sober and practical for communing with victims of biblical-level flooding.

Those shoes especially drew critical fire. "Melania is wearing stilettos to a hurricane zone," tweeted a *Wall Street Journal* reporter. "Trump is the kind of woman who refuses to pretend that her feet will, at any point, ever be immersed in cold, muddy, bacteria-infested Texas water," observed the *Washington Post*. Some rushed to defend the First Lady, wielding the usual claim that women's fashion should be beneath our notice. "I don't know why anyone should care what anyone wears when they're on their way to help people," declared Trevor Noah on his show.

But there is more going on here, and it's being ignored by detractors and defenders alike. The problem is not that Melania Trump wore an unsuitable, blithely out-of-touch outfit, although she did. The problem is that this administration turns every event—no matter how dire—into a kind of anesthetized luxury fashion shoot, which leads us to some disturbing political truths.

Fashion-magazine layouts have a particular feel to them. We know it well: stylized, blank, alluring in an anonymous way, suggestive of sex, but devoid of sensuality or personal emotion. The photographs draw us in, but the models don't return our gaze. Instead, they tend to wear a kind of frozen, faraway gaze, a look that frees us to gawk unashamedly, without fear of being caught staring. Fashion models feign ignorance of the camera lens in order to signal that we are not their interlocutors, but rather voyeurs whose desires are roused only to be rechanneled toward the items for sale (clothes, jewels, handbags, etc.).

Such photos exist to cast the fetishizing spell of the commodity over us. They create, that is, a dissociative relationship with the viewer. And while Melania Trump was known to have been somewhat stiff as a model, she has clearly mastered that squinty, middle-distance gaze, which she regularly employs as First Lady.

Melania dresses and moves as if she were awkwardly performing a theatrical role, much as Ivanka does. Their oddly stilted presence in political settings seems to transform all occasions, no matter how "presidential," into advertisements. This is not because they were both once models, but because they cannot stop posing like models. (Ironically, successful models learn to avoid such obvious artificiality, since it makes the unreality of fashion shoots too glaring.)

The Trump women evince a dazed blankness and anonymity that in turn cast doubt on the reality of everything around them. When you see Melania headed to Marine One, or dining with world leaders, or standing on a White House balcony, the entire scene looks like a magazine spread in which "real" people, equipment, and buildings are being used merely as dramatic backdrops for a fashion layout. On Tuesday, this meant that instead of being a supporting presence in the president's trip to survey flood damage, Melania became the star and the trip morphed into a simulacrum, a kind of *Vogue* shoot "simulating" a president's trip. In other words, the realness of everyone and everything else (including hurricane victims) faded and the evacuated blankness of the commercial overtook the scene.

And this is how something as apparently trivial as women's style reveals a profound truth at the heart of this administration and its relationship to America's citizens: It is as dissociative as a fashion advertisement, brought to power by manipulating and rechanneling the electorate's desires for wealth and possessions. This truth seeps out of every photographed occasion, including and especially those featuring the Trump women.

So Melania dominated the scene yesterday (witness how much we were talking about her), but it was not with her personality. Rather it was the power of the commodity that she wielded—the power of transactional commerce purveyed with utter irreality and disconnection, which it has been her role to channel, and which feels disturbingly recognizable to us in our commerce-saturated society.

Driving that home, Melania actually later donned, somewhat heartbreakingly, a black cap with FLOTUS emblazoned on it—not "America," or the awful "MAGA," or her name, or the name of the devastated city she was visiting, or that of a sports team, or even a worthy organization she could have supported, such as the Red Cross. No, Melania wore a hat with the acronym of her role written on it. A non-person-specific hat, making clear that she is just a temporary occupant of this role. She labeled herself.

That's what models—and in this case also presidents—do: They inhabit anonymously temporary, unreal worlds born of the realm of luxury logo goods. The devastation in Houston is a tragedy, but so too is this administration's blank, model's stare—its mirrored shades in the face of human sorrows. This is not just about fashion. It's about the urgency of recognizing a certain genre of hypnotizing, dehumanizing spell, and snapping ourselves out of it.

43

Is Wokeness in Fashion Just Another Illusion?

Connie Wang

Refinery29, January 30, 2018

Is fashion going through something like a #MeToo movement? Judging by the number of Instagram Stories denouncing style influencer and entrepreneur Miroslava Duma and designer Ulyana Sergeenko's flippant use of the n-word last week, it certainly seemed like we were ready for one. Photographer Tamu McPherson and fashion editor Shiona Turini expressed disappointment in their street style peers on their Instagram Stories, and outspoken fashion personalities like blogger Nicolette Mason and stylist Rachael Wang reminded their Instagram followers that incidental racism is indicative of a web of institutional racism. There was even a petition that called for Business of Fashion to remove Miroslava Duma from its BoF 500 list of the most influential fashion professionals. "In light of Ulyana's soggy apology, I keep thinking about what if there was a #metoo moment in fashion where we all began releasing stories of racial harassment?" tweeted writer Marjon Carlos.

But after the 24-hour Stories expired, it became clear that the moment had little momentum. While Duma and Sergeenko were shamed out of finishing the couture-week circuit and Duma was removed from the board of children's retailer The Tot, the repercussions failed to extend beyond just these two women. Instead of instigating a movement that exposed how deep racial discrimination runs in the industry, the incident caved in on itself. We took down two Gallianos; we did not dismantle a system of Weinsteins.

What is perhaps most frustrating is that the fact that racism exists in the fashion industry—sometimes in blatant, obvious, almost laughably tone-deaf ways—is no surprise to anyone, especially for the people who these slurs are directed. That two wealthy, white, Russian oligarchs would believe that anything—including the n-word—is available for their pleasure is, sadly, par for the course.

That said, the incident and reaction to it revealed an increasingly antagonistic paradox about the fashion industry—that it likes to see itself as eternally woke, but it's also an establishment that is undeniably elitist. In other words, fashion is a bastion for tolerance, and fashion is also exclusionary. It is true that the industry has been among the most vocal industries to openly celebrate their LGBTQ creatives and their communities of color. But it is also true that if everyone is *fashionable*, then no one actually is. In this same dichotomy, $710 feminist T-shirts can become a runway trend and Instagram catnip, but 67 percent of women, at least stateside, can't fit into its largest size.

This has also meant that for decades, "inclusion" has largely looked like only welcoming the thin, photogenic, and magnetic folks from these marginalized communities into the fold. Creating a universe on the runway and in advertisements that reflects the diversity of the world as beautiful, glamorous, and prestigious is crucial. Representation is key to social change. Seeing arbiters of culture and beauty deem non-dominant cultures as beautiful is essential. But, fashion's Achilles heel is that we seem to stop just short of real reckoning beyond simple representation and charity. Why does fashion demand boldness when it comes to style, but shirk from bold changes in thinking, behaving, and communicating?

Today, it's clear that wokeness is at odds with exclusivity. This presents a problem for those like Duma and Sergeenko who profit from their perch. Like how designers have been trained to pick and choose inspiration like toppings in a salad, they've also been trained to treat inclusivity as something "cool" to promote—Sergeenko believed using the n-word was a way to be "as cool as these guys who sing it." While I find it difficult to believe that Sergeenko or Duma used the word in a malicious way (like one of their fan's post that sprung up in their defense), their wokeness is skin-deep. The cost of projecting public wokeness while enjoying institutional exclusivity may be hypocritical, but it's not difficult to do. In the day following the controversy ignited over Duma's photo of the n-word, a transphobic 2012 video came to light in which she talked about how fashion influencer Bryanboy and model Andreja Pejic were dangerous role models for young boys. That video inspired the second Instagram apology of two days in which Duma said: "I have committed myself to a journey of personal growth, where ignorance has been replaced by acceptance, and discrimination by inclusion." If the language reads as thoughtful, it was probably because it was most likely written by a fleet of PR experts.

Duma also says something in the original video that reveals a lot about the ideology of the fashion elite: "I think a certain kind of refined culture is needed here," she muses. She may have been talking about the perceived inelegance of gender-bending, but that sentiment can be applied to nearly everything in Duma's world. Refinement is a set of gestures and a rarified presentation to express superiority and good taste. Though the definition of what is refined changes over time, the process is the same: Get the gestures and presentation down, and you're considered "in" with the fashion establishment. That is as true in 2012 as it was in 1912. And, it's definitely still true today.

So, what happens when wokeness—inclusivity, diversity, cultural sensitivity—is also considered good taste? Duma's Instagram apology demonstrates she has the rudimentary vocabulary to express "wokeness," even if their private lives may be unwoke. Some people have rationalized Duma and Sergeenko's gaffe by pointing at the fact that they are from Russia, a country where Black citizens make up less than 0.02 percent of the population. But as many others have pointed out, they travel, operate global brands, and benefit from Western consumers. So, even though they are miles away from America both geographically and culturally, Duma and Sergeenko were able to give the illusion of American "wokeness" by ticking certain checkboxes.

Consider this: Had Duma and Sergeenko not used the n-word last week, we may have believed them to be some of the good ones. Sergeenko's diverse couture week casting has won her accolades. Duma's Buro 247 has published many articles celebrating plus-size fashion, advocating for inclusivity, supporting the Women's March, and—ironically—calling out private displays of racism. That is a far cry from the private statements she gave in 2012, and it might have been evidence that she's become "woke" in the days since. Except, of course, they didn't understand what might be one of the simplest lessons in cultural sensitivity: White people do not get to use the n-word, even out of affection.

But most of these stories are indistinguishable from those on most publications that rely on aggregation and reblogging. Understanding that, it's hard then to be surprised that the outrage machine against Duma and Sergeenko replicates that system, with people screen-grabbing, reposting, and re-sharing the same feelings of anger and disappointment. At best, this educates those who may use the n-word that it is not okay to. At worst, it creates a false sense of accomplishment—that you've actually done something to change things, without having done much at all.

There's something to be said about why the fashion industry has largely relied on the ephemeral Instagram Stories to express strong personal opinions instead of Twitter, Instagram, Facebook, or other more permanent platforms. One could reason that it's because opinions are ugly and "mess up" a feed. But how can we demand permanent change, if our demands are impermanent?

It is a skill of the fashion industry that we are incredibly adroit at parroting the shape, look, and feel of anything, and make it seem attractive and desirable. That goes as much for wokeness as it does for runway trends. But unlike trends, the point of wokeness is not just that you're merely dressed in it. It's what you do with it once you're awake.

Sources and Acknowledgments

Als, Hilton. "Buying the Fantasy." *The New Yorker.* June 10, 1996. "Buying the Fantasy" by Hilton Als. Originally published in The New Yorker. Copyright © 1996 Hilton Als, used by permission of The Wylie Agency LLC.

Als, Hilton. "The Only One." *The New Yorker.* November 7, 1994. "The Only One" by Hilton Als. Originally published in The New Yorker. Copyright © 1994 Hilton Als, used by permission of The Wylie Agency LLC.

Babitz, Eve. "Hippie Heaven." Originally published in *Vogue*, October 1992, and republished in *I Used to Be Charming: The Rest of Eve Babitz*. New York: New York Review of Books, 2019. Copyright Eve Babitz. Permission by the Trident Media Group and NYRB Books.

Brubach, Holly. "In Fashion: Modernism Outmoded." *The New Yorker.* November 20, 1989. Permission by the author.

Brubach, Holly. "Ralph Lauren's Achievement." *The Atlantic.* August 1987. Permission by the author.

Campbell, Bebe Moore. "What Happened to the Afro?" *Ebony*, vol. 37, iss. 8 (June 1982): 79–85. Permission by the estate of Bebe Moore Campbell.

Carter, Angela. "The Wound in the Face." *New Society.* April 24, 1975. The Wound in the Face by Angela Carter. Published by New Society, 1975. Copyright Angela Carter. Reproduced by permission of the Estate of Angela Carter c/o Rogers, Coleridge & White Ltd., 20 Powis Mews, London W11 1JN.

Cronberg, Anja Aronowsky. "The Revolution Will Be Branded Vetements." *Vestoj.* March 17, 2016. Permission provided by the author and Vestoj.

Cronberg, Anja Aronowsky. "Will I Get a Ticket?" *Vestoj.* July 3, 2017. Permission provided by the author and Vestoj.

Dame Rogue [Louise Norton]. "Philosophic Fashions: The Importance of Being Dressed." *Rogue.* July 15, 1915.

Dame Rogue [Louise Norton]. "Philosophic Fashions: Trouser Talk." *Rogue.* April 15, 1915.

Dame Rogue [Louise Norton]. "Philosophic Fashions: Who Fell Asleep on the King's Highway?" *Rogue.* March 15, 1915.

Epstein, Eleni. "A Campaign Issue–Clothes?" *The Washington Evening Star.* September 16, 1960.

Epstein, Eleni. "Candidates in a Tie On Fashion's Slate." *The Washington Evening Star.* April 10, 1968.

Evans, Caroline. "Hussein Chalayan: Nostalgia for the Future." *032c*, iss. 9 (Summer 2005). Permission provided by the author.

Fraser, Kennedy. "Feminine Fashions: The Fall Collections II." *The New Yorker.* July 18, 1977. Republished in *The Fashionable Mind: Reflections of Fashion 1970–1982*. New York: Alfred A.

Knopf, Inc., 1981. Excerpt(s) from *The Fashionable Mind* by Kennedy Fraser, copyright © 1981 by Kennedy Fraser. Used by permission of Alfred A. Knopf, an imprint of the Knopf Doubleday Publishing Group, a division of Penguin Random House LLC. All rights reserved.

Friedman, Vanessa. "Trump vs. the Disappearing Tie." *The New York Times.* May 11, 2016. From the *New York Times* © 2016. The New York Times Company. All rights reserved. Used under licence.

Garelick, Rhonda. "Melania Trump and the Chilling Artifice of Fashion." *New York Magazine, The Cut*, August 30, 2017. Permission provided by *New York Magazine* and the author.

Givhan, Robin. "All Hail the Leader of the Fashionable World." *The Washington Post.* January 21, 2009. From the Washington Post © 2009. The Washington Post. All rights reserved. Used by permission and protected by the Copyright Laws of the United States. The printing, copying, redistribution, or retransmission of this Content without express written permission is prohibited.

Hawes, Elizabeth. *Fashion Is Spinach*. New York: Random House, 1938.

Hollander, Anne. *Sex and Suits*. New York: Alfred A. Knopf, 1994. © Anne Hollander, 1994, *Sex and Suits,* Bloomsbury Academic, an imprint of Bloomsbury Publishing Plc.

Horyn, Cathy. "Future Take Note: Raf Simons Was Here." *The New York Times.* July 4, 2004. From the *New York Times* © 2004. The New York Times Company. All rights reserved. Used under licence.

Long, Lois. "Feminine Fashions." *The New Yorker.* August 28, 1926.

Long, Lois. "Feminine Fashions." *The New Yorker.* September 10, 1927.

McBride, Dwight A. *Why I Hate Abercrombie & Fitch: Essays On Race and Sexuality*. New York: New York University Press, 2005. Permission provided by the author and NYU Press

Menkes, Suzy. "Fashion's Military Fascination: Unsettling, Romantic Esthetic." *The New York Times.* March 10, 1996. From the *New York Times* ©1996. The New York Times Company. All rights reserved. Used under licence.

Mower, Sarah. "The Mystery Man: Margiela Be Mine." *Vogue,* vol. 198, iss. 9 (September 2008): 595, 598. From Sarah Mower, *Vogue* © 2008. Condé Nast.

Sheppard, Eugenia. "Fashions from Paris: A Suit Story at Balenciaga." *The New York Herald Tribune.* March 18, 1951.

Sheppard, Eugenia. "A Mini for Men?" *World Journal.* February 1967.

Sontag, Susan. "Looking with Avedon." *Vogue,* vol. 168, iss. 9 (September 1978): 460–1, 507–8. "Looking with Avedon" by Susan Sontag, originally published in Vogue. Copyright © 1978 Susan Sontag, used by permission of The Wylie Agency LLC.

Spindler, Amy. "Coming Apart." *The New York Times.* July, 25, 1993. From the *New York Times* ©1993. The New York Times Company. All rights reserved. Used under licence.

Steele, Valerie. "Calvinism Unclothed." *Design Quarterly,* no. 157 (Autumn 1992): 29–34. Permission provided by the author and the Walker Art Center.

Thurman, Judith. "Dressed to Thrill: Alexander McQueen at the Met." *The New Yorker.* May 16, 2011. "Dressed to Thrill: Alexander McQueen at the Met" by Judith Thurman. Originally published in *The New Yorker*. Copyright © 2011 Judith Thurman, used by permission of The Wylie Agency LLC.

Thurman, Judith. "The Misfit." *The New Yorker.* July 4, 2005. "The Misfit" by Judith Thurman. Originally published in *The New Yorker*. Copyright © 2005 Judith Thurman, used by permission of The Wylie Agency LLC.

Trebay, Guy. "Suket Dhir, Men's Wear Designer, from Delhi to the World." *The New York Times*. November 6, 2016. From the *New York Times* ©2016. The New York Times Company. All rights reserved. Used under licence.

Wang, Connie. "Is Wokeness in Fashion Just Another Illusion?" *Refinery29*. January 30, 2018. Permission provided by the author and *Refinery29*.

Wilde, Oscar. "Mr. Oscar Wilde on Woman's Dress." *The Pall Mall Gazette*. 1884.

Wilde, Oscar. "Literary and Other Notes." *The Woman's World,* November 1887

Wilde, Oscar. "Literary and Other Notes." *The Woman's World,* December 1887

Wilson, Elizabeth. "Haute Coiffure de Gel." *New Statesman & Society.* December 22, 1989. Permission provided by the author.

Yaeger, Lynn. "Avant Guardians." *The Village Voice.* April 7, 1998. Permission provided by the author.

Yaeger, Lynn. "The Eastern Bloc." *The Village Voice.* October 3, 1995. Permission provided by the author.

Index